REFERENCE

RATING LAW

THE UNIFORM BUSINESS RATE

AUSTRALIA
The Law Book Company
Brisbane ● Sydney ● Melbourne ● Perth

CANADA
Ottawa ● Toronto ● Calgary ● Montreal ● Vancouver

AGENTS
Steimatzky's Agency Ltd., Tel Aviv;
N.M. Tripathi (Private) Ltd., Bombay;
Eastern Law House (Private) Ltd., Calcutta;
M.P.P. House, Bangalore;
Universal Book Traders, Delhi;
Aditya Books, Delhi;
MacMillan Shuppan KK, Tokyo;
Pakistan Law House, Karachi, Lahore

RATING LAW

THE UNIFORM BUSINESS RATE

Phil Askham, B.A., M.A., ARICS
David Mackmin, B.Sc., M.Sc., FRICS

LONDON
SWEET & MAXWELL
1995

Published by
Sweet & Maxwell Limited of
South Quay Plaza,
183 Marsh Wall,
London E14 9FT

Computerset by Tradespools Ltd, Frome, Somerset
Printed and bound in Great Britain by Butler and Tanner Ltd, Frome
and London

A CIP catalogue record
for this book is available
from the British Library

ISBN 0 421 525703

No natural forests were destroyed to make this product:
only farmed timber was used and re-planted

Acknowledgements

The authors gratefully acknowledge the help and contribution of the following rating surveyors in the preparation of this book.

David Varley, the York Valuation Office, for his help on retail property and for general editorial assistance; Pat Brennan of the Leeds Valuation Office for keeping us straight on Public Utilities, Community Properties and Miscellaneous Hereditaments; John Stephenson of Fuller Peiser for his detailed contributions on Plant and Machinery and Industrial Properties; Chris Tattersall of Lawrence Tattersall for dealing with the vagaries of licensed properties; Philip Clarkson of Storey Sons and Parker for dealing with the procedural complexities which tend to change on a daily basis; Roger Sykes of Lambert Smith Hampton for the chapter on garages and service stations; and Trevor Richards of Sheffield Hallam University for the section on mineral hereditaments.

Our thanks to Sarah Line for her perfect typing.

Preface

This book owes much to the editors and authors of Bean and Lockwood's *Rating Valuation Practice*. The publishers permission to use earlier copyright material is acknowledged.

This book on the Uniform Business Rate and Council Tax has been written for the general practice surveyor and student surveyor. The aim has been to present the current law and practice in simple terms to cover both theory and practice. It is hoped that readers will recognise the specialist nature of some aspects of rating, and will in accepting clients' instructions recognise their own limitations of knowledge and experience and will refer where necessary to the rating expert. The purpose here is to provide the surveyor with the general basis of the subject, to cover most aspects of principle but to stop short of endeavouring to cover the detail of the subject needed by the specialist rating surveyor.

The 1995 rating revaluation brings with it further complications of shifting rate burdens, where this has led to the provision of further transitional arrangements these have been covered in Chapter 3.

The authors have not incorporated all the relevant statutory instruments in the text as these in turn can be changed so easily. This book should therefore be read, where necessary, in conjunction with the appropriate regulations and orders.

The authors are grateful to a number of rating surveyors for their generous assistance in preparing this new book.

The Royalties from this book have been donated to the Royal Institution of Chartered Surveyors Benevolent Fund.

Phil Askham
David Mackmin
Sheffield 1995

Contents

1. INTRODUCTION AND HISTORY

2. PRINCIPLES OF VALUATION

3. LIABILITY FOR RATES

4. TOTAL AND PARTIAL EXEMPTIONS FROM RATING

5. COMPILATION AND ALTERATION OF THE RATING LIST

6. METHODS OF ASSESSMENT

7. Referencing of Properties

8. Assessment of Retail and Commercial Property

9. Industrial Property, Plant and Machinery, Mineral Hereditaments

10. Assessment of Licensed Premises

11. GARAGES AND SERVICE STATIONS

12. VALUATION OF PUBLIC UTILITY UNDERTAKINGS

13. COMMUNITY PROPERTIES

14. VALUATION OF MISCELLANEOUS PROPERTIES

15. COUNCIL TAX

TABLE OF CASES

TABLE OF STATUTES

TABLE OF STATUTORY INSTRUMENTS

(References are to paragraph number)

1

Introduction and History

GENERALLY

The purpose of a rating valuation is to arrive at a figure termed **1-01** rateable value on which rates, namely the Uniform Business Rate (UBR), are levied upon the ratepayer at so much in the pound in order to defray the expenses of local government. The present rating law is regarded as having originated with the Poor Relief Act 1601, which provided for the levying of taxation on "every occupier of land, houses ... towards the relief of the poor." Under this enactment occupiers were to contribute to a poor rate according to their means but no specific method of assessment was laid down. The annual value of a person's property within the parish gradually became recognised as the most satisfactory basis and this was first given statutory approval in 1836.

Throughout this book where reference is made to the principal modern enactments relating to rating and valuation a brief title only will be used (*e.g.* the 1988 Act).

The current procedure for making and amending local non-domestic rating lists and central lists is enacted in the 1988 Act as amended by the 1989 Act. These Acts are subject to more than 100 supplementary provisions set out in various statutory instruments and regulations.

The primary purpose of this book is to set out the principal matters to be taken into account in arriving at the values to be entered into the rating list. All non-domestic properties are assessed direct to rateable value as defined in Schedule 6, paragraph 2(1) of the 1988 Act as amended by Schedule 5, paragraph 38(3) of the 1989 Act. Domestic properties are subject to Council Tax under the 1992 Act and are covered in Chapter 15.

HISTORICAL: PRE-1948

1–02 Before dealing with the process of assessment, a very brief summary of the manner in which lists were made and amended prior to the operation of the 1988 Act will be given, so that the route by which current law and practice has evolved can be appreciated.

The list previously known as a valuation list was prepared by the rating authority in draft form under the 1925 Act and, after approval by the assessment committee, came into operation normally for a period of five years. Assessment committees were appointed for each assessment area.

The values in the valuation list could be amended during the quinquennium by means of a proposal. These were considered by the assessment committee, who, if they thought fit, amended the valuation list, subject to a right of appeal to quarter sessions and to higher courts on questions of law.

The 1929 Act provided for the complete derating of agricultural land and buildings and the partial derating of industrial and freight transport hereditaments. Industrial and freight transport hereditaments have been rated in full since 1963 but agricultural derating remains to this day.

Quinquennial lists were brought into effect in September 1928 and April 1933. The April 1933 list, due to the postponement of the revaluation due in September 1938 and to subsequent postponements necessitated by the 1939–45 war, ultimately remained effective until 1956.

HISTORICAL: 1948–1967

1–03 The Local Government Act 1948 made fundamental changes in rating law. In particular, it transferred the duty and responsibility of making and defending the valuation of properties for rating purposes to valuation officers appointed by the Commissioners of Inland Revenue, it abolished the central valuation committee, county valuation committees and assessment committees and established a new appeals tribunal.

From February 1, 1950, the main duties in relation to the maintenance of the list were assumed by the Inland Revenue Valuation Office.

Notwithstanding the intentions of the 1948 Act, the scheme of regular revaluations at five-yearly intervals was not adhered to. The

2

revaluation due in 1953 was not brought into effect until 1956, the 1961 revaluation was postponed until 1963 and the 1968 revaluation until 1973. A general revaluation of non-domestic properties under the 1988 Act came into effect in April 1990 with a revaluation in 1995.

Novel provisions of the 1948 Act with regard to the assessment of dwelling-houses were found to be unsatisfactory and impracticable. However, the basic concept of the 1948 Act to limit the assessment of dwellings and ensure that these did not soar to current rental levels was preserved in the Valuation for Rating Act 1953. This Act introduced a uniform basis for all types of dwelling-houses with provisions to ensure that all were valued by reference to rental levels prevailing in June 1939. Special provisions were included to cover properties which were partially residential in character (*e.g.* house and shop). These special provisions remained from 1956 to 1963, but in the 1963 lists residential properties were all assessed on the basis of full current rental values.

As the first revaluation under the 1948 Act neared completion it **1–04** was realised that a number of amendments to rating law were needed. The Rating and Valuation (Miscellaneous Provisions) Act 1955 was accordingly passed with three main purposes:

(1) To introduce a new procedure in relation to proposals and to abolish the necessity for the publication of draft lists;
(2) to provide a new method for the rating of gasboard property;
(3) to extend the exemption of rating to church-halls, etc., and to provide protection for charitable and certain other organisations.

Following the introduction of the lists on April 1, 1956, there was considerable protest from the occupiers of commercial properties which had been revalued by reference to current rental levels as opposed to dwellings which were reassessed by reference to 1939 rental levels. The effect of the new lists had been to place a disproportionately heavy burden on the occupiers of commercial properties. Although this was anticipated and was the deliberate intention, it was, nevertheless, decided that some measure of relief should be given to the occupiers of shops, offices and commercial properties.

Accordingly, the Rating and Valuation Act 1957 provided that there should be a measure of derating for non-industrial buildings. Special provisions dealt with composite hereditaments.

The Rating and Valuation Act 1959 postponed the 1961 reval- **1–05** uation until 1963 as it was considered that there would be

3

insufficient evidence of open market rentals of residential property for a 1961 revaluation.

Against this background the Rating and Valuation Act 1961 was introduced with the object of rationalising the system and ensuring that at the 1963 revaluation all properties (with very limited exceptions) should be valued, and charged rates, on the basis of full current rental values. Agricultural derating was, however, unaffected and properties occupied by charities were granted a 50 per cent remission of rates. Additionally, local authorities were given discretionary powers to reduce, further reduce, or remit rates in the case of properties occupied by charities, or other organisations concerned with recreation, education, social welfare, science, literature or the fine arts.[1]

The 1961 Act also introduced a system of formulae valuation to be used in the case of water undertakings.

1–06   The resulting reallocation of the rate burden was thought to bear too harshly on certain classes of householder and the Rating (Interim Relief) Act 1964 gave local authorities discretionary powers to remit rates in the case of elderly ratepayers of limited means.

The Rating Act 1966 enacted a more comprehensive and permanent scheme for rate rebates to be given to domestic ratepayers of limited income and enabled ratepayers of dwellings to pay rates by instalments.

The Local Government Act 1966 reorganised the system of exchequer grants and introduced a new grant to keep down the rate poundage for residential properties; it introduced differential rate poundages as between "residential properties," "mixed hereditaments," and all other properties; it postponed the revaluation until 1973; it gave authority to "tone of list" valuation and gave local authorities adoptive powers to charge half rates on empty properties.

The General Rate Act 1967 consolidated the existing rating law and did not introduce any new principles of valuation or rating practice.

HISTORICAL: POST-1967

1–07 The General Rate Act 1970 recognised the growing difficulty of finding open market rental evidence for residential property and permitted other evidence to be used.

The Rating Act 1971 extended the exemption from rating of

---

[1] See Chap. 4 for current exemptions and reliefs.

agricultural land and buildings. These amendments became necessary because of the changing nature of agriculture, the creation of
new business arrangements for farming and ensuing cases concerned
with the strict definitions of agricultural land and buildings.

The restructuring of local government in 1972 led to the need to
amend the General Rate Act 1967 to reflect those changes. The Local
Government Act 1972 extended boundaries of areas to the low water
mark, provided for precepts from the county councils, (now amended
by the Local Government Finance Act 1982 and the Local Government Act 1985), amended the provisions relating to local valuation
panels and introduced "equalising powers ... for the purpose of
reducing disparities in the rates levied in different rating areas of the
country."

The Local Government Act 1974 contained a number of significant
changes to the 1967 Act which in some cases were controversial. It
amended the rate rebate scheme and the provisions relating to the
rating of unoccupied property. It introduced controversial penal
rating surcharges on unused offices, shops, warehouses, etc. It
amended the provision relating to plant and machinery, gave power
to the Secretary of State to make provisions by order for fixing or
determining the rateable value of certain classes of hereditament
such as railway and canal premises and electricity boards, and made
provision for lists not to be altered on account of minor structural
alterations to dwellings.

The Local Government, Planning and Land Act 1980 made further **1-08**
important changes. In particular, it amended section 19 so that in any
new list only "dwelling-houses, etc.," as defined would be valued to
gross value; section 19A and 19B were added, paving the way for
valuation by reference to a date earlier than the date on which a list
would come into force, and effectively removing the provision which
enabled public houses to be revalued every time their trade went up
or down. The Act also specifically exempted fish farms, extended the
provisions relating to domestic rate relief and payment by instalments, gave the Secretary of State power to suspend the rating
surcharge provisions of the 1974 Act and included a number of
financial changes relating to rates and local authorities. In addition, it
provided for exemption for certain classes of property in enterprise
zones, extended the provisions relating to domestic rate relief and
payment by instalments, gave the Secretary of State power to suspend
the rating surcharge provisions of the 1974 Act and included a
number of financial changes relating to rates and local authorities.

Since 1975, a number of other Acts have been passed relating, *inter
alia*, to Caravan Sites (1976), Charity Shops (1976), Public Utilities
(1977), Disabled Persons (1978), the Local Government and Finance

5

Act 1982, Social Security and Housing Benefits Act 1982, Rates Act 1984 and Local Government Act 1985.

1-09 This catalogue of tinkering came to an abrupt and dramatic end with the Local Government Finance Act 1988. The key changes made by the 1988 Act included:

- The abolition of domestic rating.
- The introduction of the community charge.
- Revisions to the system of rates on non-domestic property.
- The repeal of the General Rate Act 1967.

The Community Charge or Poll Tax proved to be so unpopular that it had to be repealed in 1991 and replaced by the Council Tax[2] under the Local Government Finance and Valuation Act 1991.

The changes to the non-domestic rating system operative from April 1990 included:

- Adoption of rateable value as the rating definition for all classes of non-residential property.
- Replacement of valuation lists with rating lists and central lists.
- The introduction of the antecedent date as the valuation date for the preparation of the lists.
- Introduction of new terms such as "composite" for "mixed" hereditament, *e.g.* shops with flats above.
- Collection to be by charging authorities not rating authorities, now billing authorities for both the UBR and the Council Tax.
- Amendments to a number of established rating terms such as "tone of the list".
- Provision for Parliament to legislate through Statutory instruments.
- The creation of a central non-domestic rating list to cover certain classes of property that cover several districts such as utilities and rail track.
- The replacement of local rate poundages determined by local authorities with a nationally determined non-domestic rating multiple (NDRM), the Uniform Business Rate. Separate NDRMs are determined for England, Wales and Scotland.

The Valuation Officer (V.O.) covering the area for each billing authority is responsible for preparing and maintaining the rating lists.

---

[2] See Chap. 15.

6

Principles of Valuation

INTRODUCTION

In the majority of rating valuations, the valuer is endeavouring to **2–01** ascertain the appropriate annual value of the hereditament. This is by no means a simple task and depends upon a whole series of assumptions as to the precise definition of value, the date of valuation, and indeed what is being valued. The valuation date is prescribed for each rating list but different rules apply for subsequent alterations to the list, and in these circumstances consideration must be given to the "tone of the list" principle. The definition of value envisages a rental value—but one which is subject to a whole range of considerations determined by statute, rating practice and case law. In particular, the value has to be ascertained having regard to the principles of *rebus sic stantibus*, regarding physical condition and use.

In simple terms the following questions represent the process of carrying out a valuation for rating purposes, each element of which is considered in this chapter.

- What is the definition of value?
- What is being valued?
- What is the valuation date?
- What physical and other circumstances have to be assumed?

RATEABLE VALUE

Since 1990, all rating valuations have been carried out to rateable **2–02** value. This is a considerable simplification as before then valuations were either to gross or rateable value. The definition of rateable value is contained in Schedule 6, paragraph 2(1) of the 1988 Act and is, in part, a restatement of the definition contained in section 19 of the General Rate Act 1967:

> "The rateable value of a non-domestic hereditament shall be taken to be an amount equal to the rent at which it is estimated the hereditament might reasonably be expected to let from year to year if the tenant undertook to pay all the usual tenant's rates and taxes and to bear the cost of repairs and insurance and the other expenses (if any) necessary to maintain the hereditament in a state to command that rent."

The assumption for all rating valuations, is that the tenant will be responsible for carrying out all repairs and insurance, an assumption which accords more closely with the concept of the full repairing and insuring lease. The definition is considered in more detail later in this chapter.

ANTECEDENT DATE

2–03 The relevant date for a rating valuation, *i.e.* the date at which the level of values to be applied is fixed, was, in the past, the date the list came into effect; thus for the 1973 list this was April 1, 1973. This gave rise to particular problems at that time because it forced the Valuation Officer, in practice, to anticipate future levels of value. The 1973 list was introduced at a time of unprecedented increases in value, making forward prediction difficult in the extreme. This issue was considered in detail in *K. Shoes v. Hardy.*[1]

This difficulty should no longer arise as the Secretary of State now has powers to determine an antecedent date, a date which precedes the actual date of the introduction of the rating list. These powers are contained in Schedule 6 to the 1988 Act. Thus, for the 1990 list the antecedent date was set at April 1, 1988 and for the 1995 list April 1, 1993. This allows sufficient time for the collection and analysis of evidence prior to the introduction of the list.

---

[1] *K. Shoe Shops Ltd v. Hardy (V.O.) and Westminster City Council* [1980] R.A. 333 256. E.G. 927, 1019; on appeal [1983] R.A. 26, 266 E.G. 119, etc.

VALUATION BY REFERENCE TO "TONE OF LIST"

Whilst the value to be ascribed to a property for rating purposes is **2–04** based on the level of value prevailing at the antecedent date, rateable values need to reflect physical circumstances relating to the property and its locality, at any later date on which it is proposed to alter the list. In simple terms this ensures, for example, that where a property is altered physically, an extension or demolition perhaps, this alteration can be taken into account in the valuation. However, these "tone of the list" provisions are far from straightforward and some consideration of the historical development of the principle is required for a full understanding of the current statutory position.

Before the Local Government Act 1966 the law required that whenever the list was amended in respect of new or altered hereditaments, the new values should be on the basis of the rental values current at the date when the proposal to amend the list was made. Such a scheme was fair in an era of static values or, to a lesser extent, when regular revaluations were carried out. However, for many classes of property, rental values are not static and between 1963 and 1990 there was only one revaluation. In these circumstances, occupiers of new or altered hereditaments would have been unfairly treated had the law been strictly applied. In practice a device known as "tone of the list" valuation was widely adopted in order to obviate unfairness. This device involved basing the values to be ascribed to new or altered hereditaments on a scale of values derived from established values, as included in the valuation list, of similar properties. This approach was used in the pre-1956 and pre-1963 periods but due to the absence of any statutory backing difficulties had arisen. The Local Government Act 1966 therefore incorporated the necessary provisions which were later to be found in section 20 of the 1967 Act below:

"**20.**—(1) For the purposes of any alteration of a valuation list to be made under Part V of this Act in respect of a hereditament in pursuance of a proposal, the value or altered value to be ascribed to the hereditament under section 19 of this Act shall not exceed the value which would have been ascribed thereto in that list if the hereditament had been subsisting throughout (the relevant year), on the assumption that at the time by reference to which that value would have been ascertained:

(a) the hereditament was in the same state as at the time of valuation and any relevant factors (as defined by subsection (2) of this section) were those subsisting at the last mentioned time, and
(b) the locality in which the hereditament is situated was in the same state, so far as concerns the other premises situated in that

9

locality and the occupation and use of those premises, the transport services and other facilities available in the locality, and other matters affecting the amenity of the locality, as at the time of valuation."

2–05   Subsection 2 outlined the "relevant factors":

"(a) the mode or category of occupation of the hereditament;
(b) the quantity of minerals or other substances on or extracted from the hereditament; or
(c) in the case of a public house, the volume of trade or business carried on at the hereditament."

In simple terms, this required that the value ascribed to the hereditament should not exceed the value of that property if it had been in existence at the time when the valuation list came into force.

In effect, the section required the valuer to imagine what the property, as it stood at the date of valuation, would have been worth if it had existed in that state during the period immediately before the list came into force. Section 20 operated to set a "ceiling" on the value which could be applied to a particular property, but there was nothing to stop properties being valued at a lower level than the "tone" value, provided always it could be established that values had actually fallen since that time. Strictly speaking, it was always necessary to carry out two valuations of any property for rating purposes, a valuation based on the level of rents at the time of valuation (date of alteration to the valuation list) and a second valuation based on the level of rents relevant to the time the list came into force. The lower of these two valuations would be adopted as the appropriate assessment.

2–06   The application of section 20 still gave rise to a number of problems, in particular, the question of what is meant by the word "state". Although the section has been substantially restated as section 121 of the Local Government Finance Act this does contain some important revisions.

First, as was argued in the Yellow Discussion Paper of July 1987, where frequent revaluations are to take place, it is not necessary for the tone provisions to operate as a ceiling value. From 1990 onwards, ratepayers are unable to challenge an assessment solely on the grounds that current rental values have dropped below the "tone" level. The question of the precise meaning of the word "state" in this context was a matter which caused considerable controversy during the later years of the 1973 valuation list. During this period a number of cases were heard on the issue. The most significant of these being the case of *Addis v. Clement*,[2] which was finally decided in the House of Lords. It concerned a property just outside an enterprise zone where it was claimed that since the 1973 list came into force, values outside the zone had fallen because of the relative attractions of properties inside the zone which enjoyed a 10 year rate-free period. It was claimed that the effect of the designation of the zone was in fact a change which affected the state of the locality. Previously the view had been that the word state could only apply to changes in the physical state of the property or the locality but the House of Lords decided that "state" could be interpreted to include changes of a non-physical nature.

As a consequence, the interpretation of section 20 was somewhat modified during the later years of the 1973 list in respect of those "matters" which could be taken into account in a section 20 valuation. Reference should also be made to the cases; *Sheerness Steel*[3] and *Thorn EMI*[4] for further interpretation.

CURRENT "TONE" PROVISIONS

"Tone of the list" provisions remain to this day, but in a modified **2–07** form within section 121 of the 1988 Act. It is worth quoting these in full:

> **"Valuation according to tone of list**
> **121.**—(1) Where for the purposes of section 20 of the 1967 Act a hereditament is valued on the basis of the assumptions specified in subsection (1) of that section (basis of valuation for the purposes of a proposal to alter a valuation list to be consistent with the tone of the list), no account shall be taken of a change to which this subsection applies unless it is one which:
>
> > (a) affects the physical state or physical enjoyment of the hereditament, or
> > (b) affects the physical state of the locality in which the hereditament is situated or, though it does not affect the physical state of the locality, is nonetheless physically manifest there.
>
> (2) Subsection (1) above applies to any change in the state of the hereditament or the state of the locality in which the hereditament is

---

[2] *Addis v. Clement (V.O.); Clement (V.O.) v. Coteglade* [1984] 271 E.G. 291; [1984] R.A. 137 L.T.
[3] *Sheerness Steel Co. plc v. Maudling (V.O.)* [1986] R.A. 45; [1986] J.P.L. 613, L.T.
[4] *Thorn EMI Cinemas v. Harrison (V.O.)* [1986] R.A. 125; 279 E.G. 512; [1986] J.P.L. 844 L.T.

situated which has occurred since the time by reference to which the value of the hereditament is to be ascertained, other than one relating to a factor which is a relevant factor within the meaning of that section."

2–08 The relevant factors referred to in the section are identified in Schedule 6, paragraphs 2(5) and 2(7).

"(5) Where the rateable value is determined for the purposes of compiling a list ... the matters mentioned in sub-paragraph (7) below shall be taken to be as they are assumed to be on the (material day)."

"(7) The matters are:

(a) matters affecting the physical state or physical enjoyment of the hereditament,
(b) the mode or category of occupation of the hereditament,
(c) the quantity of minerals or other substances in or extracted from the hereditament,
(cc) the quantity of refuse or waste material which is brought onto and permanently deposited on the hereditament,
(d) matters affecting the physical state of the locality in which the hereditament is situated or which, though not affecting the physical state of the locality, are nonetheless physically manifest there, and
(e) the use or occupation of other premises situated in the locality of the hereditament."

2–09 The precise wording of subsection (7) is important because it represents a widening of the "matters" which can be taken into account. Where these were thought previously to be of a purely physical character, the new provisions refer to physical enjoyment with regard to the hereditament and matters which are physically manifest in connection with the locality.

Matters affecting the physical state of the locality will include changes to other buildings, constructions and demolitions and physical features such as roads, car parks and other items of infrastructure.

In addition, matters which are physically manifest in the locality but do not affect its physical state could include traffic and pedestrian flows, public transport, noise, fumes and vibration.

Interpretation of section 121 tone provisions will depend upon case law and will no doubt develop.

Those "matters" mentioned in section 121(7), such as the physical state of the hereditament, are to be assumed to be as they were on the "material day". The precise meaning of this term is explored in the next section.

12

THE MATERIAL DAY

This was originally defined in section 6 of the 1988 Act as either: **2-10**

  (a) the day when the Valuation Officer makes an alteration to the list,
  (b) for a proposal which challenges a Valuation Office alteration, the date of that alteration,
  (c) for other proposals the day on which the proposal is made.

This still applies to proposals made before April 1, 1992, and those made after that date in respect of Valuation Office alterations made earlier than April 1, 1992.

In all other cases it is now defined by virtue of the Local Government Finance Act 1992, Schedule 10 and regulations[5] as either:

  (a) the day of the event giving rise to the alteration or proposal or,
  (b) the day of the alteration or service of proposal.

The one exception is a proposal challenging a Valuation Office alteration when the material day will be the date of that alteration.

SUMMARY "TONE" PROVISIONS

A brief summary of the current provisions determining the date of **2-11** valuation is that, in all cases, whether valuation is for the inclusion in a rating list or for an alteration to that list the valuer must carry out his valuation having regard to the level of value existing at the antecedent date but having regard to the physical characteristics and other circumstances surrounding the property as specified in the Act at the later material day. It should be noted that the tone provisions will no longer operate as a ceiling where the general level of values at the material day happens to be lower than the level of values at the antecedent date. The volume of trade or business carried out in a public house is no longer specified as a matter to be taken into account at the material day,[6] and generally, in the case of hereditaments valued by reference to trading accounts it would appear to be

---

[5] S.I. 1992 No. 556.
[6] See Chap. 10, Public Houses.

the accounts for the period prior to the antecedent date which need to be taken into account in arriving at the value of the hereditament.

THE HEREDITAMENT

2-12 The unit of property which is the subject of rating is the hereditament. The word hereditament is referred to in section 64 of the 1988 Act and this in turn refers back to section 115(1) of the 1967 Act which defines hereditament to mean:

> "property which is or may become liable to a rate, being a unit of such property which is, or would fall to be, shown as a separate item in the valuation list."

Section 64 extends this definition to include reserved advertising rights. Every "relevant non-domestic hereditament" must be entered in a local rating list. The only exceptions are hereditaments which are exempt and those which are entered in a central rating list.

Section 64(2) defines what is included in the term relevant hereditament:

> (a) "lands;
> (b) coal mines;
> (c) mines of any other description, other than a mine of which the royalty or dues are for the time being wholly reserved in kind;
> (d) any right of sporting (that is, any right of fowling, of shooting, of taking or killing game or rabbits, or of fishing) when severed from the occupation of the land on which the right is exercisable;
> (e) any right to use any land for the purposes of exhibiting advertisements ...".

Non-domestic hereditaments are those which consist entirely of property which is not domestic or those which are composite hereditaments. The definition of domestic property is contained in section 66(1) and is considered in detail later in this book.[7]

2-13 Composite hereditaments are those which consist partially of domestic and non-domestic property, for example, flats occupied together with shops. The definition of domestic property is important as domestic property is no longer subject to the Uniform Business Rate.

The identification of the hereditament is a crucial element in rating valuation as it will influence the level of assessment and hence

---

[7] See Chap. 15.

the level of rates payable. As it is impossible to carry out a valuation until the physical and legal extent of that property can be determined, this should always be the first stage of the process.

Whilst statute defines the hereditament it does not indicate its extent which is more difficult to establish. In many cases this will present few problems but there are situations where it will be less obvious.

Generally, the hereditament will embrace the whole of the actual and potential occupation. Thus the unit of property is generally regarded as including all land, buildings and rights for which there is a single rateable occupier and which are contained within one curtilage, provided that it is possible for the occupier to pass freely from one section of the occupation to another without having to use a public road or pass over the land of another. This is a generalisation and there are exceptions to this rule, *e.g.* a golf course or an airport may be regarded as a single rateable hereditament although traversed by one or more roads.

2–14 The circumstances in which properties, although severed from one another, may be regarded as a single rateable hereditament were illustrated in *Gilbert v. Hickinbottom & Sons Ltd.*[8] In this case the Court of Appeal ruled that the Lands Tribunal had not erred in finding that two properties not physically connected or contiguous constituted a single rateable hereditament for the premises in question were a bakery which was on one side of a highway and a workshop on the other side of the highway which, *inter alia*, repaired the bakery machinery. The basis for the decision was that the workshop was functionally essential to the operation of the bakery as it was needed "on the spot" to effect prompt repairs in case of breakdown. This being so, in the special circumstances, there was one hereditament.

This decision has been followed in other Lands Tribunal cases where similar conditions applied and there were good grounds for the tribunal to decide that two properties were functionally essential the one to the other and thus only one hereditament. In several other cases claims that two properties should be regarded as one hereditament have failed.

2–15 The general rule is that the occupation of part of a hereditament creates a liability in respect of the whole unless there are circumstances which warrant the setting up of a separate assessment on the part occupied. In *R. v. Aberystwyth*[9] Lord Ellenborough C.J. said:

"There is no instance where a man has been permitted to carve out of

---

[8] [1956] 2 Q.B. 240.
[9] *R. v. Aberystwyth Inhabitants* (1808) 10 East 254.

the occupation of his house in the manner now attempted, locking up one room and then another, but using as much of the house as he found convenient. This would make a new system of occupation by subdivisions."

In contrast to the above the occupier cannot be rated for portions of a property which are neither occupied nor owned by him and are outside his tenancy. Likewise an owner cannot be rated for a whole property if he lets part of it and makes no use at all of the rest.

It must, however, be fully appreciated that the boundaries of a hereditament are not necessarily determined by the extent of the occupiers' rights. Thus, for example, if a tenant takes a whole building and occupies only half of it, if the unoccupied part is physically capable of separate occupation, then the rateable hereditament only extends to the occupied half. Furthermore, if the tenant in this example occupies the whole building and subsequently reduces his occupation by a subletting of a part of it, two separate hereditaments will have been thereby created—indeed the same result can be achieved if the original tenant ceases to occupy a part of the building and genuinely endeavours to sublet the part concerned. Such division of premises into two hereditaments will, however, only be possible if the unoccupied part is physically capable of separate occupation. A temporary void where there is an intention to reoccupy, or a void where the empty portion cannot be separately occupied, will not take the empty accommodation outside the hereditament.

2-16   In this context it is to be noted that if a charging authority become aware that part of a hereditament is unoccupied but will remain so for a short time only, then under section 44(a) of the 1988 Act the authority have a discretionary power to ask the Valuation Officer to apportion the rateable value between the occupied and unoccupied parts.

It is important to appreciate that in considering the actual hereditament it is that hereditament as it exists at a particular date, that date being the date of the proposal, which is to be considered. The Valuation Officer, in relation to the current rating list, may be presumed to have dealt with the facts as they existed on April 1, 1995 (the date on which the current list became operative), but in any challenge with regard to an assessment a proposal must be made. The date of this proposal then becomes the material date relative to which the facts must be ascertained.

A property which is divided by a billing area boundary will, all other things being equal, be assessed by the Valuation Officer as a single hereditament and the rateable value will then be inserted in the rating list of the billing area containing the larger proportion by value of the hereditament.

The hereditament also has to be considered exactly as it stands *rebus sic stantibus* and the meaning and effect of this qualification merits special attention.

REBUS SIC STANTIBUS

This principle is applicable to all properties and requires that the **2-17** premises must be valued in the condition, state and circumstances existing at the time of valuation. The basic rule was expounded by Lord Parmoor in a railway case where he ruled that: "The hereditament should be valued as it stands and as used and occupied when the assessment is made."

The following quotations from Scott L.J. in the *Robinson* case[10] aptly set out the legal requirements:

> "(1) The hereditament to be valued [...] is always the actual house or other property for the occupation of which the occupier is to be rated and that hereditament is to be valued as it in fact is *rebus sic stantibus*.
> (2)Whilst the tenant is hypothetical and the landlord who is to let to the tenant is necessarily also hypothetical, the hereditament is actual, namely the hereditament described in the valuation list with all its actualities. Two consequences follow. All the intrinsic advantages and disadvantages must be considered and weighed. It is just that particular hereditament which is supposed to be in the market with all its attractions for would-be tenants to whatever kind of human emotion or interest or sense of duty they may appeal—economic, social, aesthetic, political (for example, in order to perform a statutory duty)—and also with all its imperfections and drawbacks which may deter or reduce competition for it."

It should be noted that the principle of *rebus sic stantibus* extends **2-18** to rather more than the physical conditions, and if there are statutory restrictions affecting the hereditament these must be taken into account. Lord Buckmaster said in *Port of London Authority v. Orsett Union Assessment Committee*[11]:

> "The actual hereditament of which the hypothetical tenant is to be determined must be the particular hereditament as it stands with all its privileges, opportunities and disabilities, created or imposed by its natural position or by the artificial conditions of an Act of Parliament."

---

[10] *Robinson Bros (Brewers) v. Houghton and Chester-le-Street Assessment Committee* [1937] 2 K.B. 445.
[11] [1919] 1 K.B. 84; [1920] A.C. 273.

The principal of *rebus sic stantibus* also applies to the condition of the hereditament. Prior to 1990, this gave rise to a number of cases concerning the state of repair where the courts held that disrepair and lack of maintenance should be disregarded provided there was no inherent and irremediable defect in the structure. In extreme cases regard could be had to the actual state of repair where it was inconceivable that the hypothetical landlord would put in repair and maintain the property. Most of these cases concerned properties valued to gross value under the 1967 Act where it was clear that the hypothetical landlord was under no obligation to maintain and repair the property. Even so, it is submitted that the principles established equally apply to valuations based on the definition of rateable value where the repair obligation falls on the tenant. (See *Snowman v. McClean*.[12])

The *rebus sic stantibus* principle clearly also applies to the actual user of the hereditament and the particular effect this may have on the ultimate assessment is dealt with separately in paragraph 2–23.

THE HYPOTHETICAL TENANCY

2–19

Under the terms of the definition of rateable value a tenancy is envisaged and the hypothetical tenant is deemed to occupy the premises as a tenant from year to year, although in fact the property may be such that no tenant would take it on such a tenancy. As Ryde comments, referring to the decision of the House of Lords in *London County Council v. Erith & West Ham*[13]:

> "The effect of this decision of the House of Lords is that, even though it may be impossible in fact, and forbidden by law that the actual occupier should be a yearly tenant of the hereditament to be rated, still for the purpose of valuing that hereditament it must be supposed that the actual occupier is among the possible yearly tenants: and unless that supposition be made, most absurd anomalies result."

The nature of the tenancy envisaged is important, and in *R. v. South Staffordshire Water Works Co.*[14] it was held that "a tenant from year to year is to be considered as a tenant capable of enjoying the property for an indefinite time, having a tenancy which it is

---

[12] [1979] 251 E.G. 859.
[13] *London County Council v. Erith Parish (Churchwardens) and Dartford Union Assessment Committee* [1893] A.C. 562.
[14] [1885] 16 Q.B.D. 359.

expected will continue for more than a year but which is liable to be put to an end by notice." It is thus apparent that a reasonable prospect of the tenancy continuing may be assumed and the decision in *Humber Ltd. v. Jones and Rugby Rural District Council*[15] has made it clear that the implied lack of security of tenure cannot be claimed as a factor which would adversely affect the rent to be expected. Nevertheless, *Almond (V.O.) v. Ash Brothers and Heaton Ltd*[16] demonstrates that where there is an early prospect of disturbance owing to the exercise of its statutory powers by a local or other public authority, any effect this may have on annual value has to be reflected in the assessment.

In considering the hypothetical tenancy not only must the tenure **2–20** be considered but also the hypothetical parties to this suppositional transaction. The tenancy is an assumption and the fact that premises are owner occupied is immaterial. All possible occupiers, including the actual occupier, may be taken into account. If the hereditament is such that occupation is by the public at large or dedicated to the public in perpetuity it is said to be "struck with sterility" and in such a case it is impossible to conceive a hypothetical tenancy or any parties thereto. In some cases, *e.g.* sewage disposal works, the only possible tenant is a public authority, and although it may make no profit from its obligations, it would be prepared to pay a rent to discharge its obligations. As well as a tenant a landlord must be envisaged and it should be borne in mind that he will have capital sunk in the property. He may be forced by circumstances to accept a very low rental which represents a very small return on his capital but cases giving rise to a nil assessment are rare,[17] even in circumstances where hypothetical tenants are hard to envisage. The following extract from a decision of the Lands Tribunal[17a] makes particular reference to the parties and the part they play in the "make-up" of the hypothetical tenancy:

> "Perhaps the most practical form in which the matter can be put is that the gross value in the present case should represent the rent which a farmer of Pigeon House Farm could reasonably expect to pay for the house rather than fail to obtain it and should also represent the rent which an owner of the house could reasonably be expected to accept for it rather than keep it vacant, in other words the gross value should represent the rent at which the farmer and hypothetical owner would be likely to come to terms."

---

[15] [1959] 5 R.R.C. 23.
[16] V.O. [1967] 3 All E.R. 952.
[17] But see *British Transport Commission v. Hingley and Grimsby C.B.C.* (1961) R.V.R. 150, and *Black v. Oliver (V.O.) [1978] Q.B. 870.*
[17a] *Cosker v. Newbigging* (1951) 44 R. & I.T. 411.

RENT WHICH MIGHT REASONABLY BE EXPECTED

2-21 This is the rent which the actual property will command when subject to the hypothetical tenancy. As noted above it is the rent at which the hypothetical tenant and hypothetical landlord would be likely to come to terms. As such it is possible to arrive at a nil valuation.[18] The rent actually paid is only prima facie evidence of the annual rental value, as it is not necessarily the rent that the hypothetical tenant might reasonably be expected to give. Thus, in the case of premises let on long lease granted many years previously it was held not conclusive where evidence was tendered to show that values had increased. Lord Buckmaster said in *Poplar v. Roberts*,[19] "The actual rent paid is no criterion unless indeed it happens to be the rent that the imaginary tenant might reasonably be expected to pay. Nevertheless the actual rent paid is most important evidence." Scott L.J. said in his judgment in the *Robinson* case[20]:

> "(1) Where the particular hereditament is let at what is plainly a rack rent, or where similar hereditaments in similar economic sites are so let, so that they are truly comparable, that evidence is the best evidence and for that reason is alone admissible; indirect evidence is excluded not because it is not logically relevant to the economic inquiry, but because it is not the best evidence.
> (2) Where such direct evidence is not available, for example, if the rents of other premises are shown to be not truly comparable, resort must necessarily be had to indirect evidence from which it is possible to estimate the probable rent which the hypothetical tenant would pay."

2-22 It will be noticed that in his judgment Scott L.J. refers to the rack rent, which may be interpreted as the best rent obtainable in all the circumstances. In further quotations from the same case he said:

> "(3) Every imaginable motive affecting human nature which makes people want a thing, whether a commodity or a hereditament, creates a demand and thus affects value.
> (4) The only conceivable purpose for which the metaphor of "market value" can properly be used in cases where there is in fact no market test of actual rents is to describe the real value (expressed in terms of the statutory test) which section 22 requires the assessment committee to ascertain. If this be so, then to speak of a hereditament possessing both a market value of £x and a higher value of £x plus £y due to a special factor of demand is a contradiction in terms. In my opinion the higher value is,

---

[18] *Roberts v. Poplar Assessment Committee* [1922] 1 K.B. 25, etc.
[19] *ibid.*
[20] See above.

in that event, the market value in the only sense in which that phrase can properly be used in such a case."

It is of interest that in *Bruce v. Howard*[21] the Lands Tribunal reiterated that it had to determine "the rent which might reasonably be expected" for the subject property, as evidenced by actual letting transactions, and not a "reasonable rent," for on this basis there would be many varied opinions as to the correct answer.

In determining the rental value, the use to which the hereditament is put should be considered, as this may have a fundamental affect on the basis of assessment and/or upon the quantum of the rent which might be expected.

THE EFFECT OF USER UPON ASSESSMENT

The actual use of the hereditament is one of the relevant facts which **2–23** must be taken into account and it may have an important bearing on the value for rating purposes. However the actual (as opposed to the potential) trade, will have no direct bearing and restrictive covenants as to the use of a building should be ignored. These principles can be illustrated by the case of *Rawlinson v. Pritchard*,[22] which concerned a parade of local authority shops which had been let by tender, each shop being subject to restrictive covenants limiting its use to one particular trade in order to obtain monopoly rents. The rents so obtained varied considerably for identical shops restricted to differing trades. Principally for these reasons the Lands Tribunal felt obliged largely to disregard the rental evidence concerned.

When dealing with problems of user, where no special statutory provisions are invoked, the first and most important question is: Can the property be utilised for alternative purposes without structural alterations? If it can be so utilised, then the rents which would be obtainable for the premises "vacant and to let" can be taken into account.[23] Thus, for example, in *Hanger Motor Co. (Birmingham) Ltd v. Almond*,[24] the Lands Tribunal decided on the facts of that case that shops and motor-car showrooms in the same street must be valued on a common basis. Similarly, in *Allen's (Plymouth) Ltd v. Blackman*,[25] the assessment of a repair workshop was held to be the rent it would

---

[21] (1964) R.V.R. 381; (64) R.A. 139; 114 L.J. 410, 190 E.G. 897; [1964] J.P.L. 557.

[22] *Rawlinson (WA) & Co. v. Pritchard (V.O.)* (1958) 4 R.R.C. 178, 52 R. & I.T. 182, (1959) J.P.L. 129.

[23] See, for example, *Grand Lodge of Mark Master Masons v. Cane* (1957) 50 R. & I.T. 30.

[24] *Hanger Motor Co. (Birmingham) Ltd v. Almond (V.O.)* (1959) 6 R.R.C. 60.

[25] *Allen's (Plymouth) Ltd v. Blackman (V.O.)* (1955) 48 R. & I.T. 601.

command if available on the market for any purpose within the planning use classes and planning restrictions applicable.

2–24   On the other hand where a property can only be utilised for one purpose, and no other would be possible without structural alterations,[26] however slight those structural alterations might be, then it is the value of the property restricted to that one purpose which has to be found.

The second and more problematical question is: whether or not the actual use (that is, existing use under town and country planning enactments and regulations) can exercise a limit on the assessment where a better rent could admittedly be obtained for another use? Clearly, where the change in use is unlikely to be permitted the better rent must be excluded. Nevertheless, although the decision in *Allen's (Plymouth) Ltd v. Blackman*[27] points towards a more general limitation, in *Westbury v. Wiggins & Co. Ltd*,[28] a coal order office in a good retail position was valued as a shop, notwithstanding that planning consent for change of use from office to shop would probably have been necessary.

MODE OR CATEGORY OF OCCUPATION

2–25   The question as to whether *rebus sic stantibus* should also apply to the way in which a property is used is one that has been before the Lands Tribunal several times. It has long been settled that the valuer should look at broad categories of use, so that a shop is valued as a shop, but not as a specific type of shop. It has also been argued that changes of use should be assumed in cases where such changes would result in higher assessment and would not involve structural alterations. Following *Jeremy v. Jones (V.O.)*,[29] it is clear that changes of use may be assumed only if no structural alteration is necessary, if there are no problems in obtaining planning permission and if there is clear evidence of demand for the premises in the new use.

Leading cases on this difficult principle include *Fir Mill v. Royton*[30] and *Midland Bank v. Lanham (V.O.)*.[31] The latter case establishing

---

[26] See, for example, *Manchester Tennis and Racquet Club v. Castle* (1960) 53 R. & I.T. 186.

[27] *Allen's (Plymouth) Ltd v. Blackman (V.O.)* (1955) 48 R. & I.T. 601.

[28] *Westbury (V.O.) v. Wiggins & Co. Ltd* (1959) 5 R.R.C. 107, 52 R. & I.T. 469, 174 E.G. 235.

[29] (1982) R.V.R. 225, 261 E.G. 161, [1982] J.P.L. 455.

[30] *Fir Mill Ltd v. Royton U.D.C. and Jones (V.O.)* (1960) 7 R.R.C. 171, 53 R. & I.T. 389, 175 E.G. 1029.

[31] [1978] R.A. 1, 246 E.G. 1017, 1117.

the principle that alternative uses could be taken into account provided they are in the same mode or category, that demand exists from competing bidders, that planning consent for the alternative use might reasonably be expected to be forthcoming.

OTHER MATTERS

The statutory definition of rateable value envisages a tenancy **2-26** whereby the hypothetical tenant undertakes to pay the usual tenant's rates and taxes. These will include the uniform business rate, tenants drainage rate, water rate and other rates. The definition of rateable value assumes that the tenant is responsible for all repairs and maintenance. If this is not the case then it will be necessary to adjust and reduce the actual rent to bring it into line with the definition.

Particular problems arise in the case of blocks of offices in separate occupation where the repair of common parts such as lifts and staircases is undertaken by the landlord and subject to a service charge levied on the tenant in addition to rent. However, it seems reasonable to assume that these will be taken into account by the tenant in arriving at the rent to be paid.

3

Liability for Rates

INTRODUCTION

3-01 It has been seen that rates are primarily a charge on occupation and with some exceptions the charge is payable by the occupier of the hereditament. This chapter considers the nature of rateable occupation and other matters concerning who is liable for the payment of rates. Rateable occupation is not defined in rating legislation but its precise meaning can be determined by reference to case law.

RATEABLE OCCUPATION

3-02 As has already been indicated, rates are primarily levied in respect of the beneficial occupation of land, buildings, or certain types of incorporeal hereditaments and, as will be explained, empty rates can now be levied on empty properties in certain circumstances. There is no statutory definition of occupier, and reference is necessary to case law. In the principal case on beneficial occupation, concerned with the assessment of contractors' buildings on a building site, the Court of Appeal[1] considered that there were four necessary ingredients in rateable occupation:

(1) actual occupation;
(2) exclusive occupation for the particular purposes of the occupier;
(3) the occupation must be of some benefit to the occupier;
(4) the occupation must not be too transient.

---

[1] *Laing (John) & Son v. Kingswood Assessment Area Assessment Committee* [1948] 2 K.B. 116.

Actual occupation

Liability as an occupier does not depend upon the title or right to **3–03** occupy. A helpful definition of this was given by Lush J. in *R. v. St Pancras Assessment Committee*[2]:

> "It is not easy to give an accurate and exhaustive definition of the word "occupier". Occupation includes possession as its primary element, but it also includes something more. Legal possession does not of itself constitute an occupation. The owner of a vacant house is in possession, and may bring an action for trespass against anyone who invades it, but as long as he leaves it vacant, he is not rateable for it as an occupier. If, however, he furnishes it, and keeps it ready for habitation whenever he pleases to go to it, he is an occupier, though he may not reside in it one day in a year."

On the other hand, a person who, without having any title, takes actual possession of a house or piece of land, whether by leave of the owner or against his will, is the occupier of it.[3]

Beneficial occupation

The occupation to be rateable must be of value. However, the fact **3–04** that an occupier derives no pecuniary profits does not mean that there is no beneficial occupation. Thus, a school board were held to be liable in the case of school premises, although they were the only possible tenant and made no profit.[4] Similarly, the London County Council were held to be rateable in respect of sewage works.[5] It is clear in the case of properties where, for example, a local authority is the only possible occupier that the authority would be prepared to pay a rent in order to secure premises so as to be able to discharge its statutory obligations.

Permanence

Another element, however, besides actual possession of the land, is **3–05** necessary to constitute the kind of occupation which the 1988 Act contemplates and that is permanence. An itinerant showman who erects a temporary structure for his performances may be in exclusive actual possession, and may with strict grammatical propriety, be said

---

[2] [1877] 2 Q.B. 581.
[3] *Southwark L.B.C. v. Briant Colour Printing Co. Ltd* (1977) 244 E.G. 379.
[4] *R. v. School Board for London* (1886) 17 Q.B.D. 738.
[5] *London County Council v. Erith Parish (Churchwardens) and Dartford Union Assessment Committee* [1893] A.C. 562.

25

to occupy the ground on which his structure is placed, but it is clear that his occupation will not bring him within the scope of the Act so as to render him liable to rates. However, in certain circumstances where the owner derives a regular benefit from the showman's use of his land, the owner himself may incur a liability for rates.

The origin of the rule excluding transient occupiers from liability is almost certainly historical, for, quite apart from the obvious impracticability of endeavouring to assess such occupations and collect rates from the parties concerned, the old poor rate was not made day by day, or week by week, but for months in advance. It would therefore have been absurd to have held that a person, who came into a parish with the intention to remain there a few days or a week only, should incur a liability to maintain the poor for the next six months. The *Laing* case concerned temporary contractors' huts erected by the contractors and occupied for a considerable period; these were held to be in the rateable occupation of the contractors.

3-06   A further case involving contractors' buildings has been decided in the House of Lords approving an assessment in somewhat similar circumstances. In this case it was held that a structure placed upon another's land, even though it remained in law, a chattel and as such the property of the person who placed it on the land could form a rateable hereditament with the land.[6] This principle has been extended to permanently occupied caravans which had remained in position for over a year and were connected with electricity and to a soakaway pipe.[7] Likewise the removal of material from an abandoned colliery tip has given rise to a rateable occupation.[8]

Premises may still be fully rateable although temporarily disused. Thus, in *Southend v. White*,[9] a seaside shop was closed each year during the winter months and the owner held to be rateable for the whole period. It is obvious that in such a case the tenant taking the premises on a yearly rent fixes that rent knowing that he will close during the out-of-season months and the amount fixed is lower on this account. As rates are levied on the yearly rental value it is clear the tenant would get the benefit twice over were he to be rated only for the summer months. Again, in *R. v. Melladew*[10] a warehouseman, finding he had no goods to store in one of his warehouses, closed it and cut off the water supply. As the warehouseman would have reopened the warehouse had he at any time received sufficient custom to warrant it, he was held liable for rates (but see *Bexley*

---

[6] *London County Council v. Wilkins* [1956] 3 W.L.R.
[7] *Field Place Caravan Park Ltd v. Harding* [1966] 2 Q.B. 484; [1966] 2 W.L.R.
[8] *Ryan Industrial Fuels Ltd v. Morgan* [1965] 1 W.L.R. 1347.
[9] *Southend v. White* (1900) 65 J.P. 7.
[10] [1907] 7 K.B. 192.

Congregational Church (Treasurer) v. Bexley London Borough Council).[11] In the case of *Associated Cinema Properties Ltd v. Hampstead Borough Council*[12] housing accommodation was taken so as to be available as emergency offices in the event of the firm's offices being destroyed by enemy action. The premises were never used and although rent was paid it was held there was no beneficial occupation.

Where an owner only occupies a portion of a hereditament he is **3–07** liable for rates on the whole, but if he lets a portion of the premises and makes no use of the remainder he cannot be rated for the whole,[13] as there would be two separately rateable hereditaments, one occupied and one void. Again, where an owner leaves no chattels on the premises but puts in a caretaker to protect the premises, the caretaker is a servant of the owner and cannot be rated. Where, however, the caretaker resides on the premises for the purpose of looking after other property belonging to the owner, the owner is in beneficial occupation and may be rated.

It must be stressed that most of the decided cases as to whether or not there is actual occupation have turned on the intentions of the parties. A mere intention to occupy does not constitute occupation, but once occupation has occurred an intention to reoccupy can, in certain circumstances, be construed as continuing occupation. Likewise if any chattels are left or put on the hereditament this may constitute occupation even if the items are of little value.[14] Items abandoned on the premises will not, however, give rise to rateability.[15]

LIABILITY OF OWNER FOR RATES

Whilst in general the occupier is liable for the payment of rates, in **3–08** certain cases the owner may be rated. These cases will be considered briefly.

---

[11] [1972] 2 Q.B. 222.
[12] [1944] K.B. 412.
[13] *Phillips & Ystradgynlais R.A.* (1936) 24 R. & I.T. 27.
[14] *Appleton v. Westminster Corporation* [1963] R.A. 169; [1963] R.V.R. 374.
[15] *London County Council v. Hackney Borough Council* (1928) 2 K.B. 588.

Rating of empty properties

3–09 Adoptive powers enabling local authorities to charge "half rates" on "owners" of unoccupied buildings were first introduced in 1966. The current provisions distinguish between existing and new empty property.

(a) Unoccupied property

Liability for empty rate will commence after the hereditament concerned has been unoccupied for a continuous period exceeding three months. There are complex provisions to prevent the avoidance of this empty rate by short periods (of less than six weeks) of intermittent occupation or, in the case of new or altered properties, by postponing the completion of the works at a point where the building (which includes part of a building) could not be regarded as capable of occupation but where in the opinion of the billing authority it can reasonably be expected to be completed within three months. In the last mentioned type of case, and where new buildings are regarded as completed, the billing authority have powers to serve notices specifying the date on which the property is to be regarded as completed and, subject to the owner's right of appeal to the county court, the unoccupied period will start to run from that date.

3–10   For the purpose of these provisions, the owner of the property is that person who is entitled to immediate possession. Such owners are given similar rights as occupiers to deal with proposals, assessments, and rateable values certified by the Valuation Officer, in those cases where empty rate may be charged.

Under section 65(1) of the 1988 Act, all owners of unoccupied hereditaments that are shown in the local non-domestic rating list are liable to be rated provided the hereditament is within one of the prescribed descriptions contained within the Non-Domestic Rating (Unoccupied Property) Regulations 1989[16]:

> **"Property liable for unoccupied property rates**
> 2.—(1) The class of non-domestic hereditaments prescribed for the purposes of section 45(1) of the Act consists of all relevant non-domestic hereditaments to which none of the conditions in paragraph (2) applies.
>
> (2) The conditions are that:
>
> > (a) the whole hereditament has, subject to paragraph (3), been unoccupied for a continuous period not exceeding three months;

---

[16] S.I. 1989 No. 2261.

(b) its owner is prohibited by law from occupying it or allowing it to be occupied;

(c) it is kept vacant by reason of action taken by or on behalf of the Crown or any local or public authority with a view to prohibiting the occupation of the hereditament or to acquiring it;

(d) it is the subject of a building preservation notice as defined by section 58 of the Town and Country Planning Act 1971 or is included in a list compiled under section 54 of that Act;

(e) it is included in the Schedule of monuments compiled under section 1 of the Ancient Monuments and Archaeological Areas Act 1979;

(f) it is a qualifying industrial hereditament; ·

(g) its rateable value is less than £1,000;

(h) the owner is entitled to possession only in his capacity as the personal representative of a deceased person;

(i) there subsists in respect of the owner's estate a bankruptcy order within the meaning of Parts VIII to XI of the Insolvency Act 1986;

(j) the owner is entitled to possession of the hereditament in his capacity as trustee under a deed of arrangement to which the Deeds of Arrangement Act 1914 applies;

(k) the owner is a company which is subject to a winding-up order made under the Insolvency Act 1986 or which is being wound up voluntarily under that Act;

(l) the owner is entitled to possession of the hereditament in his capacity as liquidator by virtue of an order made under section 112 or section 145 of the Insolvency Act 1986."

S.I. 1989 No. 2261 goes on to provide a definition of "relevant **3-11** non-domestic hereditament" and "qualifying industrial hereditament" the latter clearly includes buildings used for storage but not retail properties.

It also makes provision to counter possible avoidance by periodic occupation whereby short periods of occupation are ignored for the purposes of empty rating.

(b) New unoccupied buildings

In respect of new buildings which are unoccupied, section 46A and Schedule 4A to the 1988 Act provides a mechanism for determining the day on which the hereditament is deemed to be completed, the completion notice. Where a completion notice has been served the Valuation Officer will specify the day on which the hereditament is to be treated as being complete and it must then be entered in the rating list. The owner has a right of appeal against the completion notice.

The completion notice provisions ensure that rates cannot be avoided by leaving a new building partially incomplete for an indefinite period.

(c) Other cases

In certain cases the owner of a right which forms a hereditament can be treated as the occupier for rating purposes. These include the right to use land for exhibiting advertisements and sporting rights, (the Local Government Finance Act 1988, s.65(8) & (9)). In certain circumstances, the owner of multiple moorings can be treated as the occupier (The Non-Domestic (Multiple Moorings) Regulations, 1991).[17]

RATE COLLECTION GENERALLY

3–12 Having considered in the preceding paragraphs the circumstances in which a rateable occupation arises, and the party liable for rates as a result, it is only fair to add that the ratepayer's greatest concern is: "How much will I have to pay?"

As will have been seen from Chapter 1, a rateable value has to be ascertained for each individual rateable hereditament. Assuming occupation for a full rate year, *i.e.* from April 1 to following March 31, the occupiers' rate liability will be:

$$\text{Rateable Value} \times \text{Uniform Business Rate}$$

The Uniform Business Rate legislation allows for the calculation of rate liability on a daily basis. Section 54(4) of the 1988 Act provides that the chargeable amount for each chargeable day is calculated by the formula:

$$\frac{A \times B}{C}$$

where A is the rateable value in the list, B is the non-domestic rating multiplier and C is the number of days in the financial year.

The multiplier is determined nationally by the Secretary of State. There are separate multipliers for England, Wales and Scotland. The rate is collected by each charging authority and is pooled centrally before being redistributed to each authority, roughly in proportion to its population. The multipliers are determined each year by allowing for a maximum increase year on year which is determined by

---

[17] S.I. 1992 No. 557.

reference to the Retail Price Index for the September of the preceding year. (Schedule 7 to the Local Government Finance Act, 1988).

One of the consequences of the national collection and redistribution of the Uniform Business Rate is the reduction in role of the local authority which, as billing authority now simply administers the collection of the rate.

MISCELLANEOUS RELIEFS

(a) Transitional relief

To reduce the impact of the introduction of the Uniform Business **3-13** Rate following the revaluation in 1990, special transitional arrangements were introduced for the period 1990–1995 by Schedule 7A to the 1988 Act and subsequent statutory instruments. The arrangements whilst straightforward in principle, were highly complex in their application due to the wide range of circumstances that can arise, such as splits and mergers and combinations of these. This section sets out the basic principles and outlines the changes made for the 1995 revaluation, but will not consider their detailed application.

The original transitional arrangements were due to cease in 1995 but it was clear for some time before that date that the Government would see fit to extend the arrangements into the 1995 valuation list as announced in the Department of the Environment consultation paper and confirmed in the budget in November 1994.

The transitional provisions are important because in many cases they will have a significant impact on the actual liability of occupiers. Rating surveyors must always have regard to these provisions when advising clients. Their complexity is such that most major rating consultants, and of course billing authorities, use specialist computer software to deal with the impact of the provisions as applied in more complex circumstances.

Broadly speaking, the Government proposals for the 1995 revaluation follow the lines of the transitional arrangements for the 1990 list.

The only requirement for a hereditament to qualify for transitional relief is that the hereditament has a rateable value shown in a local list on both March 31, 1995 and April 1, 1995. Thus, property newly constructed after April 1, 1995 will not attract transitional relief. Unlike the 1990 regulations however, transitional protection will not be lost following a change of occupier. It should also be noted that the *de minimis* threshold on rateable values (£500) introduced in 1990 has now been dispensed with.

Acknowledging that the impact of the revaluation is likely to be more significant for small businesses, the distinction between large and small hereditaments is retained:

	Small	Large
Greater London	below RV £15,000	RV £15,000 and above
Outside London	below RV £10,000	RV £10,000 and above

The broad principle of transition is that increases and decreases in liability will be limited to percentages set by the Government in each year. These adjustments will also take into account inflation as measured by the yearly increase in the RPI to September of the previous year. The adjustments for increases in liability for 1995/6 have been confirmed at 10 per cent in real terms for large properties and 7.5 per cent for small properties. Decreases will be limited to 5 per cent in real terms and 10 per cent for small properties.

Calculation

3–14 Transition sets an annual limit on increases and reductions in rate bills by comparing rate bills payable in the transitional period with those of the previous year. This operates by determining a notional chargeable amount (NCA) which can be compared with a base liability (BL) for the previous financial year.

Billing authorities are required to compare the full liability each year with the liability for the previous year. However, because of changes in liability which may occur during the year and further complications such as reliefs, it is impractical to compare actual liabilities, and so the measure of comparison is the NCA.

The NCA for 1995/6 is calculated by reference to the rateable value shown for the first day of the new list and this is compared with the notional 1994/5 rates bill, the base liability or BL.

Properties which are not in transition under the 1990 scheme on March 31, 1995 have a baseline which is calculated by reference to the rateable value shown in the 1990 list for that day. Properties which are still in transition have a baseline based on the transitional rate bill for that day, ignoring any charitable or other reliefs. Where the transitional bill for March 31 is altered following an outstanding appeal, the transitional bill for 1995/6 needs to be redetermined by reference to the new figure.

The BL and NCA figures are now quoted as annual amounts.

The transitional limit

This is the maximum amount by which the year on year bills can be increased or reduced and is determined by a prescribed percentage plus an allowance for inflation based on the increase in the retail price index to September in the year preceding the year for the bill to be determined. These percentage adjustments for the RPI ratio are rounded to the nearest 0.1 per cent.

Transitional chargeable amount

The transitional limit is found by multiplying the base liability by **3-15** the appropriate percentage uplift factor which is known as the appropriate fraction, AF. If this is less than the notional chargeable amount, the transitional chargeable amount will then be the transitional limit unless the property is subject to relief. Relief is applied to the limited notional bill to find the actual amount payable.

For years after 1995/6, the transitional limit will be calculated by applying the uplift factor to the transitional limit for the previous year so that the limit for one year becomes the base liability for the next. The process continues until the limit equals or exceeds the notional chargeable amount.

Simple example

The basic principles can be illustrated by the case of a small property in upwards transition. The rateable value on revaluation has increased from £3000 to £5000. It is assumed that inflation for the year to September 1994 is 2.4 per cent.

Transition	
UBR 94/5	0.423
UBR 95/6	0.432
Limit	1.075
Inflation	1.024

Normal Upwards	
RV 4/95	5000
RV 3/95	3000
NCA	2160
BL	1269
TL	1394.63
RL	1394.63

- The notional chargeable amount (NCA) for 1995/6 is £5000 × 43.2p = £2160.
- The base liability (BL) is £3000 × 42.3p = £1269.
- The appropriate Fraction (AF) is 1.075 (7.5 per cent increase) +0.024 (2.4 per cent inflation) =1.099 (9.9 per cent).
- The transitional limit (BL × AF) is £1269 × 1.099 = £1394.63.
- As the notional chargeable amount exceeds the transitional limit, the actual liability will be the transitional limit of £1394.63.

Special circumstances

This is, however, only the simplest of circumstances and there are a wide range of situations which are far from straightforward. It is not appropriate to cover these in detail in a text of this nature and it is likely that examples of the detailed calculations involved will be published by the major rating specialists. Attention is simply drawn **3–16** to those circumstances which will require special consideration.

• Changes In Initial Rateable Value

Where the April 1, 1995 rateable value changes as a result of an appeal following a material change of circumstances on or after that date the NCA will need to be recalculated and transitional limit redefined.

• Reductions After April 1, 1995

The NCA is calculated on the basis of a value certified by the Valuation Officer when the rateable value changes from April 1, 1995 as a result of a material change in circumstances.

• Splits Mergers And Reorganisation

Where the rateable value is split or where mergers occur, the notional transitional liability is found by apportioning the total liability on the day before the change.

• Mineral Hereditaments

The rate of extraction at April 1, 1995 is used to certify the notional baseline rateable value as if the same rate applied on March 31, 1995.

• Composite Hereditaments

Composite hereditaments continue to be treated as under the 1990 scheme.

Other special circumstances include:

- Statutory transfers/Local authority boundary changes
- Partly occupied properties
- Proposals as to rateable values in old lists
- Special authority (City of Westminster)
- Central lists

As a final warning then, all rating surveyors advising clients as to their liability need to be aware of the effect of transition and should always check the position with great care when dealing with a property in transition. Indeed, there can be circumstances where the backdating of an agreed reduction can actually be of no benefit to the ratepayer, even resulting in an increase in liability, as a consequence of transition.

(b) Discretionary relief

One of the reliefs from rating considered in Chapter 4 is relief for **3-17** charities. Charging authorities have a further wider discretion to provide partial relief from rating for institutions which though not necessarily charities, occupy premises for a range of non-profit making purposes. This discretionary relief can be applied to any organisation whose main objects are charitable or otherwise philanthropic, religious, concerned with education, social welfare, science, literature or the fine arts.

(c) Remission of liability

Finally, charging authorities have the power to reduce or remit the amount of rates payable in cases of hardship.

4

Total and Partial Exemptions from Rating

4-01 Liability to rates extended at one time to all property, real and personal, but with the passing of the Poor Rate Exemption Act 1840 the rating of personal property was finally abolished and now, apart from certain exceptions, *i.e.* incorporeal hereditaments such as sporting rights, advertising rights, etc., only real property is subject to assessment for rating purposes.

There are exceptions to the general rule that all property, whether freehold or leasehold, is rateable, and the various total and partial exemptions provided are set out in Schedule 5 to the 1988 Act and considered below.

Agricultural premises

4-02 Under Schedule 5.1 to the 1988 Act "A hereditament is exempt to the extent that it consists of any of the following—(a) agricultural land; (b) agricultural buildings. Agricultural land is defined in Schedule 5.2 as:

  (1) (a) land used as arable, meadow or pasture ground only,
       (b) land used for a plantation or a wood or for the growth of saleable underwood,
       (c) land exceeding 0.10 hectare and used for the purposes of poultry farming,
       (d) anything which consists of a market garden, nursery ground, orchard or allotment (which here includes an allotment garden within the meaning of the Allotments Act 1922), or
       (e) land occupied with, and used solely in connection with the use of, a building which (or buildings each of which) is an agricultural building by virtue of paragraph 4, 5, 6 or 7 below.

36

(2) But agricultural land does not include:

(a) land occupied together with a house as a park,
(b) gardens (other than market gardens),
(c) pleasure grounds,
(d) land used mainly or exclusively for purposes of sport or recreation, or
(e) land used as a racecourse."

The interpretation of these terms follows the general argument and precedents set by court decision brought under earlier legislation. Whether or not land is used as "arable meadow or pasture ground only" is, of course, a question of fact. Difficulty, however, arises over the inclusion of the word "only" in the definition and where there is occasional use for other purposes each case must be considered on its merits. The legal principle of *deminimis non curat lex* will operate where there is very limited user for other purposes. Where land was used for show purposes on one day a year it was held that no assessment was justified.[1] Land used for the exercising of racehorses between Christmas and March, such user not conflicting in any marked degree with other agricultural use, was held by the High Court to be exempt.[2] On the other hand a field used for motorcycle racing on two or four afternoons a year was held to be rateable because the receipts from this source far outweighed the agricultural value.[3]

Also excluded from the definition of agricultural land is land used mainly or exclusively for purposes of sport or recreation or land used as a racecourse. Land used as a golf course and also for grazing was refused exemption.[4] Similarly, some 29 and a half acres of land within the ring fence of a racecourse was held rateable by the Lands Tribunal, a decision subsequently upheld by the Court of Appeal.[5] On the other hand, land preserved as a grouse moor but also used extensively for hill farming operations was granted exemption by the Lands Tribunal.[6]

[1] *Honiton & District Agricultural Association v. Wonnacott* (1955) 48 R. & I.T. 589.
[2] *Jarvis and Dawson v. Cambridgeshire A.C.* (1938) 29 R. & I.T. 315. See also *Tattersalls Ltd v. Marlborough A.C.* (1930) 11 R. & I.T. 149. See also *Foster and Another v. Simpson (V.O.)* [1984] R.A. 85 (L.T.) where certain "Gallops" were held to be rateable, and *Hermans (V.O.) v. Whitsbury Farm and Stud Ltd* [1985] R.A. 54 (L.T.) where a stud farm was held to be rateable.
[3] *Wimborne and Cranborne R.D.C. v. East Dorset A.C.* (1940) 32 R. & I.T. 84, 404. See also *Eden (V.O.) v. Grass Ski Promotions Ltd* [1981] R.A. 7, L.T.
[4] *Abernant Hotel and Estate Co. Ltd v. Davies* (1954) 47 R. & I.T. 694.
[5] *Sandown Park Ltd v. Esher U.D.C.* (1952) 45 R. & I.T. 70 and 47 R. & I.T. 351.
[6] *Cutts v. Viscount Ingleby and Helmsley R.D.C.; Bell v. Viscount Ingleby and Stokesley R.D.C.* (1957) 50 R. & I.T. 269. See also *Meriden and Solihull A.C. v. Tyacke* (1950) 43 R. & I.T. 306; and *Fenwick v. Capstick and Weardale R.D.C.* (1956) 49 R. & I.T. 38.

The basis for this decision was that the predominant user was agricultural, the two uses did not conflict with one another and in fact the provision of gamekeepers also enhanced the value for agricultural purposes.

4-03 Yet another borderline use of land which is excluded from the definition is land occupied together with a house as a park. The Lands Tribunal considered the rating of a deer park of 126 acres attached to Powderham Castle and although the land was farmed as part of the owner-occupier's home farm, decided that it was rateable. It could not be regarded as other than a park in its popular sense and as defined in *The Oxford English Dictionary* and could not therefore be exempted as agricultural land.[7]

If a river flows through or adjoins farmland it has been held that the bed of the river forms part of the agricultural land which comprises the farm and thus any fishing rights may thereby be treated as exempt.[8] This is, however, not necessarily so, where the value of the fishing is substantial and the fishing rights are exercised by the farmer separately from the rights of agriculture.[9]

4-04 Under Schedule 5.10 a number of "fishing" hereditaments are exempt:

> "10. A hereditament is exempt to the extent that it consists of a right of fishing exercisable in a fishery regulated by an order which:
>
> > (a) is made under section 28(3) of the Salmon and Freshwater Fisheries Act 1975, and
> > (b) contains such provision as is mentioned in paragraph 1(a) of Schedule 3 to that Act (contributions imposed by water authorities).
>
> (2) A hereditament is exempt to the extent that it consists of a right of fishing exercisable in a fishery:
>
> > (a) which is regulated by the council constituted under section 6 of the Tweed Fisheries Act 1969, and
> > (b) as regards which a rate or assessment is levied under section 79 of the Tweed Fisheries Act 1857 or section 5 of the Tweed Fisheries Amendment Act 1859."

An allotment garden is defined in section 22 of the Allotments Act 1922 as: "an allotment not exceeding one quarter of an acre in extent which is wholly or mainly cultivated by the occupier for the

---

[7] *Earl of Devon v. Rees* (1951) 44 R. & I.T. 74.
[8] *Watkins v. Hertfordshire A.C.* (1935) 23 R. & I.T. 304.
[9] *Clay & Clay v. Newbiggin* (1956) 49 R. & I.T. 203.

production of vegetable or fruit crops for consumption by himself or his family."

Interpretation of other phrases used in Schedule 5.1 may require reference to cases decided under earlier legislation. The meaning of "land occupied with, ... , a building" is clarified by reference to paragraphs 4, 5, 6 or 7 set out below under agricultural buildings.

Agricultural buildings

The definition of agricultural building for exemption purposes is set **4–05** out in paragraphs 3 to 8 of Schedule 5.

"3. A building is an agricultural building if it is not a dwelling and

(a) it is occupied together with agricultural land and is used solely in connection with agricultural operations on the land, or
(b) it is or forms part of a market garden and is used solely in connection with agricultural operations at the market garden.

4.—(1) A building is an agricultural building if it is used solely in connection with agricultural operations carried on on agricultural land and sub-paragraph (2) or (3) below applies.
(2) This sub-paragraph applies if the building is occupied by the occupiers of all the land concerned.
(3) This sub-paragraph applies if the building is occupied by individuals each of whom is appointed by the occupiers of the land concerned to manage the use of the building and is

(a) an occupier of some of the land concerned, or
(b) a member of the board of directors or other governing body of a person who is both a body corporate and an occupier of the land concerned.

(4) This paragraph does not apply unless the number of occupiers of the land concerned is less than 25.
5.—(1) A building is an agricultural building if

(a) it is used for the keeping or breeding of livestock, or
(b) it is not a dwelling, it is occupied together with a building or buildings falling within paragraph (a) above, and it is used in connection with the operations carried on in that building or those buildings.

(2) Sub-paragraph (1)(a) above does not apply unless

(a) the building is solely used as there mentioned, or

39

(b) the building is occupied together with agricultural land and used also in connection with agricultural operations on that land, and that other use together with the use mentioned in sub-paragraph (1)(a) is its sole use.

(3) Sub-paragraph (1)(b) above does not apply unless

(a) the building is solely used as there mentioned, or
(b) the building is occupied also together with agricultural land and used also in connection with agricultural operations on that land, and that other use mentioned in sub-paragraph (1)(b) is its sole use.

(4) A building (the building in question) is not an agricultural building by virtue of this paragraph unless it is surrounded by or contiguous to an area of agricultural land which amounts to not less than two hectares.
(5) In deciding for the purposes of sub-paragraph (4) above whether an area is agricultural land and what is its size, the following shall be disregarded:

(a) any road, watercourse or railway (which here includes the former site of a railway from which railway lines have been removed),
(b) any agricultural building other than the building in question,
(c) any building occupied together with the building in question.

6.—(1) A building is an agricultural building if it is not a dwelling, is occupied by a person keeping bees, and is used solely in connection with the keeping of those bees.
(2) Sub-paragraphs (4) and (5) of paragraph 5 above apply for the purposes of this paragraph as for those of that.
7.—(1) A building is an agricultural building if it is not a dwelling and

(a) it is used in connection with agricultural operations carried out on agricultural land, and
(b) it is occupied by a body corporate any of whose members are (together with the body) the occupiers of the land.

(2) A building is also an agricultural building if it is not a dwelling and

(a) it is used in connection with the operations carried on in a building which, or buildings each of which, is used for the keeping or breeding of livestock and is an agricultural building by virtue of paragraph 5 above, and

(b) sub-paragraph (3), (4) or (5) below applies as regards the building first mentioned in this sub-paragraph (the building in question)."

Sub-paragraphs 3 to 8 of paragraph 7 clarify certain aspects of the meaning of "occupied" and "occupier" whilst paragraph 8 clarifies the construction of "agricultural land" and "agricultural building". Paragraph 8(5) defines "livestock" as including "any mammal or bird kept for the production of food or wool or for the purpose of its use in the farming of land".

These provisions remove much of the debate over factory farming processes such as poultry broiler houses: see for example, *Prior (V.O.) v. Sovereign Chickens Ltd.*[10] Most such buildings will now be classed as agricultural buildings if the various conditions in the Schedule are satisfied.

Fish farms

Fish farms are exempt under paragraph 9: **4–06**

> "9.—(1) A hereditament is exempt to the extent that it consists of any of the following:
>
> > (a) land used solely for or in connection with fish farming,
> > (b) buildings (other than dwellings) so used.
>
> (2) In determining whether land or a building used for or in connection with fish farming is solely so used, no account shall be taken of any time during which it is used in any other way, if that time does not amount to a substantial part of the time during which the land or building is used.
> (3) 'Building' includes a separate part of a building.
> (4) 'Fish farming' means the breeding or rearing of fish, or the cultivation of shellfish, for the purpose of (or for purposes which include) transferring them to other waters or producing food for human consumption.
> (5) 'Shellfish' includes crustaceans and molluscs of any description."

Privileged property

This may be briefly described as property occupied by persons or **4–07** organisations entitled to diplomatic privilege or immunity. Rates cannot be recovered from ambassadors or their servants in respect of property occupied by them by virtue of the Diplomatic Privileges Act 1708, see also Diplomatic Privileges Act 1964 and Diplomatic and other Privileges Act 1971; the premises are therefore treated as exempt. Diplomatic immunity is now extended to international organisations (such as United Nations Organisation, North Atlantic Treaty Organisation, etc.) by virtue of the International Organisations (Immunities and Privileges) Act 1950. Diplomatic immunity

---

[10] [1984] R.A. 73 (C.A.).

is now also extended to Commonwealth countries and the Republic of Ireland by the Diplomatic Immunities (Commonwealth Countries and Republic of Ireland) Act 1952. In all these cases where properties are treated as exempt, a contribution in lieu of rates will be paid by the Treasury as in the case of Crown occupation.[11]

Charitable and other organisations

4–08 Relief from Rating in respect of premises occupied by charities is covered by sections 43 and 47 of the 1988 Act. Section 43 deals with mandatory relief which is given as a right and section 47 deals with discretionary relief.

The effect of section 43 is to reduce the chargeable amount per chargeable day to one-fifth where the ratepayer is a charity or are the trustees of a charity and the hereditament is used wholly or mainly for charitable purposes. This amounts to relief of 80 per cent of rates payable.

Section 47 allows a charging authority to give relief of up to 100 per cent provided "a decision of the charging authority concerned operates to the effect that this section applies as regards the hereditament concerned." This discretionary power applies where the conditions in section 47 are met namely that one or more of the following applies:

> "the ratepayer is a charity or trustees for a charity, and the hereditament is wholly or mainly used for charitable purposes . . . ;"

> "the hereditament is not an excepted hereditament, and all or part of it is occupied for the purposes of one or more institutions or other organisations none of which is established or conducted for profit and each of whose main objects are charitable or are otherwise philanthropic or religious or concerned with education, social welfare, science, literature or the fine arts;"

> "the hereditament is not an excepted hereditament, it is wholly or mainly used for purposes of recreation, and all or part of its is occupied for the purposes of a club, society or other organisation not established or conducted for profit."

These charitable reliefs extend to shops used for fund raising

---

[11] See para. 4–11.

purposes by charitable organisations. The hereditaments are not exempt it is the ratepayers who enjoy relief.[12]

Churches and chapels

The exemption of places of public religious worship is covered in **4–09** paragraph 11 of Schedule 5:

> "11.—(1) A hereditament is exempt to the extent that it consists of any of the following:
>
> > (a) a place of public religious worship which belongs to the Church of England or the Church in Wales (within the meaning of the Welsh Church Act 1914) or is for the time being certified as required by law as a place of religious worship;
> > (b) a church hall, chapel hall or similar building used in connection with a place falling within paragraph (a) above for the purposes of the organisation responsible for the conduct of public religious worship in that place.
>
> (2) A hereditament is exempt to the extent that it:
>
> > (a) is occupied by an organisation responsible for the conduct of public religious worship in a place falling within sub-paragraph (1)(a) above, and
> > (b) is used for carrying out administrative or other activities relating to the organisation of the conduct of public religious worship in such a place."

This exemption only applies in respect of the purposes specified, if the hereditament is used for purposes other than public religious worship a liability will arise.

OTHER EXEMPTIONS

Schedule 5 exempts a number of other organisations or classes of **4–10** hereditaments specifically:

- Certain property of Trinity House such as lighthouses, buoys, beacons.
- Sewers and accessories to a sewer such as manholes, pumps, within the meaning given by section 343 of the Public Health Act 1936.

---

[12] See also Chap. 3.

- Land, structures and appliances occupied or maintained by a Drainage authority as defined by the Land Drainage Act 1976.
- Parks which have "been provided by, or is under the management of a relevant authority ... and is available for free and unrestricted use by members of the public."
- Hereditaments "intended to be occupied or used solely for the purpose of affording protection in the event of hostile attack from the air ..."
- Hereditaments in enterprise zones described as such under Schedule 32 to the Local Government, Planning and Land Act 1980. These enjoy a 10 year rate free period. This exemption in many cases is now elapsing.
- Swinging moorings.
- Certain hereditaments used wholly for the benefit of the disabled.

Crown occupation

4–11 It is a principle of law that unless the crown is specifically mentioned it is not bound by statute. Therefore, as the Crown is not mentioned in the Act of 1601, occupation by the Crown has been deemed not rateable, and this was upheld in *Jones v. Mersey Docks*.[13] Since then, it has been provided by section 64(3) of the Rating and Valuation Act 1925 (section 37 of the 1967 Act) that no gross value is to be determined and entered in the valuation list in respect of properties in Crown occupation.

The 1988 Act has made no material changes to the rules relating to occupation by the Crown.

4–12 *Ryde on Rating* gives the following five propositions as having been established:

> "(1) The Crown, not being named in the Statute of Elizabeth, is not bound by it.
> (2) No rate can be imposed in respect of property in the occupation of the crown by itself or by its servants, whose occupation amounts to the occupation of the Crown.
> (3) No rate can be imposed in respect of property occupied by persons who occupy for public purposes which are required and created by the government of the country, and are, according to the theory of the constitution, administered by the Crown.
> (4) The exemption attaches although the property can be used for purposes of imperial government in a particular locality only, and although it can be provided and maintained by funds raised by local rates.

---

[13] [1865] 11 H.L. Cas. 443.

(5) Property occupied for 'public purposes' is not exempt, unless it comes within the foregoing propositions."

The exemption applies to all premises occupied for the purposes of **4–13** the general administration of the country and which is a public purpose of the imperial government as distinct from a public purpose or duty of a local government authority. Thus, military purposes, administration of the law and other general administration of the country being positive functions of the imperial government give rise to the exemption but when the hereditament is used for the administration of justice, police purposes or other Crown purposes and is maintained by a local authority the hereditament must be entered in the list (Schedule 64).

In practice the Treasury will in most cases make a contribution in lieu of rates (Schedule 59).

Hospitals and other premises transferred to the State under the National Health Service Acts no longer rank as Crown property and are therefore valued in the normal way.

Premises occupied by visiting armed forces are by virtue of the Visiting Forces Act 1952 and the Visiting Forces (Application of Law) Order 1954 to be treated as premises occupied by the Crown. A normal contribution in lieu of rates is paid in these cases.

Property occupied by the Atomic Energy Commission, by virtue of the Atomic Energy Authority Act 1954, is regarded as occupied by or on behalf of the Crown. Again a contribution in lieu of rates is paid.

Extra-parochial properties

It has always been fundamental that a person shall be rated only for **4–14** his possessions within the parish where the assessment accrues. It has followed that land on the seaward side of low-watermark, not being within the parish, was not rateable.

The position was modified by section 72 of the Local Government Act 1972 which provides that:

"... every accretion from the sea, whether natural or artificial, and any part of the sea-shore to the low-watermark, which does not immediately before the passing of this Act form part of a parish shall be annexed to and incorporated with:

(a) in England, the parish or parishes which the accretion or part of the sea shore adjoins, and
(b) in Wales, the community or communities which the accretion or part of the sea-shore adjoins, in proportions to the extent of the common boundary.

45

Every accretion from the sea or part of the sea-shore which is annexed to and incorporated with a parish or community under this section shall be annexed to and incorporated with the district and county in which that parish or community is situated."

The matter is of particular importance in connection with pleasure piers, tunnels and mines which extend under the sea.

Land struck with sterility

4-15 Land dedicated to the use of the public, *e.g.* public highways, is regarded as exempt from rates as there is no rateable occupier. Similarly, public parks and recreation grounds dedicated to the public in perpetuity are "struck with sterility" and thus are not rateable (see also Schedule 5, Public Parks).

5

Compilation and Alteration of the Rating List

THE LOCAL RATING LIST

A local rating list is conclusive on all matters concerning liability to **5–01** pay rates in respect of a hereditament other than the identity of the occupier. All exemptions for rating are given effect by exclusion from the local or central rating list. A list also shows not only changes in rateable value but the date from which such changes take effect. Lists show the address of the property, a brief standardised description, and the rateable value and date on which the latest alteration (if any) took effect.

Local rating lists were compiled initially on April 1, 1990, and are due to be compiled on April 1, in every fifth year thereafter. A local list comes into force on the day on which it is compiled, and it is the duty of the Valuation Officer to maintain the list.

Under paragraph 8(1) of Schedule 9 to the 1988 Act a person may at all reasonable times and without payment, inspect the local rating list which is held at the local Valuation Office. Copies may be taken of documents or extracts in all cases subject to the payment of a reasonable charge.

Section 41 of the 1988 Act authorises the Valuation Officer for a billing authority to compile local rating lists, he must take such steps as are reasonably practicable to ensure the list is accurately compiled.

To facilitate the preparation of a new list, the Valuation Officer is empowered under Schedule 9, paragraph 5(1) of the 1988 Act to serve a notice upon any occupier or owner of a hereditament requiring him to supply information as is required by him for the purpose of carrying out functions conferred or imposed on him by the Act. This information can, and is most likely to include information concerning occupation and ownership of the hereditament, information relating to recent alterations and improvements, details of tenancies and where relevant, details of trade or throughput. Information about capital transactions arising from the sale of an interest in property may not be asked for by the Valuation Office and cannot be utilised in court proceedings but it is available to the Valuation Officers.

Not later than December 31 preceding a day on which a list is to be compiled the Valuation Officer shall send to the billing authority a copy of the list he proposes to compile. The authority must take such steps as it thinks most suitable for giving notice of it. Also once the list has been compiled a copy must be sent to the authority who must deposit it at its principal office.

ALTERATION OF LOCAL RATING LISTS

5–02 Once the list has come into force it may be altered for broadly four reasons:

(1) An interested person may successfully argue that the original entry was wrong.

(2) An interested person may successfully argue that the entry needs altering because factors affecting the hereditament have changed.

(3) The Valuation Officer may conclude that the entry needs altering; normally because the factors affecting the hereditament have changed. An interested person may also successfully argue for a rateable value other than that inserted in the list by the Valuation Officer.

(4) An interested person may successfully argue or the Valuation Officer may conclude that an entry should be deleted from the list, or that one not included, which ought to have been, should be added.

"An interested person" in the majority of cases means either the occupier of a hereditament or another person (other than a mortgagee not in possession), having in any part of the hereditament either a legal estate or an equitable interest, such as would entitle him (after the cessation of any prior interest) to possession of the hereditament or any part of it, and lastly, any person having a qualifying connection with any person previously described.

An interested person or billing authority may make a proposal within the period specified by government in the regulations. In

1990, proposals could be made between April 1, 1990 and October 1, 1990; the regulations for the 1995 list set down no time-limits.

Alterations of lists are covered currently by the Non-Domestic Rating (Alteration of Lists and Appeals) Regulations 1993, and the Non-Domestic Rating (Alteration of Lists and Appeals) (Amendment) Regulations 1995.

Alteration of the list by the valuation officer

Where the Valuation Officer is satisfied that the list requires **5–03** alteration this can be done without making a proposal (s.41, 1988 Act) as was required under the 1967 General Rating Act. Once the Valuation Officer has altered the list the billing authority and the ratepayer must be notified of the alteration within six weeks. The billing authority should then, as soon as is reasonably practical, alter its copy of the list. The Valuation Officer is also required to serve notice on the ratepayer stating the effect of the alteration, and explaining the right to make a proposal seeking reversal of the alteration or further amendment of the list, and that if successful, this will be back dated to the date of the Valuation Officer's present alteration of the list. The notice will also explain that in the interim rates will be payable on the basis of the altered rateable value contained in the list. A Valuation Officer is not obliged to serve notice of alteration on a ratepayer in respect of alterations made:

- to correct clerical errors,
- to reflect a decision that a proposal is well founded,
- in response to an agreement made following a proposal,
- due to a change in the area of the billing authority or,
- when directing into the list a decision of a Valuation Tribunal or the Lands Tribunal in relation to the hereditament concerned.

Effects of an alteration to the list—effective dates

A change in the amount a ratepayer is liable to pay will follow from **5–04** the date with effect from which the list is altered. The Non-Domestic (Alterations of Lists and Appeals) (Amendment) Regulations came into force on July 9, 1994, and have significantly altered the 1993 Regulations. These regulations are now so complicated that they need the services of a specialist in rating to unravel. Those involved must refer to the Regulations themselves and be aware of their significance for rate liability, especially in transition cases. Valuation Tribunals have wide ranging powers with respect to effective dates.

ALTERATION OF THE RATING LIST BY PROPOSAL

Who may make a proposal?

5–05 The right to make a proposal to alter the list is available to the ratepayer, *i.e.* the occupier (or, if the hereditament is unoccupied, the owner), and to any other person who has a legal estate or an equitable interest in any part of the hereditament, such as would entitle them (after the cessation of any prior interest) to possession of the hereditament or any part of it. "Third party proposals" are no longer provided for since the rateable value of one hereditament in an area no longer has such a direct bearing on the rates paid by other ratepayers, although it remains open to any third party to draw the Valuation Officer's attention to any circumstance he believes might cause the Valuation Officer to alter the list.

Apart from its rights as an owner/occupier, the billing authority may make a proposal for the inclusion of a hereditament not already included in the list. The billing authority may also make a proposal in respect of any hereditament within its area where it believes here has been a material change of circumstance, or where a relevant decision of the local Valuation Tribunal, Lands Tribunal or Court of Appeal warrants the making of a proposal. In certain circumstances it may be possible to become a party to another's proposal.

When may a proposal be made?

5–06 When a new list is compiled an interested person, if aggrieved by:

    (a) the value shown in the list, or;
    (b) any statement made in or omitted from that list in respect of a hereditament,

may at any time, serve a proposal for the alteration of the list so far as it relates to that hereditament. An alteration of the rating list by the local Valuation Officer may take place, for example, on completion of a new property or because of structural alterations or improvements. A proposal can also be made at any time if the property is affected by a "material change of circumstances", *i.e.* a change in:

- Matters affecting the physical state or physical enjoyment of the hereditament.
- The mode or category of occupation of the hereditament.
- The quantity of minerals or other substances in or extracted from the hereditament.
- The quantity of refuse or waste material which is brought onto and permanently deposited on the hereditament.
- Matters affecting the physical state of the locality in which the hereditament is situated or which, though not affecting the physical state of the locality, are nonetheless physically manifest there.
- The use of occupation of other premises situated in the locality of the hereditament.
- Any part of the hereditament ceasing to be, or becoming liable to be included in the list.

A proposal can also be made if a decision of the Local Valuation Tribunal or Lands Tribunal has a bearing on the valuation of the property.

How to make a proposal

The form of proposal is not prescribed in the Regulations, but **5–07** information is specified as to how they should be made. Any proposal must be made in writing, stating the name and address of the person making it and the capacity in which they do so. It must identify the property to which it relates, the manner in which it is proposed that the list be altered, and include a statement of the reasons for believing the list to be incorrect. In the case of a proposal on the ground of a material change of circumstances, a statement is required of the nature of change and date on which the person making the proposal believes the change occurred. If the proposal disputes the accuracy of an alteration by the Valuation Officer, the proposal by the interested person must state the date on which the Valuation Officer issued the relevant notice, and if the proposal disputes the date from which an alteration should have effect the date proposed in its place should be stated. A proposal should normally deal with one hereditament only, but may deal in certain circumstances, with more than one. In all circumstances proposals must be served on the Valuation Office.

Action of valuation officer on receipt of a proposal

5-08 A Valuation Officer will acknowledge receipt of a proposal to its maker and is required within six weeks, starting on the day on which a proposal is served, to send a copy of the proposal to each of the following:

- Any ratepayer in relation to any hereditament to which the proposals relates (if they did not make the proposal).
- The billing authority for the area where the authority has served notice on the Valuation Officer that it wishes to receive a copy of the class of proposals into which it falls.

Invalid proposals

5-09 The proposal may be invalid if it is made outside the time-limits, or if it fails to specify one of the prescribed grounds; or if the Valuation Officer is not persuaded that the grounds specified apply. In these circumstances the Valuation Officer is required, within six weeks of the service of the proposal, to serve a notice on the person making the proposal stating that it is invalid. The Valuation Officer's notice must give the reasons for the decision, and must advise the proposer of their rights of appeal to the Valuation Tribunal against the decision not to take the proposal any further. If a proposer wishes to exercise that right they should make their appeal by serving notice in writing on the Valuation Officer within four weeks of the service of the Valuation Officer's notice. Unless the Valuation Officer is persuaded of the validity of the proposal he will transmit the contents of the proposal to the Clerk of the Local Valuation Tribunal, together with the reasons for believing it to be invalid. Until the appeal as to validity is determined, the Valuation Officer will not process the proposal in the normal way previously referred to. However, if the Valuation Tribunal decides that the proposal is valid the standard procedures as to serving copies of the proposal on other interested parties, agreed alterations, etc., will have effect as if the proposal had actually been served on the Valuation Officer at the date of the Valuation Tribunal's decision. It should be noted that a failure to treat a proposal as invalid does not prevent any party, including the Valuation Officer, from arguing on an appeal to the Valuation Tribunal that the proposal was invalidly made.

Agreements and withdrawals of proposals

Where the Valuation Officer is satisfied that a proposal is well **5–10** founded and that the list should be altered to give full effect to the alteration proposed, then the Valuation Officer must serve notice on the proposer informing the proposer that the list is to be so altered. The Valuation Officer is required to alter the list within six weeks of the service of that notice.

Because the pursuance or non-pursuance of an appeal may affect subsequent appellants' rights, the circumstances in which appeals may be withdrawn is now expressly provided for. Unfairness would otherwise result if a departed occupier could withdraw a proposal without the new occupier's agreement, since a later proposal could not be backdated to the same extent. Thus, where a proposal has been made by a departed occupier it may not be withdrawn except with the written agreement of the present occupier. In other circumstances however, the maker of the proposal is free to withdraw it at any time before a hearing of a relevant appeal by the Valuation Tribunal.

Where the Valuation Officer and the interested persons agree in writing on an alteration to the list, at any time before the hearing by the Valuation Tribunal, the Valuation Officer will, within six weeks, alter the list to give effect to the agreement. The following must be parties to such a written agreement:

- The Valuation Officer.
- The maker of the proposal.
- The occupier at the date of the proposal if they did not make it (however, where the occupier made the proposal but is no longer in occupation of any part of the property, and the Valuation Officer has taken all reasonable steps to find that occupier but has failed to do so, that person's agreement is not required).
- Any other interested person who would have been eligible to make the proposal, and has within three months, beginning on the day the proposal was served on the Valuation Officer, served notice on the Valuation Officer to the effect that they wish to be a party.

Where written agreement has been reached the Valuation Officer is required to alter the list within six weeks of the day on which all parties have agreed.

Where the Valuation Officer does not believe a proposal is well **5–11** founded; it is not withdrawn and no written agreement is reached, the disagreement between the parties must, no later than the expiry of the six months beginning on the day on which the proposal was served, be transferred by the Valuation Officer as an appeal to the Valuation Tribunal. The Valuation Officer is required to transmit to the Valuation Tribunal a statement of:

- The entry in the list (if any) which it is proposed should be altered.
- The date of service of the proposal.
- The names and addresses (where known to the Valuation Officer) of persons who would have to be a party to any written agreement on an alteration to the list, all of whom have taken action to become a party to appeal.
- The grounds on which the proposal was made.

This transfer of information is generally in electronic form, however, a hard copy of such information will normally be sent to the Valuation Tribunal as soon as is reasonably practical.

DETERMINATION OF RATING APPEALS

The valuation tribunal

5-12 The Valuation Tribunal is a lay Tribunal wholly independent of the Valuation Officer and the billing authority which exists to resolve all rating and Council Tax appeals. The members are local people serving in a voluntary capacity and they need not be professionally qualified but are experienced in hearing appeals. The Tribunal is advised on points of procedure and law by its Clerk, a salaried employee, who is not a member of the Tribunal. A Tribunal may determine appeals on the basis of written representations or a hearing.

Proposals may be withdrawn at any time before a formal hearing of an appeal by the Valuation Tribunal or consideration of written representations. All appeals may also be settled between the parties by written agreement of every party at any stage before a Valuation Tribunal hearing commences or it begins to consider written representations. If written agreement is reached between the parties an appeal will be deemed to have been withdrawn when the Valuation Officer notifies the Clerk to the Tribunal that agreement has been reached. Either on written application of a party or on the decision of a chairman, a pre-hearing review may be held by one of the Valuation Tribunal's chairman in order to determine the extent to which the facts can be agreed. This procedure could prove useful in respect of more complex cases and may avoid the need to postpone a hearing where, for example, one party is not in possession of evidence to be used by another.

Notice of hearing

Where an appeal is to be determined at a hearing the Clerk to the Tribunal will give each party at least four weeks notice of the date, time and place of the hearing.

The Clerk is also required to post notices advertising the date, time and place of the hearing outside the office of the Valuation Tribunal and an office of the relevant billing authority. These notices will state a place where a list of the appeals to be heard can be inspected.

Representation and conduct of the hearing

All parties to a hearing may appear in person with assistance from **5-13** anyone else they choose: counsel, surveyor, solicitor or other representative. A Tribunal cannot award costs and the parties would each have to meet their own costs in preparing and presenting their case and attending the hearing.

A Tribunal would generally be constituted by three members, however, exceptionally and only where all parties who appear agree, its function may be discharged by two members.

The hearing will generally be held in public unless a party applies for a hearing in private, and convinces the Tribunal that it would be prejudicial to their interests. The Tribunal has the power to require evidence to be given by oath or affirmation.

Where proceedings arise from a Valuation Officer's alteration of a local rating list or, where the Valuation Officer has refused to process a proposal on the grounds that it was invalid, the Valuation Officer will normally begin the hearing. In all other cases the parties will be heard in such order as may be decided by the Tribunal. Any party may examine any witness before the Tribunal and may also call witnesses. So far as appropriate, the Tribunal will try to avoid undue formality in its proceedings. It has powers to adjourn or postpone a hearing and to hold site visits to inspect the hereditament in relation to which the appeal is brought, or a comparable hereditament. A Tribunal may proceed to determine an appeal in the absence of a party unless that party has sought and been granted an adjournment. An appeal may also be dismissed where the Valuation Officer is a party and every other party, apart from the Valuation Officer, fails to appear.

Evidence

5-14 Lists of comparable properties may be exchanged before the hearing or consideration of written representations take place. If the Valuation Officer intends to support his assessment by using rental information obtained under paragraph 5 of Schedule 9 to the 1988 Act, notice to that effect must be served on all parties to the appeal. The notice will specify the information to be used and the hereditament to which it relates and inform the parties of their right, provided at least 24 hours notice is given, to inspect at any reasonable time and take extracts from the documents or any other media in which the information is held.

Any person on whom such a notice is served may serve notice on the Valuation Officer before the hearing of one or more hereditaments (to a number no greater than that used by the Valuation Officer) which they believe to be comparable in character or otherwise relevant to their case and requiring the Valuation Officer to permit them at any reasonable time specified in the notice to inspect and, if they require, make a copy of any document that is in the possession of the Valuation Officer and to produce at the hearing, or submit to the Tribunal, such documents as they have informed the Valuation Officer they require.

Decisions of the tribunal/orders

5-15 The decisions of the Tribunal will be by a majority. Where the Tribunal comprises two members and they are unable to agree the appeal will be remitted by the Clerk for determination by a Tribunal consisting of different members.

The Tribunal will give its decision in writing signed by the chairman and it will be notified to all the parties as soon as reasonably practical. The Tribunal is required to give reasons for its decision.

Following a decision on an appeal concerned with an entry in a local rating list the Tribunal may direct the Valuation Officer to:

(a) alter the rating list in accordance with its decision and any relevant regulations,
(b) alter any determination or certificate issued in respect of the transitional arrangements.

The Valuation Officer is required to give effect to such an order within six weeks of it being made.

Where the Tribunal decides that a rateable value should be greater than the amount shown in the list at the date of the proposal and greater than that contended for in the proposal, the resulting order may require that the list be altered only with effect from the day on which the Tribunal's decision was given.

In the case of, for example, proposals for temporary reductions in rateable values the Tribunal can order that an alteration should only take effect for the duration of the circumstances which give rise to the alteration.

Review of decisions

The Tribunal shall have power on written application by a party to **5–16** review or set aside their decision on the grounds that:

- the decision was wrongly made as a result of clerical error;
- that a party did not appear and show reasonable cause why they did not do so;
- that the decision is affected by a decision of or an appeal from the High Court or the Lands Tribunal in relation to an appeal in respect of the hereditament which was the subject of the Tribunal's decision.

An application for a review may be dismissed if it is not made within the period of four weeks beginning on the day on which the notice was given.

Other functions

The Tribunal is also able to deal with appeals against completion notices and appeals against certification as set out in the relevant Regulations.

Appeals

There is a further right of appeal against the Valuation Tribunal's decision in respect of appeals relating to:

- the validity of a proposal;
- the proposed alteration of a rating list and certifications;

but there is no such appeal possible in respect of completion notices (here the Valuation Tribunal's powers to review a decision are broader).

Where any party to an appeal (except in relation to a completion notice) is aggrieved by the decision of the Valuation Tribunal that person will be able to appeal to the Lands Tribunal.

Appeals to the Lands Tribunal should be initiated within 28 days of the date of the Valuation Tribunal's decision or order.

Payment of rates pending appeal

5-17 The ratepayer will be required to pay the full amount shown in a rate bill until the proposal/appeal is agreed or withdrawn or any resulting appeal has been determined.

However, where a reduction in rateable value is backdated and overpaid rates are refunded by the billing authority, interest may be payable on the sum involved.

Costs

A Tribunal cannot award costs to the parties, so they will have to meet their own expenses in preparing a case and attending the hearing or any expenses of a representative.

Conduct of hearings

5-18 When the proposal has been accepted by the Valuation Officer, the Valuation Officer will normally meet the proposer and or the proposer's representatives informally to discuss the proposal. At this meeting it is customary for matters of fact to be agreed. These facts should include the description of the property, dimensions, details of construction, areas, and the point of disagreement.

It may well be, and often is the case, that at this point the proposer wishes to withdraw or the parties reach agreement. If agreement is reached then the Valuation Officer will alter the list. If agreement does not prove possible then the case will proceed to a hearing before the Valuation Tribunal.

Style of presentation at valuation tribunal

In any Valuation Tribunal hearing time is important (there may well be 20–30 cases listed in one day), therefore reasonable brevity is appreciated. There is no basic difference in the documentation to be produced at a Valuation Tribunal to that for a Lands Tribunal hearing, but in the latter case more time may well be spent in detail, as a result of separation of advocacy and evidence, and in cross examination. In a Valuation Tribunal it is not usual to read through lengthy documents, it being sufficient to draw attention to important points and to leave the members to peruse the documents on their retirement. Similarly these Tribunals do not welcome lengthy extracts from reported cases but it is useful to have copies of the reports available for reference (a telephone call to the Clerk and perhaps to the Valuation Officer beforehand will often ensure that additional copies are available without copying). The case should be kept as simple as possible and should concentrate on the really important points. The members of the Valuation Tribunal are not usually professionally qualified, and do not always appreciate obscure points and abstract ideas; they do, however, understand rental evidence, and like comparables to be quoted. During the case, notes should not be read but the members should be observed to see that they have taken the point; if not the point must be put another way.

Before the hearing the case will have been carefully prepared. It is **5–19** not usual in a Valuation Tribunal for either party to be legally represented, or to call any additional expert witness. A surveyor/ valuer appearing for a ratepayer will act as both advocate and witness on behalf of his client, and the Valuation Officer usually appears in person. Proceedings are on the whole informal.

For those not familiar with Valuation Tribunals it will be useful to consider the presentation of a case in stages.

Stage 1. The purely formal introduction in which the parties are identified by name, qualifications stated, and reference made to the formal initiating documents. A brief outline of the matters in dispute is given and copies of all plans, schedules and other papers to which reference may be made are handed up. At this stage the court appreciates a few minutes to scan the papers and may raise a few minor points to facilitate their understanding of them. The party making the proposal should be the first to speak, and deal with the above matters, but sometimes when a ratepayer is not represented professionally the court will ask the Valuation Officer to start as this may speed up the hearing by early presentation of essential points.

Stage 2. The case is opened. Attention is drawn to the disputed points and a point of view stated. An outline should be given of matters to be dealt with later in formal evidence.

Stage 3. Formal evidence. This evidence includes the details of the property concerned, areas and descriptions, plus schedules of rents (if any are available), and supporting evidence in the form of leases and forms of return, inferences to be drawn should be clearly stated. Schedules of comparables should be presented together with the valuation on which it is proposed to rely. Opportunity to criticise the opposing parties' valuation should be taken, even though it will not yet have been given in evidence. Matters of fact, or opinion, on which the case rests must be dealt with in evidence at this stage. When the witness has finished giving evidence it is the turn of the opposing parties to cross examine on that evidence, and quite often the court will themselves raise questions. It should be possible, after cross examination, to give further evidence to clear up any point which the questioning has left obscure—but not to introduce fresh points.

Stage 4. The concluding statement. This is the opportunity to present arguments based upon the evidence, and to present a summary of the case, leading up to the final submission asking the court to decide the desired alteration in the assessment. Repetition of the evidence is not needed; again brevity is to be welcomed.

5–20   It will now be the turn of the other party to present their case which will take a similar form, except that it will not be necessary to go over the formal preliminaries, nor to repeat agreed facts.

Normally the Tribunal will then permit the proposer a last word in reply to the objection before retiring to consider their verdict. It is dangerous to leave to this point any submission of consequence— some courts will take the line that they have heard enough and may not always give the proposer this last word!

Once the written decision is received the question of any further appeal to the Lands Tribunal can be considered; the formal steps necessary are given in the notice of decision. Time-limits must be observed.

Conduct of lands tribunal appeal

5–21   If the case does proceed to the Lands Tribunal the parties may appear in person, or be legally represented. The Tribunal does not permit valuers to appear as advocates for their clients, but they are called as expert witnesses.

Although the presentation of a case in the Lands Tribunal is essentially similar to that before the Valuation Tribunal, the separation of function as between advocate and witness does alter the preparation of the case. The proceedings constitute an entirely fresh hearing. For this reason every fact and opinion will have to be re-presented although this will mostly be a repetition of the Valuation Tribunal hearing, and all documents will have to be produced again.

In the first instance a lawyer will have to be instructed. If time is short the valuer/surveyor can make the formal appeal by sending the necessary notice to the Tribunal, but further proceedings should be left to the lawyer. At this point the lawyer will know nothing about the case. It is therefore up to the valuer/surveyor to prepare adequate notes for guidance. These notes will contain a full history of the case, a copy of all relevant formal documents and the correspondence which has been exchanged, and a comprehensive report on all negotiations and the Valuation Tribunal hearing. In this way all points of issue will be before the lawyer, in a convenient form, and their advice can then be given on the merits of the case and the form in which they would like the formal evidence to be prepared.

The formal evidence will be covered by the "proof of evidence" **5-22** which the valuer will then prepare. It is useful to break this down into logical component parts starting with a fresh page for each part. The first stage will give the name, qualifications, and experience of the witness, and then list all the formal stages of the appeal with dates and references leading to formal production of copies of all these relevant documents. It is helpful to list all the plans, maps and documents to which reference will be made later in evidence and to hand these in to the Tribunal before the hearing gets under way; all documents should bear a readily seen reference number (usually the initials of the witness and a serial number).

The various documents will be almost the same as those already produced in the Valuation Tribunal but will have been tidied up and perhaps amplified to bring out more detail if desired. Lands Tribunal hearings are not subject to the same pressure on time, and therefore it is possible to give more detail. Some of the documents will have been exchanged before the hearing, and some may have been prior agreed. Agreement on facts is always welcomed, and expected, by the Tribunal.

Next will come a detailed explanation of all the plans, maps, schedules and any other documents, which will be formally produced to the Tribunal, and the witness will comment on these. The witness will produce the valuation and speak in support. The witness will then set down their opinion on all matters in dispute.

The object of this is that the counsel at the hearing can ask pertinent questions of the witness, who will answer in accordance with the proof of evidence. The actual proof will not be handed in to the Tribunal (note the difference in procedure from a planning appeal), nor will the witness actually have it with them in the witness box. They will of course have available all the copies of the documents, and the file, for reference.

An expert witness can expect searching cross examination on his or her evidence, but may not be examined on matters to which they have not referred —although advocates are past masters in the art of linking exploratory questions to evidence! It will be for the lawyer to make the case and present the argument, using the facts and opinions established by the witness.

The nature of the hearing before the Lands Tribunal is such that **5-23** witnesses in rating matters are normally experienced rating practitioners. Surveyors acting for ratepayers need to fully brief their clients on issues of costs which may be awarded to the successful party and may be substantial. A decision to proceed with such an appeal should not be taken lightly and should only be recommended by those with specialist rating experience. These experts will have a full working knowledge of the legislation and all relevant regulations.

The authors' opinion is that only surveyors with detailed knowledge of the legislation and regulations and several years of rating valuation experience should take on appeal work at this level. These experienced surveyors are well versed in Lands Tribunal procedures, experienced in preparing proofs of evidence and experienced in appearing as expert witnesses. The younger surveyor should concentrate on gaining this experience by acting as an assistant and sitting in on a number of hearings before taking on their own "low value" cases.

6

Methods of Assessment

GENERALLY

As a general rule, the ultimate aim of the rating valuer is to arrive at **6–01** an estimate of the current annual rental value of a property in terms of rateable value. It may be said, therefore, that a rating valuation is an opinion as to the rental, in terms of money, which a property will command at a given time and on certain assumptions, the assumptions being those appropriate to the definition of rateable value already considered in Chapter 2.

No book can convey to beginners sufficient information to enable them to place an unassailable assessment upon a property. It may, nevertheless, convey to them those principles which will help them to interpret the market and thus form a sound opinion of value. The essential starting-point is a knowledge of transactions in the market, together with a knowledge of the properties to which those transactions relate and further as much information as possible of the circumstances surrounding those transactions. This knowledge must be acquired in practice, and is perhaps best acquired in an office where the everyday business includes negotiation of lettings, for in this way the intimate details of the lettings become known.

Apart from certain exceptions, there are no specific statutory **6–02** provisions which precisely define methods of arriving at rating assessments. The exceptions include a range of classes of hereditaments such as public utility undertakings which by their very nature are difficult to assess by conventional means. For many years it has been the practice to value such undertakings by formula. The powers to prescribe the values in these cases are retained in Schedule 6, paragraph 3 of the 1988 Act. These include:

- water service companies and statutory water companies
- the electricity supply industry

- British Gas
- British Telecom (certain hereditaments only)
- British Railways Board (now Railtrack, *et al*)
- London Underground
- Docklands Light Railway
- Tyne & Wear Metro
- British Waterways Board
- statutory docks and harbours.

These powers also apply to similar competing companies in the private sector such as Mercury Communications. Many of these hereditaments will appear in a central rating list which can be updated annually.

6–03 There are four principal methods of approach in common use for the purpose of determining rating assessments:

1. Comparison

(a) Direct estimate of rental value based on the actual rent of the property, an identical property or a similar property; and
(b) Comparison with assessments ascribed to identical or similar properties, particularly where the "tone of list" provisions of the 1988 Act apply.

For the purposes of both methods (1)(a) and (b) there are several methods of comparing properties which are not identical but are merely similar. The most common for buildings is to compare accommodation, floor areas or gross roof covered areas. Capacity capabilities or capacity output capabilities are also used as effective methods of comparison where applicable.

2. The Contractor's Method

i.e. to arrive at effective capital value and apply a percentage thereto as representing the rent a tenant would pay.

3. The Profit Basis

Applicable to commercial undertakings where there is a monopoly or an element of monopoly, which involves an analysis of the revenue account of the undertaking.

4. The Output Basis

Used largely for mineral producing hereditaments, which, following the royalty payments between landlords and tenants under mining leases, relates the assessment to the actual output or average annual output.

These methods will now be considered in greater detail.

COMPARISON

Rent at which let

The purpose of the exercise being to find the annual rental value, it is **6–04** obvious that the rent being paid is the most important evidence, as it reflects all the advantages and disadvantages of the property. It is to be assumed that the tenant, before renting, considered what other premises were available and judged that the subject property and rent were the best proposition. At the same time, the landlord having maybe let the property before, or occupied it, must be aware of the value. It follows that unfettered negotiations between landlord and tenant bring into being a rental bargain which may be accepted in normal circumstances as the best evidence of value. Scott L.J. emphasised this in his dictum in the *Robinson*[1] case when he held that "Where the hereditament is let at which is plainly a rack-rent . . . that evidence is alone admissible." Nevertheless, the circumstances of the letting must be carefully considered to ascertain whether the property is, in fact, let at what is "plainly a rack-rent". If there is evidence to show that this is not the case, then Lord Buckmaster's dictum in *Poplar v. Roberts*[2] is apposite when he said: "the actual rent is no criterion unless indeed it happens to be the rent the imaginary tenant might reasonably be expected to pay". The rent which is actually passing must therefore be accepted with reservation and particular care taken to ascertain whether there are any factors which tend to show that the rent is not a *bona fide* indication of current annual value. Examples of factors which must be considered and taken into account are as follows:

(1) The date of origin of the rent is of prime importance, for it is obvious that rents negotiated many years ago may not be indicative of current value where rents generally have risen

---

[1] [1937] 2 K.B. 445.
[2] [1922] 2 A.C. 93.

substantially in the intervening period. This point is the more important now, in view of the requirement in section 121 of the 1988 Act that values shall accord with "tone of list".[3]

(2) Whether the landlord and the tenant are in any way related such that the rental agreed upon is affected thereby. Similar considerations apply where there is a lease between associated companies.

(3) Where the letting is linked to a financial transaction, for instance the tenant obtains capital for his business by selling the freehold of the property and then renting back the premises from the purchaser at a percentage of the sale price.[4]

(4) Whether the tenant gets the benefit of restrictive covenants in leases of other premises by the same landlord such that he derived a valuable trading monopoly.[5]

(5) Whether the tenant has surrendered an existing lease in exchange for a new lease at a reduced rental to reflect the value of the lease surrendered and whether a tenant has paid a premium in lieu of rent.

(6) In certain cases an excess rent may be offered for goodwill or offered by a tenant to induce letting, any such excess rentals must be ignored. Such cases will not arise in the case of rents agreed in accordance with Part II of the Landlord and Tenant Act 1954.

(7) Similarly, rents determined under Part II of the last-8mentioned Act are intended to exclude any effect of improvements carried out voluntarily during the currency of the preceding lease by the tenant or a predecessor in title or within 21 years of the determination of the new lease rent, (see later regarding adjustment of rent for improvements).

(8) Where the rent has been agreed, or determined by an arbitrator or independent valuer at a rent review, the rental must be interpreted in the light of the rent review clause and adjusted if necessary.

In all such cases it is best to treat the rent passing as suspect and check this against the rents for similar premises not thus affected. Various adjustments may be necessary to bring an actual rent into line with the rating hypothesis as expressed in the definitions of value to be used, and these will now be considered.

---

[3] See, e.g. Laws Shoes Ltd v. McMillan; Moores Grocers Ltd v. McMillan [1967] R.A. 258.

[4] Tracadero (Swanage) Ltd v. Perrins (1958) 51 R. & I.T. 140.

[5] Rawlinson v. Pritchard (1958) 52 R. & I.T. 182.

ADJUSTMENTS OF RENTALS

Lease rents

Whether any adjustment is necessary to a rent reserved in a lease for a **6–05** term of years merely for the reason that it is not a letting "from year to year"[6] will depend upon the circumstances of the particular case. Many attempts have been made over the years to justify departing from the actual rent as a starting-point. Whilst a few attempts have succeeded, a study of modern decisions leads to the conclusion that only where it can be definitely proved that the lease rent was high, because the tenant anticipated inflation increasing rents during the term of his lease, will the Tribunal accept that the lease rent requires a reduction on account of the actual tenant's greater security compared with the position of the hypothetical tenant.[7] It is useful to note the position of the hypothetical tenant, for example, envisaged in *R. v. South Staffordshire Waterworks Co.*,[8] and quoted by the Tribunal in a relevant case[9]:

> "A tenant from year to year is not a tenant for one, two, three or four years, but he is to be considered as a tenant capable of enjoying the property for an indefinite time, having a tenancy which it is expected will continue for more than a year, and which is liable to be put an end to by notice."

Further care is necessary in areas of rental growth when analysing **6–06** rents which may be uplifted above normal market levels to secure longer lease terms without review. Similarly in declining areas where a landlord may accept a lower rent to obtain the security of a lessee with a good covenant.

Further adjustments that may be necessary will depend upon the respective liabilities of the landlord and tenant under the actual lease although, given that the definition of rateable value accords more closely to the concept of the full repairing and insuring lease, common now in many commercial situations, adjustments for repairs will be necessary only where they fall to be the responsibility of the landlord. The most common adjustment is for repairs but there may be other circumstances which warrant an adjustment as detailed below.

---

[6] *National Car Parks v. Burrows* [1979] R.A. 85.
[7] *Humber Ltd v. Jones and Rugby R.D.C.* (1960) 53 R. & I.T. 293.
[8] [1885] 16 O.B.D. 359.
[9] *Phillips Bros Character Shoes Ltd v. Childs* (1959) 52 R. & I.T.

Premiums

Where a tenant has paid a premium on entering in return for a reduced rental, or the tenant undertakes to spend a considerable sum in putting the premises into repair, then the annual value of this liability must be computed.

The usual practice is to spread the premium over the term of the lease or over the period to the first rent review if the latter is to be to full market rental. It is to be noted that where a premium is paid, the addition for repairs should be made after the rent has been increased to allow for the annual value of the premium (see example 2 below).

Improvements

6–07 When a tenant spends a sum of money in carrying out permanent improvements to the property this increases the "virtual rent" at which the property is held and, assuming that the money concerned has been wisely expended, the open market rental of the property may also be increased. It will, however, be appreciated that not every item of tenants' expenditure can be regarded as an improvement, and there are cases, admittedly rare, where for reasons personal to the occupier works are carried out which actually have the effect of reducing the open market rental value of the property concerned.

Thus in practice, the valuer seeking to use the actual rent and expenditure as the basis of a valuation of the hereditament to which it relates must very carefully scrutinise such expenditure before drawing conclusions as to its effect on value. In an analysis of a number of rental transactions in an area, for example, of shops in a shopping centre, where an overall impression is required a more approximate or rule-of-thumb approach is perhaps permissible.

The almost universal rule-of-thumb approach was until recently to regard, say, 6 per cent of the capital sum expended as the additional value attributable to the improvements, for although the tenant might have only a relatively short lease, say, 14 years, the improvements would continue to enhance the property beyond the lease term, and moreover the prudent business tenant could obtain compensation under the Landlord and Tenant Act 1927 and 1954 or a renewal of tenancy at a rent which disregarded the additional rental value so created. Such a procedure also had the advantage of ensuring similar treatment whether the improvement were made by the tenant or the landlord.

6–08 Nevertheless, in a decision where the adjustment of shop rents to their "equivalent gross value" in the process of analysing rental evidence in a shopping street, was at issue the Lands Tribunal stated:

"The dispute as to the addition for improvements can be put shortly in this way. The Valuation Officer arrives at an annual amount by applying the dual rate tables at 6 per cent and 3 per cent to the known capital cost. He uses the dual rate tables because he considers that the great bulk of the improvements were carried out to suit the needs of particular tenants and would not ensure to the landlord a return on the expenditure after the expiration of the leases. He therefore considers that the addition to the rent should include provision for a sinking fund. Mr Hopper for the ratepayers considered this unnecessary and he took a straight 6 per cent. In his opinion that is the way the hypothetical tenant would approach the problem. But our view is that at this stage the valuer in endeavouring to find out only what rent or rental equivalent is being paid for the property by the actual tenant—and we think the use of the dual rate tables correct."[10]

Example 1

A shop in a first class position is let on a 25 year lease with rent reviews after 5, 10, 15 and 20 years to full rental value. The lease rent if £10,000 per annum exclusive of rates on full repairing and insuring terms. The tenant paid a premium of £5,000 on entering.

		Analysis in terms of 1995 rateable value
		£
Rent reserved under lease		10,000
Annual equivalent of premium		
$\dfrac{£5,000}{\text{Y.P. for 5 years at 5\% and 3\%}}$		
$\dfrac{£5,000}{4.1954}$	=say	1,192
Equivalent rent		£11,192

Dual rate methodology may be criticised on theoretical grounds but is expected to prevail in practice for some time.

---

[10] *Trevail v. C. & A. Modes Ltd* [1967] R.A. 124.

Example 2

A small office building let for 21 years on a full repairing and insuring lease at £7,500 per annum. Rent reviews after 7 and 14 years to full rental value excluding any effect on rents of tenants' improvements. The tenant spent £5,000 on installing central heating and additional toilets.

	Analysis in terms of 1995 R.V.
	£
Rent reserved under lease	7,500
Add amortised capital outlay on improvements	

$$\frac{£5,000}{\text{Y.P. for 21 years at 6\% and 3\%}}$$

$\dfrac{£5,000}{10.54}$ =say	474
Equivalent Rental	£7,974

Rates

6–09 In the case of inclusive rents it will normally be appropriate to reduce the actual rent by the amount of rates payable at the relevant time, but the guiding principle must be the considerations which influenced, or can be deemed to have influenced, the tenant when the rent was negotiated. For example, if the tenant can be deemed to have anticipated the possible effect of a revaluation, then this factor must be reflected.[11]

The effect of the quantum of rates upon rental negotiations is therefore a factor which should always be borne in mind, and especially so when the tenant undertakes to bear the rates. In circumstances where a tenancy was negotiated at a time when the tenant was influenced by a relatively low rate liability and that rate

---

[11] *London County Council v. Wand* [1958] J.P.L. 53.

liability has substantially altered since the commencement of the tenancy, there may be some justification for a rent-rates equation.

The principle of the equation of rents and rates is a very old one and **6–10** is referred to in *R. v. Hull Dock*[12] when it was held that:

"The whole worth of land is made up of what is paid in rent and what is paid in rates and other outgoings. Land intrinsically worth £40 a year can only pay a rent of £30 per annum if it is to pay £10 per annum in other ways and in estimating rent both landlord and tenant look to the value of the thing on the one hand and to the outgoings on the other, and the outgoings must be deduced from the value before the rent can properly be fixed."

The theory was considered in *Railway Assessment Authority v. Southern Ry.*[13]

"Briefly the principle is that the hypothetical tenant when considering the rent he can afford to offer will have regard to the anticipated amount of his rate liability, that if the rate liability is high he will be able to offer less rent and vice versa."

Mathematically the appropriate equation may be set down as follows:

Rent actually paid	+	Rate liability at time of negotiating tenancy	=	Rent which might have been negotiated had change in rate liability been anticipated	+	New rate liability based on assessment as computed

The logic of the equation is sound and the "rent plus rates" issue is one for annual press discussion whenever rate poundages rise. It is important to tenants particularly after a revaluation. However, the principle is not generally used although it may be used to apportion the divisible balance between rent and rates at the end of a "profits" valuation. In general, following the introduction of the Uniform Business Rate changes in liability have become far more predictable, limited as they are to the increase in the Retail Price Index. In times of low inflation as has been the case throughout the 1990 list, rate increases may be acceptable, however a return to high levels of inflation could again make the issue of the rent-rates equation one of great significance.

---

[12] *R. v. Hull Dock* (1824) 3 B. & C. 516.
[13] (1936) 24 R. & I.T. 53.

RENTS OF SIMILAR PROPERTIES

6-11 Where a property is not let the next best evidence is clearly the rent of an identical property, but again the rents of identical properties must be carefully analysed as in the case of the rent actually paid. Where there are no identical premises which are let, then the property must be compared with the most similar property which is let and the rent paid for the comparison adjusted to have regard to the relative advantages and disadvantages of the two properties.

It must, however, be borne in mind that identically built premises may not be of the same value, *e.g.* one may have better amenities, and all such factors must be taken into account. This is particularly so in the case of shops where position is of paramount importance.

It is obvious that to compare premises, unless they are of identical construction, it is necessary, amongst other things, to compare their relative size or accommodation, whether expressed in the number of rooms or floor area. Whilst the latter may in some cases be deceptive, it is of obvious importance in the case of factories or warehouses. In certain cases, however, it is possible to make a more direct comparison by capacity expressed in certain units, *e.g.* modern cinemas and theatres may be compared according to their seating capacity, or squash courts according to the number of courts, it being clear that the profit-making capacity, and hence the value to the hypothetical tenant, is directly related to such factors. In deciding upon the rate per unit to be adopted, it is clear that very many factors must be considered and the valuer must exercise very careful judgment and must have regard to all the advantages and disadvantages peculiar to that property. Any factors over and above the average, for example, especially good laboratories in the case of a school, can be added for as an extra.

ASSESSMENTS OF SIMILAR PROPERTIES

6-12 In the same way that rents can be devalued and the results used for the valuation of similar properties, values appearing in the rating list can be analysed and the unit prices so adduced applied to value hereditaments of the same type.

Obviously from the point of view of the Valuation Officer such an approach is of no help at the time of a general revaluation. Nevertheless, such values may assist the ratepayer or his valuer, for figures appearing in the new list can be regarded as admissions of opinion of value on the part of the Valuation Officer.

However, when a rating list is established, accepted or settled values are equally of assistance to the Valuation Officer who may use them in support of disputed values or to assist in the valuation of new or altered hereditaments. This being particularly relevant in "tone of list" valuations.

The result of the "tone of list" provisions in the 1988 Act has been to make much less important, particularly as the date of a revaluation recedes into the past, the effect of the Court of Appeal's decision in the well known *Ladies' Hosiery* case,[14] in which the appellants made a definite admission that the property would have commanded a rent equivalent to the assessment and relied on comparison to prove unfairness. Eve L.J. said:

> "The one concrete fact which emerges is the correctness of the assessment of the appellant's premises, and when that is once recognised as established, there is really nothing more to be said. It is quite impossible for the court in these proceedings to substitute for the correct figure another figure which, by their own evidence, they have proved to be incorrect. It may be that want of uniformity, and consequent unfairness, can be established, and that it is due to under-assessment of comparable premises, ... but, if so, this must be established by proper proceedings, directed to the raising of the assessments of those other premises ...".

This case, although decided under the 1925 Act procedure, undoubtedly still carries weight and in several cases the Lands Tribunal, although to some extent sympathetic towards the appellant's case, refused to reduce an assessment because of the rule laid down in the *Ladies' Hosiery* case.

In other cases where the Tribunal has found a disparity between **6–13** rents and assessments they have drawn an inference that the rents quoted were excessive ones and favoured a comparison with other assessments on the grounds that the rental evidence tendered did not yield a basis which had been followed. A somewhat similar line has been taken by the Lands Tribunal where the parties have produced little or no rental evidence. In several cases the Tribunal has relied upon the experience of the Valuation Officer and the general acceptance of his assessments as justification for the basis used, and has concerned itself with the question of whether the appeal hereditament is fairly assessed in relation to that general basis.

---

[14] *Ladies Hosiery and Underwear Ltd v. West Middlesex Assessment Committee* [1932] 2 K.B. 679.

However, the *Ladies Hosiery* decision is still relevant in the case of disputes as to assessments appearing in a new rating list.

THE CONTRACTOR'S METHOD

6-14 Certain classes of hereditament (and parts of hereditaments) are such that there is virtually no direct evidence of rental value to be derived from lettings, and no reliable or relevant indirect evidence which can be adduced from other assessments or from the accounts or profits which an occupier could anticipate. Examples of the miscellany of properties to which these remarks apply include fire stations, municipal baths, colleges, schools, sewage works, specialised industrial undertakings, and much rateable plant and machinery.

In some circumstances it is frequently necessary to have recourse to the contractor's method, *i.e.* taking interest on capital value or capital cost as representing the annual rent. The method is thus founded on the philosophy that capital value and annual value are related alternative forms of expenditure. Thus, Buckley L.J. said in the celebrated case of *Liverpool Corporation v. Chorley Union Assessment Committee*:[15]

> "In looking for the hypothetical tenant the corporation is to be regarded as within the class of persons to be considered. If they did not own this land, they might wish to rent it for the purpose for which they bought it. What would it be worth their while to pay as rent? It was worth their while to pay a sum whose annual value, had it been invested, would have been so much. They have foregone that annual income as the price of having the land. Had they rented instead of buying, that annual sum is some evidence of the amount which it was worth their while annually to pay. In the absence of evidence, the price paid is, I think, evidence to be regarded."

Whilst in this case the learned judge referred to "price paid" these words must not be taken out of context, for unless the price or the cost are of recent origin they may not represent modern capital values, and may therefore not be a suitable starting-point for a present-day valuation.

6-15 At first sight the method looks deceptively simple but for reasons which will be discussed below, and elsewhere in this book, there are considerable difficulties in its practical application. For this reason the method is regarded as "the valuer's last resort" and it should not be used, except perhaps as a check valuation, where there is an

---

[15] [1913] A.C. 197.

alternative method of valuation reasonably available. To quote from Lord Herschell's judgment in *London County Council v. Erith Parish (Churchwardens) and Dartford Union Assessment Committee*:[16]

> "It is perfectly legitimate to take into consideration the annual cost to which the owners would be put in acquiring the ownership of rateable hereditaments, as some guide, under the circumstances, as to what rent they would be willing to pay for them if they were not the owners. It is not at all conclusive, but merely an element to be considered."

In other words, the fact that the occupier is willing to pay £x capital for his property does not necessarily mean that he will pay 3 per cent of £x in terms of a rent. The motives of an owner as opposed to a tenant may differ. Furthermore, it is important to bear in mind that whilst there are two parties to every transaction, namely, a hypothetical landlord and a hypothetical tenant, the assessment must not exceed the rental which the tenant would pay for the premises *rebus sic stantibus*. For example, a commercial tenant's rental bid will be limited by the potential profitability of his business on the hereditament, and the fact that the site has a high value for development purposes will be completely immaterial to his rental bid. If a valuable site is occupied by poor buildings which do not exploit its potential, then the dormant site value which is not released must be ignored. Likewise, the buildings must be looked at carefully, especially where these are old, as the automatic assumption that "where there's a cube there's a value" can result in grievously wrong valuations.

However, the Lands Tribunal tends to agree that for the right hereditament it may be the most acceptable method: see *Eton College v. Lane and Eton Urban District Council*.[17]

THE METHOD

There is a large body of case law concerned with the application of the contractors method of valuation and it is now generally accepted that this is a five stage process which can be summarised: **6–16**

(1) estimation of construction cost of buildings;
(2) adjustment of cost to reflect differences between the hered-

---

[16] [1893] A.C. 562.
[17] [1971] J.P.L. 577.

itament and the theoretical alternative to arrive at "effective capital value";

(3) estimation of the land value;

(4) application of the decapitalisation rate to the value of the buildings and land;

(5) final adjustments to reflect what the prospective tenant is willing and able to pay.

see *Gilmore (V.O.) v. Baker Carr (No. 2)*[18] and *Imperial College of Science and Technology v. Ebdon (V.O.) and Westminster City Council.*[19]

6–17   As will be seen, there are two principal elements in a valuation via capital value, namely:

(1) the capital sum;

(2) the rate or rates of interest to be applied;

and it will be necessary to give further consideration to each of them. Dealing first with the capital sum, this can be arrived at in a number of different ways including:

(a) recent price paid;

(b) recent price paid plus recent actual building or construction cost;

(c) (in the case of older hereditaments) the modern cost of replacement *less* suitable allowances for disabilities and other matters;

(d) (in the case of older hereditaments) by recourse to the "substituted building theory".

Obviously the best evidence of capital value of a property is the recent price paid for it. Equally obviously, except in a comparatively few cases involving, for example, the sale of large houses for use as nursing homes or schools, such evidence will not be available. Nevertheless, where the property has been the subject of a modern transaction of this nature the price paid will prima facie be the best evidence of capital value.

6–18   Similarly, where a local authority purchases a site and proceeds to erect a fire station on it, the total cost will give a good indication of the capital value of the property to its occupier. It was perhaps cases of this nature which Lord Cave had in mind when in the well known

---

[18] (1963) 10 R.R.C. 205, (1964) R.V.R.
[19] [1984] R.A. 213.

case of *R. v. School Board for London* he referred to "interest on the cost".[20]

However, even when actual recent costs are available it is necessary for the valuer to proceed with caution—thus unforeseen costs such as unexpectedly costly foundations may need to be excluded. Costs are also sometimes incurred in respect of "future requirements" which have little or no bearing on the immediate annual value, so that the valuer may have to adjust the actual cost in respect of such excess capacity or other form of "surplusage".[21] Nevertheless, abnormally high expenditure is not necessarily to be ignored in whole or in part merely because it is abnormal,[22] nor can all unproductive expenditure be omitted if it was voluntarily undertaken and foreseen.[23]

6–19 One major problem which arises from this method is how to deal with the cost of ornamentation, particularly ornamentation in excess of the generally accepted standard. The normal argument runs that in the commercial world of speculative property development it is seldom worth the developer's trouble and expense to provide excess ornamentation as he is unlikely to get any appreciable increase in rent as a result; accordingly, if an owner-occupier indulges in such excess expenditure it will not add to the rental value and should be ignored. This reasoning is to a large extent supported by the (1902) *Oxford University* case,[24] where it was shown that the buildings concerned were erected out of money given or bequeathed and were partly in the form of memorials, so that although the premises were of benefit to the University it was under no obligation to provide such expensive or ornate buildings, and probably the University would not have done so had it been spending its own money. On the other hand the valuer must not lose sight of the fact that ornamentation can be a factor of importance and factories and showrooms are sometimes built for advertising reasons to a standard far beyond what is functionally necessary. In practice, therefore, careful judgment must be exercised in deciding to what extent expenditure in this category should be scaled down or excluded.[25]

6–20 When older hereditaments are being valued it will be clear that the two methods so far described will need to be modified. If the property had been created, say, 10 years ago it would be theoretically possible

---

[20] *Imperial College of Science and Technology v. Ebdon (V.O.) and Westminster City Council* [1984] R.A. 244.
[21] *R. v. South Staffordshire Waterworks Ltd* [1885] 16 Q.B.D. 359.
[22] *Liverpool Corporation v. Llanfyllin Union* (1889) 2 Q.B. 14.
[23] *ibid.*
[24] *Ryde and Konstam Rating Appeals* (1894–1904).
[25] *Davey v. God's Port Housing Society Ltd* (1958) 51 R. & I.T. 651.

to take the historic cost and scale this up to allow for changes in land values and building costs over the intervening period. Nevertheless, what appeared to be sound expenditure 10 years ago may look less so now and be positively unsound in five years time! Thus the owner may not have been prepared to erect the same structure at an increased cost 10 years later. Accordingly, only the expenditure which the owner could reasonably be expected to incur at the date of valuation can be properly considered at that time. Moreover, requirements of occupiers are constantly changing, as are building methods, so that the older the premises, the more likely they are to suffer in varying degrees from obsolescence due, for example, to bad planning, poor natural lighting, inappropriate ceiling heights, excessive wall thickness, inefficient methods of heating, etc. Thus it would be a hopelessly misleading exercise to value a multi-storey 1870 warehouse, built in the era of cheap labour and the horse and cart, on the basis of its present-day replacement cost, especially when today we use large articulated lorries and fork lift trucks and suffer high labour costs.

Nevertheless, the valuer has to start his valuation from a factual basis, so that as opposed to actual capital cost or estimated replacement cost the concept of an "effective capital value" has been developed. In the case of method (b) described above, "effective capital value" would be represented by the actual cost *less* the relevant exclusions described. In the case of older hereditament there are two alternatives and these must now be considered.

6–21 The simplest approach is to determine the physical characteristics of the hereditament (the area of land occupied, the appropriate area measure of the buildings for costings and the various plant items), and on these data to estimate the modern cost of replacement. Once such a cost has been found the valuer must exercise his judgment as to the extent to which this figure must be reduced to allow for disabilities, obsolescence and "surplusage" previously referred to—applying the same factor to both land and buildings.[26] As will be seen from examples given later in this book, in some circumstances, notably in the case of schools and university buildings, very substantial reductions of 70 per cent or more are sometimes appropriate.

The "substituted building theory" is a more sophisticated solution to the same problem of determining the "effective capital value" of an old or obsolete hereditament. In essence the starting-point is to consider the existing premises and then redesign them in modern terms, omitting excessive wall thickness, excessive room heights

---

[26] *Dawkins v. Royal Leamington Spa Borough Council and Warwickshire County Council* [1961] J.P.L. 264.

and wasted space such as unnecessary passages. From this exercise the valuer then ascertains the cost of a modern building whose sum total of usable capacity, having regard to size and function, approximates to that of the older building with its disadvantages. To the cost is added the site value, and from the sum of the two figures a deduction must be made to compensate for the disadvantages of the actual hereditament, in order to arrive at its "effective capital value". This approach to the question is supported by *Hall v. Seisdon*,[27] where it was held that evidence might be given to the estimated cost of a modern system of sewage disposal as an indication of the rent that a tenant would pay for accommodation of equal advantage to that of the property in question, although in the event the method was not adopted by the court. It was similarly not adopted by the Lands Tribunal in the (1959) *Oxford University* case[28] concerning the valuation of colleges, nor in the case of *Shrewsbury School*,[29] in both of which cases the estimated replacement cost of the actual buildings less allowances for obsolescence, etc., was preferred as a basis. However, the method was adopted by the Tribunal in the case[30] of four old county schools where the nature of the existing buildings was to some extent conducive to its use, and it is of particular interest that it was adopted, with reservations, when the question of the assessment to be ascribed to Shrewsbury School again came before the Tribunal.[31] Costs of construction per square foot of gross internal area derived from modern buildings were applied to the floor area of the school buildings, substantial deductions being made from the effective capital value so found.

THE DECAPITALISATION RATE

Prior to 1990 the selection of the appropriate decapitalisation rate **6–22** gave rise to more dispute in valuations using the contractor's method than all other elements put together and the importance of the correct rate to be used is obvious when a deviation of 1 per cent may affect the resultant net annual value or gross value by 20 per cent.

Following the 1988 Act, however, the interest rate to be adopted is

---

[27] *Hall v. Seisdon* (1912) 77 J.P. 17.
[28] *Magdalen College, Jesus College and Keble College, Oxford University v. Howard and Oxford C.C.* (1959) 5 R.R.C. 122.
[29] *Shrewsbury Schools Board of Governors v. Shrewsbury Corporation and Plumpton* [1960] J.P.L. 653.
[30] *Dawkins v. Royal Leamington Spa Borough Council and Warwickshire County Council* [1961] J.P.L. 264.
[31] *Shrewsbury School (Governors) v. Hudd* [1966] R.V.R. 559.

prescribed by statute so there is no longer any uncertainty. Even so it is worth briefly considering some of the case law on this issue as it does serve to illuminate the theoretical basis of the method as a whole.

The result of the valuation is to be the rent that a tenant might reasonably be expected to pay rather than build or buy outright, and in theory it would thus be the going rate at which funds may be borrowed in the market. There are cases in which specific departures from this principle have been made, and these will be referred to below. Furthermore, a factor limiting the rate is the possibility of the tenant deciding to occupy as owner rather than lessee. Lord Herschell in *London County Council v. Erith Parish (Churchwardens) and Dartford Union Assessment Committee*[32] observed:

> "It is said that a practice prevails of taking 5 per cent on the cost in the case of buildings as a basis for arriving at the rental. Such a rule of thumb may be all very well where the premises would be likely to find competing tenants, but it is not by any means necessarily so applicable where it is thought that the owner would be likely to give a higher rental than anyone else. It would often be obvious that he would never be willing to pay the rent arrived at in such a fashion, inasmuch as it would be more advantageous for him to become the owner."

6–23 In more recent times three broad categories of hereditament valued by reference to the contractor's method have become discernible—namely:

(1) commercial and specialised industrial properties;
(2) local authority properties built under a statutory duty;
(3) properties occupied by charitable and educational organisations.

So far as commercial properties are concerned the established rule for many years was to use 4 per cent on the value of land (including site improvements), 5 per cent in the case of buildings and rateable plant and machinery to calculate net annual value. But it is increasingly common to use the same rate for land and buildings. Occasionally 6 per cent has been utilised in respect of plant items having a short economic life. Before 1990, appropriate higher rates of interest were used when valuation was to gross value, but the rates were not adjusted on account of the investment characteristics of the

---

[32] [1893] A.C. 562.

industry concerned. In the case of *Metropolitan Water Board v. Chertsey Assessment Committee*[33] where the undertaking could borrow at a very low rate of interest, an attempt to utilise the low rate of interest in the contractor's test was rejected. Likewise it has been held that disabilities should not be allowed for by utilising a lower rate of interest,[34] a reduction in the "effective capital value" or an end allowance from the net annual value being the more appropriate way of valuing the necessary adjustment.

Prior to statutory prescription, rates per cent, determined by the **6-24** Lands Tribunal in respect of local authority properties included 3 per cent (to net annual value) to take account of the local authority's n.oral duty to provide a swimming pool,[35] and 4.5 per cent (to gross value) taken to reflect a statutory duty to provide schools.[36] Examples of decisions concerning properties occupied by educational organisations include 3.5 per cent applied to universities[37] and 3.5 per cent accepted both at the 1956 and 1963 revaluations in respect of Shrewsbury School.[38] In each case the percentages were to obtain gross value.

Further examples of the use of this method will be found in subsequent chapters of this book.

For the 1995 rating list the prescribed rates of interest are 3.67 per cent for educational hereditaments and hospitals and 5.5 per cent for all other cases. These can be found in the Non-Domestic Rating (Miscellaneous Provisions) (No. 2) Regulations.[39]

Generally, whilst the adoption of the contractor's test is often the only means of arriving at an assessment, it should be used with care, especially when valuing converted premises and buildings where the owner has had continually to expend capital on modernising, for it is seldom in such cases he can realise at a figure closely related to his previous expenditure. This method may be used when valuing extensions to existing buildings, but care must be used to match up to the value of the extension with that accorded to the existing buildings by using an appropriate percentage. When a tenant under-

---

[33] [1916] 1 A.C. 337.

[34] *Birchenwood Gas & Coke Co. Ltd v. Hampshire* [1959] J.P.L. 362.

[35] *Woking Urban District Council v. Baker* [1959] J.P.L. 440.

[36] *Dawkins v. Royal Leamington Spa Borough Council and Warwickshire County Council* [1961] J.P.L. 264.

[37] *Oxford and Cambridge Colleges Appeals* (1968). See *Downing College, Cambridge University v. Cambridge CC and Allsop & Newnham College, Cambridge University v. same; Churchill College, Cambridge University v. same; King's College, Cambridge University v. same* [1969] J.P.L. 281; [1968] R.A. 603; 208 E.G. 80 S.L.T.

[38] *Shrewsbury Schools Board of Governors v. Shrewsbury Corporation and Plumpton* [1960] J.P.L. 653.

[39] S.I. 1994 No. 3122.

takes building extensions it may be appropriate in certain circumstances to treat this expenditure in the same way as a premium and spread the cost over the remaining period of the lease as noted in paragraph 6–05. The contractor's test is used extensively when dealing with plant and machinery and is further utilised in appropriate cases for valuing the indirectly productive portions of public utility undertakings for apportionment purposes.

THE PROFIT BASIS

6–25 Although inquiry into the receipts and profits of a business is not generally admissible, where there is no rent paid and no comparable premises to provide rental evidence, it may in certain cases be appropriate to make an analysis of the receipts and expenses of the undertaking and from these compute a figure which the hypothetical tenant might reasonably be expected to pay by way of rent. Lord Davey in *Cartwright v. Sculcoates Union*[40] said in justification of such a method when dealing with licensed premises:

> "You have to find out in the best way you can what is the rent which a tenant may reasonably be expected to give, and if the best way under the circumstances is to ascertain the use which a tenant might expect to be able to make of the premises, the facility afforded by the premises for the carrying on of a trade appears to me to be a primary and elementary consideration of the case. If you are able to take into account the fact that the premises command a trade, you must surely ask what trade? Is it a large trade or is it a small trade, and I do not know myself any better test of what they may be expected to command than the trade which they actually do command. It is not that you rate the profits, it is not that you rate a man's skill ... but you have to ascertain to what sort of trade the hypothetical tenant, as he is called, may reasonably expect to be able to do on these premises, as an element in determining the rent he would be willing to give."

Such a method will not be used where more direct evidence is available, for in such circumstances evidence as to trade was rightly rejected.[41] In appropriate cases, however, it will be used in preference to the contractor's test.

6–26 Generally speaking, the type of property for which such a method is used enjoys some degree of monopoly either statutory or factual; included will be public utility undertakings, licensed premises, leisure centres, and racetracks. It might be noted that the High Court

---

[40] [1899] 7 Q.B. 667.
[41] *Dodds v. South Shields* (1895) 2 Q.B. 133.

approved its application to a zoological garden[42] as it was considered the character and position were unique and gave a virtual monopoly to the premises. Factual monopolies exist in such hereditaments as Cheddar Caves for which an entrance charge is made, and foreshore hereditaments where there is revenue from car parking, deck-chairs and the grant of exclusive trading rights. A further example of hereditament of this type was Blackgang Chine, in respect of which a composite valuation partly by reference to the accounts was approved by the Lands Tribunal.[43] Yet another type of hereditament for which this method has been approved is caravan sites,[44] the monopoly or quasi-monopoly in such cases being attributable to the town planning permission.

With regard to public utility undertakings it was held in *Kingston Union v. Metropolitan Water Board*[45] that the profits basis was the correct and proper method to be applied except where there are special circumstances to warrant resorting to some other principle.

The broad outline of a valuation by this process is as follows:

Per annum	£
Gross income	—
Less Working expenses (except rents and rates)	—
	——
Divisible balance	—
Less Tenant's share	—
	——
Rent + Rates	—
	——

The final figure is divided between rent and rates and the division will take account of the prevailing rate poundage at the time of valuation. There are other complications which in practice enter into a valuation on this principle (*e.g.* renewals in the case of public utility undertakings), but further details of the intricacies of the method are given when dealing with valuations of the appropriate types of property.

---

[42] *Surrey County Valuation Committee v. Chessington Zoo Ltd* [1950] 1 K.B. 640.
[43] *Isle of Wight U.D.C. & G. W. Woodward v. A. B. Dabell and Others* (1958).
[44] *Chichester R.D.C. v. Southern Caravan (Parks) Ltd* L.V.C./21 and 148/ 1952.
[45] [1926] A.C. 331.

THE OUTPUT BASIS

6-27 This method, which is applied almost exclusively to the valuation of mineral-producing hereditaments, consists of applying a tonnage rate, or rate per metre cube, to the actual or average annual output. The rate used will follow the usual royalty rent charged in the district under mineral leases. Further details of this method are given in Chapter 9 in the section on mineral-producing hereditaments.

7

Referencing of Properties

The purpose of referencing is twofold. The first is to obtain an **7–01** accurate picture of the property to be valued and the second to obtain an accurate picture of the relationship that property has to the area in which it is located. Before a property can be valued it is necessary for a survey to be carried out. Such a survey is generally referred to as "referencing"; in other words, to schedule or reference all relevant details of accommodation, size, structure, amenities and other factors which will enable the valuer to express his valuation by accurate comparison of one property with another.

When dealing with most hereditaments, *i.e.* shops, warehouses, factories, etc., it is usual to analyse actual rents paid (after adjustment to the statutory definition) into some yardstick, *e.g.* per square metre of floor area, and also to apply a similar method when actually valuing to rateable value. Correct measurements are, therefore, necessary for all properties.

Although referencing of small properties may be regarded as elementary, it is nevertheless most important and a task that fully repays care and provides a permanent record that can readily be consulted. When dealing with larger and more valuable premises the task calls for experienced staff who have often dealt with actual valuations and are thus able to express facts in such a form that enables the valuer to use valuation methods in a more ready manner. This particularly applies in referencing rateable plant and machinery.

Whilst descriptions and full measurements are essential, and plans highly desirable (and in many cases indispensable), it is a useful practice, particularly in the case of unusual properties, or properties distant from the surveyor's office, to have a photographic record to help recall the exact nature of the property concerned.

Whatever the class of property, there are certain facts which must **7–02** always be recorded, *e.g.* age, type and construction of the building, public services connected thereto, whether frontage roads are made up and taken over by the highway authority, whether any other persons not occupying the property have any rights of way over the property, general use of the property, and any other factors which would influence the mind of a tenant in bidding a rent for the property.

Additionally, it may be necessary to take note of improvement work carried out by the tenant, such as installation of a shop-front and plastering the walls, for example, where a shop has been taken as a "shell", in order to find the virtual rent at which the tenant sits. Similarly with offices let as a shell. With regard to particular classes of property, special factors are set out below.

Shops

7–03 The importance of accurate measurements of the accommodation is most clearly shown in this class of property. The variation in pitch or positional value between one shopping area and another underlines the need for accuracy. Traders are quite aware of the relative value of floor areas and, of course, frontage display is undoubtedly the most important factor. Internal floor areas are always used and the references should include a scaled or sketch plan of the layout of the whole of the accommodation, with detailed measurements of each part. The frontage is the most important of all measurements and so that the valuer can properly break down the evidence of rentals paid and correspondingly build up the valuation of other shops, it is necessary for the referencer to set out the calculation of the floor areas in the recognised manner of zone depths for the shop proper. For further details of referencing of shops see Chapter 8.

Offices

7–04 As in shops, the internal floor area method of measurement is invariably used. In many of the modern suites of offices the tenancy is for whole floors of open area, so leaving the tenant a choice of his own layout or division of sub-offices by the erection of prefabricated light partitioning capable of removal and not included in the rent charged by the owner. It will facilitate comparison between such offices and those where the offices are divided by permanent and solid brick walls if in each case the net office areas are calculated (*i.e.* passage and walls excluded).

Particular note should be made of the entrances, access, layout, natural lighting, sharing with other tenants of passages, toilets, etc. It may be necessary to exclude common passages, etc., where, for example, a floor is divided up and let as suites, although the value subsequently applied to the reduced areas may require to be adjusted (if justified) by an analysis of the available rental evidence. The proximity of public transport and car parking facilities should be noted.

In many cases the landlord provides services, *e.g.* cleaning and lighting of passages, toilets, supply of central heating, etc., and full details of these should be noted on the survey so that the valuer can make any necessary allowance once the details of the lease have been checked relating to the provision of service charges. Similar details need to be noted for owner occupied properties for the purpose of proper comparisons with tenanted properties.

Miscellaneous business and commercial properties, factories, etc.

In the case of such properties, it is essential that floor plans are drawn, **7–05** either in line sketch form at an approximate scale of proportions, or in scaled details of external measurements or greater detail showing wall thickness. In any case, the layout at a glance is of great importance. All measurements should also include floor heights and, in single-storey buildings or top floors of multi-storey buildings, the height is also important, on account of loss of heat. Construction and general structural condition must be noted as in most cases the tenant is presumed to be liable for all repairs, and any unusual structural defect or excess maintenance costs must tend to depreciate the annual letting value to the tenant.

Many industrial and commercial buildings are not purpose-built for the actual or present-day normal user and, therefore, any abnormal costs due to bad or uneconomic layout or siting must lessen the rental value. Therefore, the referencer must be careful to note these points.

Rateable plant and machinery is deemed to be part of the whole hereditament and the economic suitability must be noted in addition to the usual measurements of capacity. Basic knowledge of mechanical and electrical engineering is, of course, a valuable aid in properly describing each item of rateable plant and machinery so that the valuer's task is eased enabling the whole hereditament to be appraised without hindrance. All rateable plant and machinery must be adequately described for the benefit also of identification in official records as it will be appreciated that the Valuation Officer must supply on the ratepayer's request, a schedule of all plant and machinery included in the assessment. A separate summary sheet should, therefore, be kept showing the description and situation of each item.

As a final remark, the referencer should always adopt the practice of recording every fact of structure, measurement, layout and siting in such detail that together with a plan can provide such a picture of the property that it can be understood by the valuation court and others who may have to make decisions without the opportunity of actual inspection of the property.

Construction

7–06 The referencer should note the key information relating to the construction of the property. The following points should be checked and noted:

- Year of construction, or approximate age
- Type of construction with details of:

Roofs	–	design and materials
Walls	–	method of construction and materials
	–	wall facings and cladding
Floors	–	domestic—board and joist or solid
Finishes	–	type and quality
Services	–	mains supplies
		heating and ventilation, air conditioning.

The flooring in a factory or warehouse is of great importance as affecting the load that may be carried and its ability to withstand fire. The most common form of flooring in such buildings is, of course, concrete with a cement screed or granolithic finish. Upper floors are commonly of hollow block or "pot" flooring or reinforced concrete. For light assembly work concrete is of no great advantage, as it is found that it is not beneficial to the health of workers as the heat from the body is attracted to the floors. Nevertheless, it is more sanitary, as it is easily cleaned and washed down and is, of course, fireproof.

In recent construction, thermoplastic or polyvinyl tiles were used in domestic, commercial and industrial premises as a finish on concrete or other types of floor structure.

Currently floors tend to be left unfinished, *i.e.* in shell form, for the occupier to select a finish of their choice. Hi-technology conventional schemes must now provide adequate trunking facilities for communication and computer wiring and generally this will be incorporated in a raised floor.

The very high energy costs in the 1970s made occupiers of properties insulation conscious. Good design and insulation can save substantial amounts on running costs in all types of property and careful note should be made of heating and air conditioning systems and standards of insulation and energy conservation.

FACTORS AFFECTING COST

The two most important factors in determining cost are design and **7–07** construction. Most valuers will be familiar with the effects of design on cost from work associated with fire insurance valuation. The simpler the design the lower the cost per square metre. Architectural embellishments or unusual shapes, etc., will all add to the total cost. Similarly the materials and quality of finish will affect the total cost.

Cost estimation

The old traditional method of estimating the cost to build was by **7–08** obtaining the cubic content of the building and applying a rate per cube according to the type of construction. Increasingly, estimates of costs of construction are based on "gross internal area" or "gross external area" appropriately priced. Of necessity these methods only give an approximate figure and any factor out of the ordinary, such as an inaccessible site, must be allowed for.

Where pricing is to be based on floor areas care must be taken to apply the current price per m^2 to the appropriate floor measure which is generally gross internal or gross external depending upon type of property. Needless to say the area of all floors must be taken. Definitions of areas are to be found in the R.I.C.S. Code of Measuring Practice.

Whilst the quality of construction must always be noted, actual costs of construction are generally only needed where a contractors approach has to be used for valuation purposes. The referencer will also need to be aware of variations in running costs between one type of construction and another as tenants become increasingly concerned about total occupation costs. Very high running costs could lead to lower rental bids.

Estimating heights

7–09 In many cases, such as chimneys, it is necessary to estimate heights without the use of instruments. Where the height of a building is required it is usually possible to add the heights of the different floors, plus an allowance for the actual floors. Where this is not possible recourse may be had to counting the lengths of rainwater pipe (usually six feet or two metres) and the courses of brickwork which can be measured at ground level and a standard checked of courses per metre. Generally speaking, the occupier of the factory or premises is able to furnish information on difficult elements such as heights of chimneys.

MEASUREMENT OF BUILDINGS

7–10 Where measurements are used to compare buildings the usual method is to use square areas. The areas used may represent:

(1) The Net Internal Area (NIA) (formerly variously referred to as room area or carpet area or Effective Floor Area).
(2) The Gross External Area (GEA) (sometimes referred to as Reduced Covered Area (RCA) or gross floor space).
(3) The Gross Internal Area (GIA), the area inside the main walls.

Unfortunately, up until the present time there has been a marked lack of standardisation of practice in the computation of areas, and much dispute has arisen as to what should, or should not, be included. The Royal Institution of Chartered Surveyors code does, however, recommend the use of certain standard definitions. It is to be hoped that these terms will in time supersede the alternative descriptions in brackets.

It is usual to express areas in the case of shops, offices, flats and industrial premises as so many square feet or square metres. The expression "feet super" (abbreviated to f.s.) is still used, whilst in some parts of the country areas may still be referred to by the square yard. The changeover from imperial measure to metric has been slow and still not complete, and both units of measure may be necessary. Both the Inland Revenue and valuers in private practice still hold records of properties in imperial measures which are then simply converted to metric equivalents. Site areas should, of course, be given in hectares but acres are frequently quoted.

7–11 In the case of cold storage chambers and furniture depositories it is not unusual to compare premises according to their internal net cubic capacity. The following notes accord with generally accepted practice over many years.

1. Net Internal Area—sometimes referred to as room areas or carpet areas

This method is almost universally adopted in the case of business premises. The area is taken of each room, allowance being made for piers, staircases, etc. Thus the net areas arrived at represent the true effective or carpet area. It is obvious that the hypothetical tenant would give little or no extra rent for passages and corridors and the value of these is taken as being included in the rate per metre used for the rooms. If there are lobbies of any particular value, these can be added as an extra. WCs, etc., are not usually measured, and are taken as being represented in the rates per metre. Where they are better than the average, an extra can be made. When entering measurements in a notebook it is usual to write the measurements parallel to the road first, *i.e.* frontage, so that it is easy to check sizes afterwards and to facilitate comparisons.

2. Gross External Area—sometimes referred to as reduced covered area (RCA)

This is the area found by taking the length and breadth of a building between the outside faces of the walls and multiplying by the number of storeys, so as to get the equivalent area of covered space were the premises all on one floor. Thus, where there is a cavity wall, the area would be greater than that of a property identical but with solid walls.

This method of measurement does not allow for waste space and bad planning.

3. Gross Internal Area or area within the main walls

The same remarks apply as in the last method, except that the measurements are taken either from the internal structural face of the main walls, (or outside and the thickness of the walls deducted).

Net Internal Area is the preferred method but during referencing plans should be prepared to show internal and external measurements and the location and size of structural elements such as pillars.

In the case of commercial buildings the location of core facilities should be noted.

91

LOCATION AND OTHER FACTORS

7-12 The chapters dealing with the main classes of hereditaments detail further class specific issues that need to be noted by the referencer when inspecting a property for rating valuation purposes. The following points summarise the key matters that may need to be considered:

- **Location:** minor variations in location can make substantial differences to the rental bids that tenants will make in the open market. This is very pronounced in the case of central area shops, but can be significant for most types of property. Factors such as general and special accessibility, public transport and road communications will all be key points in the mind of a tenant.
- **Highways:** specific note should be made of existing and planned highways and of any height, weight and width constraints as well as restrictions on parking.
- **Planning:** the actual consent for the property should be checked as should any proposals of the local planning authority which might influence tenant's interest in a property. Permission for the construction of an out of town shopping centre may have a major impact on current open market rental bids for town centre retail units, even before the new centre has been constructed and let.

8

Assessment of Retail and Commercial Property

SHOPS AND STORES: GENERAL PRINCIPLES

The valuation of retail properties is one of the most common yet **8-01** exacting tasks which will fall to the rating valuer. It will prove difficult because of the many factors, which must be studied and reflected in the assessment.

At the time of a general revaluation the difficulties are increased by the limited amount of relevant modern rental evidence available and the differing bases upon which individual rents have been negotiated. Consequently an accurate basis of assessment will be dependent upon the skill of the valuer, both in the realistic devaluation of the available evidence and upon the selection and application of the resultant data.

The mention of the word "basis" may perhaps suggest that a large number of shops will be evenly priced at so much per square foot or per square metre, as the case may be, but in practice the basis will generally vary from parade to parade, and even within individual parades.

The reasons for variations may be manifold and sometimes will not be apparent to the casual visitor to a town but may be readily appreciated by the shop specialist or the experienced local practitioner who will be aware of the idiosyncrasies of a fickle shopping public.

Basically, however, the value of shops will vary in accordance with the three fundamental factors, quantity, quality and position, the latter being of paramount importance.

Shops are of various types and in a region will fall into the following **8-02** categories according to position: regional or main shopping centres, secondary shopping centres, local shopping centres, local shopping parades, isolated shops (including corner shops and village shops).

In a smaller town there may only be the last three of these groupings.

It might also be noted that walk round stores, departmental stores, superstores, retail warehouses and some out of town shops, do not readily fit into any basis which may be appropriate for smaller shops and therefore will need special consideration and treatment.

Further reference to these specialised categories will be made, but whatever the type of establishment, the valuation will centre round the referencing and the analysis upon which the basis is founded, and the thoroughness and accuracy of these operations will make or mar the valuation.

REFERENCING

8-03 Whilst the actual survey of the property may be entrusted to a well trained assistant a detailed inspection by the valuer is essential. Particular observation should be made of the quality of the structure, including the internal and external finish, as this is something which may be hard to express adequately on paper and needs to be seen to be fully appreciated. Observation must, however, be primarily directed towards the quality of the trading position and an endeavour made to assess its relative popularity by comparison with other positions. These observations will later be checked against the basis which emerges from rental and other evidence.

A most detailed survey is necessary and nowadays it is essential to prepare a plan of all the floors. These plans are most useful for making comparisons, and for production before Valuation Tribunals, etc. The general practice is for the assistant inspecting to have a notebook faintly ruled with squares, as for graph paper, enabling the referencer to sketch in the premises as measured, and for a proper plan to be drawn up in the office. Notebooks are sometimes ruled up with spaces for address, terms of lease, size of rooms, etc., but as in practice the information obtained seldom fits into the fixed rulings, this is of doubtful advantage. A "checklist" of questions to be answered may be useful.

At the same time as taking measurements a careful note should be made of the position of the shop, as, obviously, this is fundamental to its value. It is always a useful operation, if circumstances permit, to make a block plan of the whole surrounding area of the shop to be valued. If this is done to, say, a scale of 1/500, it is possible to show the shop depths of all the adjoining shops. Upon this plan can be recorded positions of bus stops, pedestrian crossings and other extraneous factors which may have some bearing upon values. Some sites have a good advertising position, whilst others may have a poor position for the purpose of attracting passers-by. It is not unusual to find that opposite sides of a road have different values. This may be due to a difference in width of pavement, the presence of multiple shops, a break in continuity caused by the presence of offices, one-way traffic, location of public car parks, etc. All such items as these plus names and trades of adjoining occupiers' can be shown upon the block plan, which is undoubtedly the most convenient way of recording these facts.

Where available large scale ordnance survey sheets or "Goad" **8–04** plans of important shopping centres can be used as the basis for this essential part of the referencing process. In this last mentioned event the information needs to be checked and if necessary updated. A photographic record can also be useful. In all cases the date of the inspection and the name of the surveyor or referencer should be recorded on the measurement sheets, the location survey or the photograph as the case may be. Whatever the derivation of the block plan it will provide a most useful overall check upon the relativity of the valuations, provided that other factors such as quality of structure and finish are not overlooked when making comparisons. Such a plan will also prove most useful as a ready source of information in the Valuation or Lands Tribunals.

It must never be overlooked that the value of a particular shop is dependent almost wholly upon its trading potential. For many retail trades this in turn will, in no small measure, reflect its prominence or advertisement value within its particular centre. Thus, the amount of display or glass frontage is of considerable importance, and this gives added value to shops with a return frontage. The amount of display varies according to the trade carried on. Note should be made as to the fascia and type of front—whether wood and glass with a tiled stallboard or modern metal and glass with low stallboard, whether the display is affected by stanchions or piers, etc.

With some the trades aspect is important. Jewellers like to be on the sunny side of the street for instance, in order to make their wares show to better advantage. Confectioners are best situated close to places of amusement and so forth. These detailed factors will affect the trading capacity of the shop, and hence its rental value.

Having inspected the exterior and noted the details already referred **8–05** to and the trade carried on, the assistant should proceed inside the shop and note the materials used in the construction of the walls, floors and ceiling, the ceiling height, lighting, heating, etc. Particular note should be made of any disadvantages, *e.g.* awkward plan shape, a difference in floor level, whether the shop space is spoilt by piers or a staircase, etc. Day lighting to the rear of the shop is most desirable. If the sketch plan is prepared to scale the question of zoning or of taking different parts of the shop at different rates can be left until all the data are available. Some shops have a basement or upper part, and the use to which these are put along with the convenience of the access should be noted in addition to the consequential details. The actual use is, of course, important, but it must always be remembered that the actual occupier is not the only occupier (the property must be regarded as vacant and to let). It is equally important to consider and note whether the actual use is the best possible use, though both town planning and any other publicly imposed restrictions must be borne in mind. Size is only one factor, and two shops built identically will have different values if in one case the basement is adapted by having a good floor and panelling so that it can be used as a showroom, and the other basement is only fit for storage. The accessibility of the subsidiary parts is most important as affecting their value. Upper parts, for instance, are generally not suitable for selling space unless there is a fairly wide and easy staircase, escalator or passenger lift. If the upper part has a separate entrance and is self-contained and let off, a separate assessment must be placed upon it.

8-06 The difference in value between old shop premises and new shop premises may be significant though certain very old premises may themselves have a premium value for certain trades on account of their antiquity.

One point which requires careful attention when referencing a property within a parade of shops arises from the *rebus sic stantibus* rule. Thus, the dividing wall frequently found at the rear of the ground floor sales space may be of a chattel non-structural nature, a demountable partition, or a permanent structural wall. In the case of the structural wall the property has to be valued on the assumption that this physical barrier cannot be altered.[1] Thus, according to the circumstances of the local letting market for shop property, such a wall might not have an adverse effect upon the rent the hypothetical tenant might reasonably be expected to pay for the hereditament. Strong evidence will be required, however, to prove that a tenant's alterations actually reduce the value of the shop.

A factor of importance particularly in the case of larger shops is a rear access incorporating availability of vehicular access and rear entrance for goods.

---

[1] *Lewis Vitners t/a Smokey Joe v. Speight (V.O.)* [1984] 274 E.G. 1177.

CONSIDERATION AND DEVALUATION OF RENTALS

The second important contributory step in the valuation of shops is **8-07** the appreciation and devaluation of the rental evidence. The basic evidence of rents may be available on forms of return or may be known to the private practitioner. Whatever rental information is known, it will generally need to be augmented by further detail as to the background of the rental negotiations, and with supplementary details of happenings since the negotiations (e.g. improvements).

The type of inquiries which should, if possible, be made in relation to rental transactions are as follows:

(1) Whether the occupier had a lease previously, so that the present tenancy constitutes a renewal. If so, further questions arise, such as:

what was the former rent and when was this negotiated? was the old lease surrendered prematurely for a new lease at a lesser rent than full market rental? was there capital expenditure by the lessees during the currency of the old lease which may have influenced negotiations?

(2) Whether any personal relationship or any business relationship exists between the landlord and the tenant.

(3) Was there any premium paid? Were there any improvements contemplated at the time of the rental negotiations, and were these carried out and at what cost? Were the premises in disrepair such that the lessee was obliged to expend a capital sum at the commencement of tenancy?

(4) Are there any clauses in the lease strictly limiting the trade to be carried on. If so, does the same landlord control other properties in the block or vicinity enabling a local trading monopoly to be conferred? Is there thus created an artificial monopoly which has influenced the tenant to pay a greater rent that the open market rental?[2]

(5) Did the lease negotiations amount to a capital transaction? i.e. did the lessee own the premises and sell out to a lessor willing to lease them back to him?

(6) Did the rent arise from the exercise of a rent review? If so

---

[2] *W. A. Rawlinson & Co. Ltd & Others v. J. F. Pritchard (V.O.)* (1959) 52 R. & I.T. 182. See also *Dyer v. Mullard* (1958) 51 R. & I.T. 794.

what were the assumed terms of the transaction as stipulated within the lease?

8–08   The object of these inquiries is to find out how much weight should be attached to a particular rent as evidence of value or to what extent the rent should be adjusted. The best evidence is generally that which has been freshly negotiated between parties entirely unrelated in either a personal or business capacity for a first tenancy (*i.e.* not a renewal) for a short term (as opposed to a long lease) and without fine, premium or other incidental capital commitment.

In practice, there is usually very little rental evidence which is in this perfect category and it is frequently necessary to use less ideal evidence which may need some adjustment to bring it into line with the statutory definition.

Full explanation as to the adjustment of rentals for repairs, premiums and improvements was given in Chapter 2 and these principles, as necessary, should be followed up in dealing with shop rentals.

Further factors which may have a bearing upon shop rentals are as follows:

1. Goodwill. A tenant may by trading for many years create personal goodwill which will increase the rental value to that particular occupier. Such goodwill cannot be taken into account for rating. In fact almost all renewals of shop leases will today be negotiated within the statutory rights conferred on the tenant by Part II of the Landlord and Tenant Act 1954. Under these provisions the value of goodwill attaching to the premises by virtue of the tenant's occupation has to be excluded from the agreed rent.

2. Tenants' improvements. Tenants may carry out improvements to their properties during the currency of a lease. Where the tenant was under a contractual obligation to his landlord to carry out the improvement concerned, the value of the improvement will be taken into account when the new rent is determined on renewal. On the other hand Part II of the Landlord and Tenant Act 1954 as amended provides, that on the occasion of renewal within 21 years (or more) after a tenant has, otherwise than in pursuance of an obligation to the landlord, effected an improvement, the value of the improvement must not be taken into account when determining the rent under the new lease. Accordingly, where a lease has been renewed under the provisions of the Landlord and Tenant Act 1954, the value of former improvements made by the tenant will not necessarily be included within the agreed rent so that an adjustment must be made to bring the rental evidence into line with the statutory definition. The increasing complexity of rent reviews and renewals is such that considerable care needs to be exercised when analysing rents agreed on review or renewal to ascertain the extent to which they do or do not reflect the added value of tenants' improvements.

Having selected the rents which may be accepted as indicative of **8–09** rental value and having adjusted them, as necessary, to the terms as required by the legislation, it is then necessary to devalue them, *i.e.* apportion them in such manner that a fair proportion is allocated to each contributory part of the premises, *e.g.* basement, storage accommodation, offices, living quarters (if any) and shop itself. This stage in the process is important, since the effect of allocating insufficient rental to the other parts (known as ancillaries) is to inflate the value attributed to the shop, and it is the value of this portion (*i.e.* the shop) which the valuer is most particularly seeking to establish. This "stripping off" process should be applied on an individual basis and not at a pre-determined scale of values, for the sake of apparent uniformity, as such an inflexible process may produce distorted results.

Particularly difficult problems arise where the ancillary space includes sales on basement or upper floors, as the value of such space will tend to reflect the position of the shop in the same way as ground floor sales space. Devaluation in such circumstances requires considerable experience, and several "trial" devaluations may be necessary before the figures provide a proper relative balance as between the various constituent parts of the property.

It may seem today to be a statement of the obvious (although the **8–10** principle was slow to be recognised) that where rental evidence and observation indicate that different basic values should be applied in valuing front ground floor sales space of shops in different sections of a street or shopping centre, then any selling space on other floors should be devalued (and subsequently valued) reflecting such differentials. However, the same exact fractions may not necessarily be appropriate to other shopping areas, each location being dependent upon local conditions and analysed evidence.

A further point not to overlook at this stage is to be prepared to make some allowance, if appropriate, for return frontages so that should a corner shop be amongst the rental evidence, the basis evolved for single fronted shops is not inflated on this account. Return frontages may be dealt with by pricing at so much per foot run or by percentage enhancement of the shop value. Whatever method is used, it should reflect the relative importance of the side road. If the side road is in fact a busy shopping street special treatment such as additional zoning from that frontage may be appropriate which will make the devaluation of the rent of any such shop particularly complicated.

When all the rents have been devalued thus far, it is then open to the valuer to divide the various rents as allocated to shop portions by their respective areas and thus obtain a rent per square foot or a rent per square metre for the shop. Rent schedules may thereupon be produced to record in convenient form the details of rents and their devaluation.

Whilst for large shops of say 20,000 square feet (2,000 m²) it is useful to devalue in the manner described above (*i.e.* on an overall basis), in the case of smaller shops this may lead to widely differing results, particularly if the shops devalued are of differing depths. It is to overcome and minimise the difficulty, and endeavour to arrive at a common basis, that the system of devaluation and valuation by zoning principles was devised.

THE ZONING METHOD

8-11 It is obvious that the front part of a shop is more valuable than the rear portion as the purpose of a shop is to sell goods, and the front with its display is thus of greater importance. The value will decrease towards the rear as these portions will not be so suitable as selling space. In order to allow for this reduction in value a method of comparison called the zoning system has come into general use, the shops being divided into belts or zones to which different values are allocated. The front zone, which is taken as the most valuable, is normally called Zone "A", the next zone back "B", and so on. Many valuers use zones 20 feet deep, whilst others adopt a depth of 15 feet for the front zone, with perhaps 25 for the others, but the depth to be used should have regard to the normal depths of shops in the area. There are no rigid rules, except that the same zoning depths must be used throughout the street or sector, the theory being to endeavour to adopt the system of zone depths which best suits the local circumstances. Generally, but not invariably, the more important the shopping street and the more valuable the shops concerned the greater the appropriate Zone "A" depth. As the Lands Tribunal stated in a decision[3] concerning large shops in Southampton's main shopping street:

---

[3] *Trevail v. C. & A. Modes Ltd; Trevail v. Marks & Spencer Ltd* [1967] R.A. 124.

"There is no hard and fast rule. Sometimes it is thought best to have two zones (A and B) and a remainder; sometimes to have three zones (A, B and C) and a remainder; and sometimes, as was the case in Above Bar, Southampton, to have one zone (A) of 60 feet and a remainder. Once a decision on this point has been reached, the same zones must be adopted for all the shops in the street whether for devaluation or valuation."

It is to be noted that a Zone "A" of 60 feet would only seem to be justifiable in exceptional circumstances, if it is not to offend the theory behind the system that the rental value of sales space diminishes as the shop depth increases. In normal circumstances a Zone "A" depth exceeding 25 feet would be unusual.

The decision of the Lands Tribunal referred to above is an **8-12** important one as the Tribunal took the opportunity to include in its decision a detailed exposition of the zoning method and its application.

Practice varies as to the relative values to be attributable to the different zones, though it is normal to "halve back", the second zone being taken as one half the value of the first, the third at half the second, and so on, but practice differs as to the value to be attributed to the remainder as, for example, one-eighth of the Zone "A" price may be absurdly little, and be less than storage value.

It may be noted here that "just as depth affects remainder prices, so shallowness affects Zone 'A' prices; therefore it may be proper to 'gross up' the Zone 'A' price of a shop not having the depth adopted for Zone 'A' in that sector of shops" (as per the Tribunal's decision in the Southampton case referred to above).

Nevertheless, the valuer must never lose sight of the fact that zone depths, and the relativity of zone values, should preferably not be determined by an arbitrary decision. It will probably be necessary for the valuer to make some trial devaluations of the best available rental evidence, before deciding upon the combination of depths of zone and relativities of zone values which best fit the physical and economic characteristics of the shops being valued.

Having made the point in the previous paragraph certain practical **8-13** constraints must be noted. First, if a parade has been fully referenced in the past using a particular pattern of zoning, unless actual rental evidence points to a resultant serious distortion, the likely pragmatic approach will be to continue as before. This decision appears to have been reached by the Valuation Office Agency for, in spite of metrication, zoning depths remain the equivalent of the old imperial standard.

Secondly, analysis can be carried out between revaluations of established assessments. If this is done, particularly by a ratepayers surveyor, it would be impractical to deviate widely from the then accepted system on which established values have been determined.

Two practical observations are appropriate at this juncture. First, the zoning principle is widely adopted by the profession as an aid to rental valuations albeit that whereas rating valuation is inevitably carried out on the basis of metric areas, the profession when dealing with rental valuation adheres to areas expressed in square feet. Secondly, the most common zoning combination used is on the basis of 20' 0" depths, halving back, and using three zones and a remainder.

Further comments upon the zoning method, and particularly its application to large shops will be found in paragraph 8–24.

8–14   The whole selling area on the ground floor is often expressed in the terms of Zone "A", (abbreviated to "area ITZA") and the following example for a shop of 20 feet frontage will make this clear:

Zone	Area (ft)		
A	20 × 20	=	400 ft super/37.2 m²
B	20 × 20	=	400 ft super/37.2 m²
C	20 × 10	=	200 ft super/18.6 m²

In terms of Zone "A"

"A"	=	400 sq. ft. or 37.2 m² of "A"
"B" 400 × ½	=	200 sq. ft. or 18.6 m² of "A"
"C" 200 × ¼	=	50 sq. ft. or 4.6 m² of "A"
	=	650 sq. ft. or 60.4 m² of "A"

Then if the R.V. of the shop portion represented by the rent is, say, £10,000 the value per square metre in terms of "A" will be £165.56.

i.e. $\frac{£10.000}{60.4}$ (or $\frac{£15.58 \text{ per sq. ft. } i.e. \ (£10,000)}{650}$). This can be checked as follows:

37.2 m² at £165.56 per m²	=	£6159
37.2 m² at £82.78 per m²	=	£3079
18.6 m² at £41.39 per m²	=	£770
		£10,008 = say £10,000

The application of the zoning to a specimen parade of shops in a small town will now be illustrated. For simplicity this example is worked through in imperial measurement.

Figure 8.1.

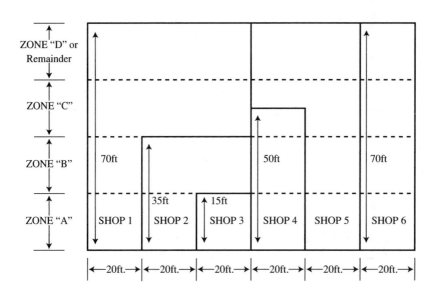

Shop number 1 is owner-occupied, and it is desired to arrive at a basis from the rented shops in order to assess this one and others adjoining for which no rental is paid.

The zones used are "A" 15 feet, "B" and "C" 20 feet deep, with "D" **8–15** (remainder), and "B" is taken at one-half the value of "A", "C" at one-half the value of "B", and so on.

Shop No. 1   In terms of Zone "A"

Zone "A" 20 ft. × 15 ft. = 300 sq. ft.	300 sq. ft.
Zone "B" 20 ft. × 20 ft. = 400 sq. ft. at ½	200
Zone "C" 60 ft. × 20 ft. = 1,200 sq. ft. at ¼	300
Zone "D" 60 ft. × 15 ft. = 900 sq. ft. at ⅛	112
Total in terms of "A"	912

Shop No. 2

Zone "A" 20 ft. × 15 ft. = 300 sq. ft.	300 sq. ft.
Zone "B" 20 ft. × 40 ft. = 800 sq. ft. at ½	400
Total in terms of "A"	700

103

Shop No. 3

Zone "A" 20 ft. × 15ft. =	300 sq. ft.	300

Shop No. 4

Zone "A" 20 ft. × 15ft. =	300 sq. ft.	300 sq. ft.
Zone "B" 20 ft. × 20ft. =	400 sq. ft. at ½	200
Zone "C" 20 ft. × 15 ft. =	300 sq. ft. at ¼	75
	Total in terms of "A"	575

Shop No. 5

Zone "A" 20 ft. × 15ft. =	300 sq. ft.	300 sq. ft.
Zone "B" 20 ft. × 20 ft. =	400 sq. ft. at ½	200
Zone "C" 20 ft. × 15ft.		
40 ft. × 5 ft. =	500 sq. ft. at ¼	125
Zone "D" 40 ft. × 15 ft. =	600 sq. ft. at ⅛	75
	Total in terms of "A"	700

Shop No. 6

Zone "A" 20 ft. × 15 ft. =	300 sq. ft.	300 sq. ft.
Zone "B" 20 ft. × 20 ft. =	400 sq. ft. at ½	200
Zone "C" 20 ft. × 20 ft. =	400 sq. ft. at ¼	100
Zone "D" 20 ft. × 15 ft. =	300 sq. ft. at ⅛	37
	Total in terms of "A"	637

Shop	R.V. justified by rent	Areas in terms of Zone "A"	Rents in terms of Zone "A"
1	Owner-occupied	912	–
2	£9,000	700	£12.86
3	£3,750	300	£12.50
4	£7,200	575	£12.51
5	£9,300	700	£13.28
6	£8,500	637	£13.34

It will be observed that a level of a little over £12.50 per square foot is indicated. The higher values occur, however, in the case of units 5 and 6 where there is a substantial remainder. If an alternative notation of zones A and B plus remainder is used a more even set of results is achieved thus:

Shop No. 5 in terms of Zone "A" = 775 sq. ft. = £12.00 per sq. ft.
Shop No. 6 in terms of Zone "B" = 675 sq. ft. = £12.59 per sq. ft.

8–16   As these values per square foot agree more nearly with the others, it would seem reasonable to adopt a basis of £12.50 per square foot and apply this to all the shops, treating Zones "C" and remainder as being of equal value.

Shop No. 1 will then be:

Zones "A", "B" and "C" as before	—	800 sq. ft.
Remainder 900 sq. ft. at ¼	—	225 sq. ft.
Total in terms of Zone "A"	—	1,025 sq. ft.
1,025 sq. ft. at £12.50 = £12,969; say	—	£12,975 R.V.

Irregularities in shape, such as are present in the rear part of Shops Nos. 1 and 5, may, where rental evidence or circumstances indicate, warrant a disability allowance or other adjustment, but eligibility for such allowance is not automatic and will depend entirely upon the individual circumstances.

It is most unlikely that a parade of shops would devalue as conveniently as those shown above, and the facts are assumed so as to illustrate the method of procedure. In practice the rents would devalue to varying rates per square foot and this may be due to different planning, flank windows, better shop fronts, etc., and unless these factors are noted when the property is surveyed, the reasons for the varying amounts will not be appreciated. Other factors which will account for some differences in rental are the probable variation in the dates when the rents were fixed (except in the case of new parades or precincts), the relationship between the parties and the good or bad bargain they have made.

It may appear that when all rents are devalued in terms of Zone "A" **8-17** there is still a wide gap between the relative rents of the small unit lock-ups and the relative rent of the larger shop or the shop with more subsidiary accommodation. If this is so, one should try with these small units to ascertain by what percentage the relative rent is inflated over and above the relative rents of more ordinary sized shop units. In this way, it may emerge from an examination of the devalued rents of several such small unit shops that these merit special treatment by way of percentage addition when making valuations using the "common basis" applied in the block or immediately locality.

Although the zoning method as described above is by far the most widely used when valuing shops for rating purposes at the present time it is not inviolate or sacrosanct and other methods may be used. The profession's reluctance to use the zoning method for large stores may give some impetus to the use of alternative methods. The most usual alternative is an overall rate expressed in terms of price per square metre or per square foot.

To summarise, the valuer must select the method considered to be the most suitable for all the shop properties which are to be valued.

Thus, not only must the method yield values which are consistent with and supported by the rents used as a basis, but it must also be capable of applying such values fairly to all the shops to be valued, since it is, as always, fundamental that "as you devalue so you must value".

8–18   It is, of course, necessary to value premises at their value at the time of the valuation, and therefore evidence of a rent entered into several years previously, when conditions were different, may be no guide. Thus, particular attention should be paid to the more recent evidence, and in some offices graphs are kept showing the rates per square foot represented by tenancies entered into during the year, so that one can see if rents are rising or falling and by how much.

Reference has already been made to the fact that improvements carried out by the tenant must be taken into consideration. It may be, however, that money has been spent unwisely and that to take a percentage on the outlay as representing the increase in rental value would be unfair. Again, money may be spent in pursuance of a long-term policy, and it may be that the improvement may not be immediately effective. In such cases a low rate of interest should be used. In other cases money may have been spent to maintain the existing rental value.

It must be noted here that proper application of the available rental evidence may be secured not only by appropriate use of the zoning or overall methods, but also by end-adjustments such as are referred to later.

THE VALUATION

8–19 Thus far, the valuer has concentrated upon the referencing, ascertaining all the facts relative to the property, and the devaluation of the rental evidence, the latter operation being an endeavour to arrive at a starting basis for the valuation. Thereafter it rests with the valuer's judgment to build up a valuation which will fit all the facts and which will be supported by the available rental evidence. If the valuer does the exercise properly then the value ascribed will stand the test of comparison with assessment of other shops in the vicinity and will take account of every factor, advantageous or detrimental, which may have some influence on the rental likely to be negotiated in the open market.

Mention has already been made of the many important points to be considered in valuing shop premises, but it is as well to emphasise that these points should be taken into account and adjustments made after a provisional calculation has been undertaken using the zoning method or overall method, and after due allowance has been made for return frontages, etc. A few of the points to be borne in mind are the direction of foot traffic, zebra crossings, busy corners, crossing places, one-way traffic streets, no-waiting restrictions, churches, bus stops, railway stations, markets, etc., all of which affect the number of persons who will pass by, and hence the number of potential customers.

The popularity of a shopping location may be gauged, to some extent, by observation of density of shoppers and by taking a census of passers-by, but this latter method may be misleading and should therefore be used with caution. In such cases local distortions such as date, time of day, weather, etc., have to be allowed for. Moreover, the number of passing pedestrians is not the only factor to determine value, for example passing students and old age pensioners may not have the same spending power as others.

It is emphasised that the valuer should never be a blind slave to arithmetic, an arithmetical calculation should be made and then adjusted boldly, if necessary, where individual factors point to a value either higher or lower than that produced by an arithmetic approach. Mention has already been made of various categories of shops, and brief notes of factors relative to these will be recorded. The question of end adjustments for quality, quantity, etc., are considered later.

Isolated shops

In some respects these present particular difficulty because, if not **8–20** actually let, the valuer is driven to comparison with others in different situations and with different potentialities. Even when actually let, there is often complication because the rental may include living accommodation. Notwithstanding these difficulties, the value ascribed should bear comparison with shops in blocks and parades and with assessments of other isolated shops. It should be borne in mind when dealing with this type, that much will depend upon the degree of isolation which the shop enjoys, *i.e.* the density of houses in the vicinity and the absence of other shops and superstores. The assessment might therefore be expected to vary with the degree of monopoly arising from the absence of presence of competition in the locality.

Local shopping parades

8-21 These will present no great difficulty if there are useful rents within the block to give a guide, but may present comparison problems if this is not the case. Particular difficulty may be experienced if these are local authority shops and are let on tenancies which have been secured by means of competitive tender. The wide variations of rental which emerge if there are also restrictions governing the trades to be pursued and the complications of devaluation are such that a more satisfactory approach will be by way of careful comparison with other shops for which less tainted rental evidence is available.

Considerable care should be taken to ensure that shops of this class are valued in such a way that comparison one with another and with other similar blocks can be made. This does not mean that a uniform basis should be adopted, but merely that differences made should be fully justified and readily capable of reasoned explanation.

Local shopping centres

8-22 These will exercise all the skill and care of the valuer to produce a satisfactory pattern of values. Most local shopping centres tend to be a mixture of old and new properties in which a proportion of the old shops may have been modernised in varying degree, with the result that there are very wide variations of quality to contend with. Added to this there will often be comparatively little really satisfactory rental evidence. Zoning principles will almost certainly assist the valuer in devaluing rents to a reasonably uniform basis and if used intelligently will help in building up a consistent pattern of assessments. The degree of success will depend upon the quality of the referencing, the selection and appreciation of the rental evidence and its scientific devaluation, and also upon the skilful application of valuation principles to take account of all the differences in quality and position as well as mere size.

Regional and main shopping centres

8-23 As with local shopping centres similar principles will be followed out, but with higher values. If a position is known to be the finest in town one must not be misled by rental evidence of doubtful authenticity into fixing assessments which show a lower basis than in local or secondary positions. There will, however, be room for marked variations to take account of quality of structure and positional differentiations. There should be a constant endeavour to ensure that there is a proper appreciation of all the relevant factors and that an intelligible pattern of values is built up which accords with common sense. Most shopkeepers and business people and many from amongst the ordinary shopping public could grade the quality of trading positions in a town with a fair degree of accuracy and the valuer should tend to follow this common-sense lead, picking up rental evidence wherever possible to support an overall pattern. The use of shopping counts in this connection has already been referred to above. In the case of modern covered shopping centres rents may have been fixed on a "turnover" basis. Usually a small fixed sum is payable together with a percentage of gross takings. Such rents can vary greatly depending on the trade and often do not represent what would otherwise be open market rents.

Departmental and walk-round stores

The assessment of shops in this category is specialist in nature as **8–24** inevitably there is precious little, if any, rental evidence and there is difficulty in attempting to relate these to any basis appropriate for smaller shops. Difficulties of this sort are frequently overcome by some form of quantity allowance but the justification and degree of adjustment are controversial.

"Case" decisions in respect of large stores have not shown any consistent ruling and this has been justified by the fact that each case should be treated on its merits and in relation to the evidence proffered. These two points were reiterated by the Lands Tribunal in what may be regarded as a leading decision[4] relating to the valuation of very large departmental or walk-round stores for rating purposes. The Tribunal commented:

> "... we would emphasise again that the zoning method was the only method of valuation advanced at the hearing. We have therefore had no alternative but to adopt that method and within the four corners of the evidence we are satisfied with the conclusion at which we have arrived. But we are not satisfied that our answer does in fact represent the rent which a tenant could reasonably be expected to pay. We think the difficulties we have expressed above in dealing with the question of quantity allowance are only a surface illustration of a doubt which lies deeper, and which was expressed by the Tribunal as early as 1958 in *British Home Stores v. Brighton County Borough Council*, viz.,[5] whether in cases such as this the zoning method is not being stretched a good deal beyond its capabilities. The complexities of the calculations

---

[4] See n. 3 above.
[5] *British Home Stores Ltd v. Brighton C.B.C., & Burton; Fine-Fare Ltd v. Burton & Brighton C.B.C.* (1958) R. & I.T. 665.

necessary if one is to try to find the value of a store with over 43,000 square feet from rental evidence relating to shops with an area of only 2,000 or 3,000 square feet, and the consequences which follow from a variation in price or other valuation details, incline us to the view that some other less complicated method of valuation of 'large' shops or stores should be tested."

8-25   In 1980 the Lands Tribunal decided an appeal[6] in respect of a department store occupied by John Lewis where the zoning method was used in the absence of any rental evidence of comparable stores. An opinion based on zoning is only acceptable where direct rental evidence is lacking.

As a result of "sale and leaseback" transactions in recent years, more direct evidence (albeit suspect) is available. Accordingly, at the present time the market does tend to attempt direct comparison of values as between large stores by the pricing of overall net floor areas. Rating valuations should and generally do follow the market.

Hypermarkets, superstores and retail warehouses

8-26 This category of retail establishment has evolved in the last two decades. It owes its origin, at least in part, to the grocery superstore and exploits the fact of extensive and increasing car ownership combined with the inconvenience of parking at traditional shopping centres. At the outset the properties used were usually traditional warehouses with some (often limited) car parking. However, as the demand for such shopping facilities has increased, specialised purpose-built properties often with extensive parking have been created to meet the demand. Occasionally such new properties are arranged in groups or enclaves thus sharing communal car-parking.

Apart from age and general suitability it is possible, largely because of town planning controls, to categorise such properties into user groups in terms of a decreasing car parking requirement as follows:

(1) Food retailers (highest value and largest parking requirement).
(2) D.I.Y. retailers.
(3) Furniture, carpets, electrical and miscellaneous retailers.

Value, however, is the result of supply and demand so that currently, values are dependent upon the availability of competing stores and of suitable sites which can be developed for this purpose. Where the absence of competition occurs, a quasi monopoly can arise

---

[6] *Lewis (John) & Co. Ltd v. Goodwin (V.O.) (1980) RAI.*

which will be reflected in higher rental values. Other factors influencing value are location, local population, accessibility, prominence, degree of adaptation, closeness of other complimentary retail warehouse operations, etc.

The commercial market for such properties is almost invariably quoted on the basis of a rent per square foot of "gross internal area" inclusive of car parking and it is thought that the valuation profession may well follow this lead. Rating valuations again follow the market though may be expressed in terms of net internal area. The units may or may not include car parking.

ADJUSTMENTS FOR DISABILITIES AND QUALITY

There are five basic problems to be looked at under this heading. They **8-27** can for convenience be categorised as follows:

(1) Shops where the "remainder zone" on the ground floor is of considerable depth and area.
(2) Shops where a substantial part of the sales space is on floors other than the ground floor.
(3) Shops considerably larger than the normal range of size where the quality of the accommodation is superior by reason of the basic structure and superior building services (lifts, escalators, heating, comfort, cooling, air conditioning, fire precautions, and for customer toilets, etc.).
(4) Shops which by virtue of (1) or (2) above have a floor area considerably in excess of the typical units in the particular shopping centre.
(5) Shops whose potential value is reduced by factors which reduce efficiency below normally perceived expectations. Such factors include, bad layout, awkward plan shape, lack of basic facilities such as delivery bays, changes in floor level, intrusive structural columns, etc.

Reference to several of these matters has already been made earlier in this chapter but whatever difficulties may be involved in valuing large shops, the main problem is usually one of deciding whether or not an end addition or allowance is to be made on account of differences in character or size between the store in question and other properties in the area, including of course those from which the values adapted were derived. Particular regard must be had to analysis of all relevant rental evidence to ascertain whether any light is cast upon the justification or otherwise of making such end adjustments.

8-28   Such additions or allowances are normally made in respect of the whole premises in the absence of any special circumstances affecting only part of the hereditament.

The basic concept of a quantity allowance is founded upon the economic principle that bulk can normally be obtained more cheaply than small parcels. Arguments against quantity allowances are mainly threefold. First, that the economic principle outlined above does not necessarily apply to land which, so far as peak position land is concerned, is almost always limited in supply and this limited supply tends to be matched with substantial demand. Secondly, that the zoning principle is specifically designed to deal with quantity so far as shop depth is concerned, and that extra frontage (unless excessive in relation to depth) only ensures a well-balanced shop which contributes to value rather than detracts from it. Thirdly, market conditions, *e.g.* for superstores, can sometimes result in unfulfilled demand for suitable units resulting in premium values rather than the reverse. There is the further point that in attempting to compare small shops with large stores, there is often a vast difference in quality. The small shops may be brick structures with plastered walls and ceilings and boarded floors. The large shop will probably be a steel-framed structure with perhaps special block ceiling, expensive plaster-faced or veneer wall panels and granolithic floor finish; air conditioning, sprinkler system, space heating, escalators, lifts, etc. The appropriate quality differential may therefore have to be balanced against any quantity allowance which might otherwise be justified.

8-29   Upon the question of quantity allowance, the following extract from a decision[7] may be said still to contain the current views of the Lands Tribunal on this problem:

> "We do not accept therefore the submission that there is a presumption in favour of a quantity allowance for large shops when valued on the zoning method; but we do accept that, as the method was originally based on factual rental evidence, it requires comparatively slender evidence to establish that in any particular shopping centre quantity is still allowed for in the market. Once that is done, it must be answered by positive evidence to displace it."

The Tribunal also stated that evidence relating to information derived from rents of properties elsewhere may be of assistance in

---

[7] See n. 3 above.

certain circumstances improving or disproving the need for such allowance.

Before leaving these problems a brief reference is appropriate to the value of sales and ancillary space on other floors. In the John Lewis case (referred to above), virtually all values were expressed as a fraction of Zone "A" price, which is not unusual. However, the particular divisors used in that case are not universal and in an earlier case[8] the Lands Tribunal stated that although the position affected the whole of the premises to some extent, nevertheless, no mathematical relationship could be regarded as appropriate. It nevertheless approved a pricing of the first floor which amounted to one-sixth of the Zone "A" pricing.

It should also be mentioned that in the large departmental or **8-30** walk-round store, the basement floor, provided access and lighting are good, is often worth virtually as much as first floor sales space on account of the preference of the shopping public to walk down rather than up.

There are, however, few general principles. Each individual hereditament has to be looked at against the facts of the case, such as available rental evidence, the size of the hereditament in relation to the importance of the shopping centre and the size of other units in that centre. Thus, allowances for quantity allowances were not given to walk-round stores in Brighton's principal shopping street! However, where allowances are given the range is seldom if ever in excess of 20 per cent, with typical cases warranting 5 per cent to 7.5 per cent.

LICENSED BETTING OFFICES

It should be noted that a betting office (which possibly enjoyed an **8-31** element of quasi-monopoly value), was valued by the Lands Tribunal[9] on the same basis as shop and warehouses in the same vicinity.

---

[8] *Sheffield C.C. v. T. B. & W. Cockayne Ltd and Donall* (1958) 51 R. & I.T. 810.
[9] *Jack Swift Ltd v. Dixon* [1968] R.A. 43.

OFFICES AND WAREHOUSES

Generally

8-32 The valuation of these two broad categories of commercial property is one of the most common problems faced by the valuer.

Both categories of property have been the subject of marked changes in market requirements in recent years due, in particular, to the impact of the growth of motor traffic and the improved network of roads outside central urban areas. Thus, in some cases offices without adequate car parking are increasingly difficult to let, and the growth of distribution warehouses in locations convenient to the motorway network, with a corresponding decline in central city areas, or based on the docks, are well known phenomena.

Offices

8-33 These, broadly speaking, fall into two groups: those to which the public may resort, such as bank and building society offices, and those whose primary purpose is purely the provision of office accommodation. These two classes will be considered separately.

The first class is almost invariably ground-floor premises with direct access from the street, and is closely akin to shops. It is obvious that were an insurance company to take a shop as offices, as often occurs, then the value can be little different from that of the adjoining shops. As the shopkeepers would be in competition for a tenancy, the premises would not be secured at a lower rental because they were to be used as offices instead of a shop. It is, however, less usual to zone offices as is done with shops, unless they are equally suitable for either purpose. It must not be overlooked, however, that the beneficial occupation that is being rated is that of the premises in their present structural condition, *rebus sic stantibus*, with all their disadvantages and advantages and if they are not structurally adapted, *e.g.* shop windows, etc., for any other purpose than, say, for offices, the latter occupation is the one to be looked at. Offices are normally taken at a flat rate per metre net internal area, perhaps placing a higher figure on the front public offices than on the private portions at the rear. Banks prefer to secure corner premises on account of their greater prominence and any enhancement in value due to such an advantage must be reflected in the assessment. Likewise, in some cases the superior construction and finishes of, for example, a bank or building society, together with any adaptation of the basement as strong rooms will warrant special consideration. On the other hand the valuer will need to bear in mind that when considering the cost of building improvements, etc., banks frequently regard the annual equivalent of expenditure in the light of the low rates of interest they pay for money they hold on deposit.

Finally, it should be borne in mind that due to the widening **8-34** clientele and services involved in modern banking many of the old "fortress type" branches are obsolete. Some premises lend themselves to modernisation, but an older property located in a shopping street may not only have to be valued on an overall basis, rather than on the zoning principle, but also at a substantial discount.[10]

The second class is offices usually let in suites of rooms, office floors or office blocks, which are typically found in the central areas of the town. In most cases the offices will have been let with the landlord being responsible for certain services, *e.g.* lighting and cleaning the staircases, and maybe the provision of central heating, and in some cases the landlord may also be responsible for rates.

If this is the case, the following 1990 example will illustrate the method of analysing the rents to ascertain the appropriate rateable value:

A recently erected building which on the ground floor and basement is a departmental store is as to the upper part let in suites of offices. There are suites of offices on each of the first, second and third floors and on each floor two of the suites are about one-third larger than the others. Rents include services which comprise central heating, lift with attendant, lighting and cleaning of common parts. Tenants are responsible for inside repairs. The Uniform Business Rate is assumed to total 50 pence in the pound.

First Floor   — 2 suites at £12,000 4 suites at £9,000
Second Floor — 2 suites at £11,000 4 suites at £8,000
First Floor   — 2 suites at £10,000 4 suites at £7,500

---

[10] See *Halifax Building Society v. Payne* [1961] R.V.R. 85.

Floor	Suite Nos.	Inclusive rent	Adjustment for repairs	Total adjusted rent-roll
1	1 & 6	12,000	600	22,800
	2, 3, 4, 5	9,000	450	34,200
2	7 & 12	11,000	550	20,900
	8, 9, 10, 11	8,000	400	30,400
3	13 & 18	10,000	500	19,000
	14, 15, 16, 17	7,500	375	28,500
			Total Net Rents	155,800

Services	£
Wages, national insurance, uniforms	15,000
Fuel, boiler insurance and sundries	10,000
Lift, power and insurance	1,100
Lighting of common parts	1,040
Cleaning materials	520
Miscellaneous expenses	520
	28,180
Add cost of supervision of services	2,820
	£31,000

	£
Net inclusive rentals	155,800
Less services	31,000
Rateable value plus rates	£138,100

RV+Rates = £138,100
Therefore:

$$RV = \frac{138,100}{1.5} = 292,067$$

The relationship between rateable value and the gross inclusive rentals is expressed by the fraction:

$$\frac{92,067}{155,800} = 59\%$$

so that if this percentage of the gross inclusive rental of each suite is taken the rateable value is found.

The following assessments emerge:

Floor	Nos.	Inclusive rent	59% for RV
First	1 & 6	11,400	6,726
	2–5	8,550	5,045
Second	7 & 12	10,450	6,165
	8–11	7,600	4,484
Third	13 & 18	9,500	5,605
	14–17	7,125	4,204

Notes

In practice, having arrived at the equivalent net values of the various suites the results would be analysed at a price per square metre for it is seldom found in real life that the rental evidence in a building, let alone in an office area, throws up a consistent pattern. Moreover, the rateable values would doubtless be rounded.

The repairs adjustment is an estimate of the probable annual **8–35** expense which is preferable to a percentage of rents which include services and rates.

It is more usual, however, in office blocks for the tenant to be responsible for the rates, and often in new blocks the letting is of "office space" which the tenant himself has to fit out with partitions, wall finishes and decorations. If this is the case, there may sometimes be justification for using the actual rents plus a percentage of the expenditure on adaptation as the equivalent rental for assessment purposes. However, the presence of partitions does not automatically enhance the market rental value, for partitioning requirements are very much personal to the actual occupier whose own needs may alter from time to time. Thus, in practice there is often no discernible difference between the rent obtained for a partitioned floor and that for open office floor space.

The useable floor area is, of course, the most important item affecting the rental value, as offices, when to let, are nearly always advertised as being of so many square metres. Thus, whenever actual rents do not provide the assessment, the valuation will be by reference to the area, an appropriate basis per square metre being derived from rents elsewhere.

8-36 Other factors which should be specially borne in mind when comparing office suites one with another are as follows:

Prestige	A combination of those qualities that impress the outsider of the importance of the occupiers.
Position	A convenient central commercial location is usually desirable, although there is a continuing trend in some congested commercial centres for prime offices to be located away from the traditional centre because these locations provide greater accessibility.
Facilities & Services	The presence or otherwise of such items as central heating, forced ventilation, air conditioning, modern lifts, adequate toilets, underfloor ducting, etc.
Car Parking	The availability or otherwise of adequate car parking.
Access	Whether convenient or prominent. The general impression given by the main office entrance.
Shape	A convenient office plan shape is an advantage.
Lighting	Whether good natural lighting or whether overshadowed by other buildings.
Floor	In buildings without lifts the higher the floor the lower the rental value.

Finally, it should be noted that in recent years in the office sector, other changes in information technology have had a significant bearing on office specification. But this pace of change also brings in its train rapid technological obsolescence. Deep floor and ceiling voids which were the norm by the end of the 1980s, are no longer an essential requirement now that fibre optics are overtaking the use of heavy heat generating coaxial cabling used in computer networks. Clearly the flexible and energy efficient office is capable of commanding higher rents in the present economic climate.

Warehouses

Warehouses exist for the temporary storage of materials and **8–37** merchandise their location being as diverse as the purposes of their occupiers and the items stored. (Retail warehouses are dealt with earlier in this chapter at 8–26). Where they exist as distinct hereditaments, unattached to a factory or a retailing operation, the main factors which govern their attraction and hence value, are accessibility for road transport and design features which facilitate cheap efficient handling.

The modern standard warehouse is thus often seen as a clear span single storey building of six metres eaves height with level floor to enable full use of fork lift trucks, and with tailboard delivery and despatch bays protected by a roof canopy. There will usually be both a concrete yard for goods vehicles with some on site car parking. The building will have a sprinkler system and will contain offices, toilets, etc., but will not necessarily be heated. Larger units will have a surrounding site security fence and perhaps other refinements. Location-wise, such properties are typically within easy reach of the motorway/trunk road network.

Such properties are to be contrasted with storage buildings adapted from properties formerly used for some other purpose, frequently manufacturing, and indeed their forbears of yesteryear, some of which still exist. These earlier warehouses were frequently located near to ports, canals, railways or in the centre of towns. Usually constructed of brick and slate with stone staircases, timber floors and low headroom, they employed loopholes and simple hoists to handle bulk goods.

Throughout this wide range of property types there is usually sufficient rental evidence to form the basis of a valuation albeit that in the case of very large and/or specialised premises it may be necessary to resort to the contractors test. Valuation is almost invariably effected by pricing the various categories of floor space at a price per square metre.

In practice, the rental value of warehouses may not differ very **8–38** greatly from premises used for light industry, but special consideration may apply in ports, etc., where there tends to be surplus of warehouse accommodation due to the changing times and this will particularly apply in respect of premises which due to their construction, size and/or lack of natural lighting are unsuitable for letting for other purposes.

It is sometimes the case when premises of any kind become out of date for their original purpose, they are taken over for warehouse purposes. The minimum rental which they command for this purpose is sometimes referred to as "storage value" or "warehouse value" and generally denotes the lowest level of value to which premises will normally fall.

Cold stores

8–39 These are a special type of store which are in greater demand now that many commodities are preserved in "deep freeze".

This type of warehouse used to be costly to build because of the high cost of cork slab insulation and because of the special construction necessary. Nowadays, however, by limiting the store to a single storey height and utilising unit construction methods and expanded polystyrene as the insulating material the cost of such stores has been dramatically reduced.

Moreover, as with warehouses, modern handling methods utilising fork lift trucks and palletisation have revolutionised the industry and it is not now unusual to find new chambers with 4–7 metres height. Methods of stacking animal carcasses in cages have now enabled even meat to be economically stored and handled in this way. Nevertheless, in older type cold stores, where, by reason of the size and design of the chambers, fork lift trucks cannot operate economically, manual handling is still found on occasion. Such stores are at a very substantial economic disadvantage and their values must be discounted to reflect this fact.

Valuation is usually by pricing floor space (some rents are occasionally found) or in the case of modern specialised properties resort may be had to a contractors test.

9

Industrial Property, Plant and Machinery, Mineral Hereditaments

VALUATION OF INDUSTRIAL HEREDITAMENTS

The valuation of industrial property is a lifetime's study. This **9-01** chapter provides an outline only of the knowledge needed to undertake this task competently. Changes in building and manufacturing technology, and the application of ever higher environmental standards have been rapid during the last 20 years, and seem set to continue in the future at an even faster rate. During this period manufacturing industry has suffered a relative decline and there has been considerable consolidation into larger and more specialised units. Warehousing has similarly undergone significant changes. "Logistics" is the current term for the storage, transport and delivery of goods; a task now frequently undertaken by specialist contractors rather than manufacturers.

It is against this background that the approach to the valuation of industrial properties for rating purposes is set out. A knowledge of current practice and historical context in the industry concerned is also required.

Since 1990, all industrial property has been assessed direct to rateable value, and from the 1995 revaluation onwards the last traces of industrial de-rating in Scotland will disappear. There will be a revaluation in Northern Ireland in 1997 but there will continue to be 100 per cent de-rating of industrial properties in the meantime.

The vast majority of industrial properties are valued on a "comparative" or "rental" basis. Specialised properties are valued on the "contractor's" basis. Both methods of valuation are briefly discussed later in this chapter, but there are a number of common factors which should be taken into account in valuing by either method. This list cannot be exhaustive, but among the foremost are the following:

Location

9–02 In recent years the location of industrial property has become increasingly important and it is now, perhaps, the greatest influence on rental and land values. The need for good access to the motorway network, and where appropriate, rail facilities, is now self-evident. There is an increasing need for a manufacturer to have location in mind in satisfying the needs of customers, for example in the increasing demand for "just-in-time" delivery.

Industry, has in the past, tended to concentrate close to the source of raw materials, skilled labour or port facilities. Whilst these factors may still be of importance, they may have become less compelling in recent years. In cases where the reason for the location of a factory is not self-evident, it is appropriate to examine the need for the location of a factory in a historic *and* a current context.

The construction and layout of the buildings

9–03 The quality and layout of the buildings is also a prime consideration in the value of industrial property. A careful inspection will indicate whether the buildings are appropriate for the work being undertaken, but of equal importance is an understanding of the needs of the industry concerned. In assessing these it is clearly of assistance to be able to compare the operational requirements of an industry as a whole rather than one example which may not be typical. In other words, the current standard appropriate to the industry will provide a benchmark by which individual units can be judged.

Many factories have developed over a long period of time, and consequently the original layout has been modified, in some cases to the detriment of the flow of goods through the various production processes. With the aid of flow diagrams it is possible to examine where compromises have been made, and where the existing layout may be wholly unsuitable for present requirements. In many cases older factories may be totally unfitted for modern transport requirements and will contain a number of obsolete and possibly redundant buildings.

Adaptability and redundancy

With changes in technology and product range, together with the **9–04** tendency towards miniaturisation of components and plant and machinery it is necessary to consider, in the case of older buildings, whether they are suitable for modern requirements. The fact that a building is old, will not in itself render it obsolete, but excess or restricted height, multi-storey accommodation and excessive or redundant overhead crane capacity, may indicate that a particular building is not suitable for current manufacturing requirements. It is as well to consider, particularly in the case of older buildings:

(a) What is the current use of the building?
(b) How well does it fulfil that use?
(c) Are there any plans to replace it?

Although in the rating context properties have to be considered vacant and to let, the more specialised the nature of the property, the more necessary it is to consider adaptability and redundancy.

Age and layout

In order to sum up the points made in the previous two sections, old **9–05** buildings are likely to be less valuable in the rental and capital market because their mode of construction renders them less adaptable to current requirements and more costly to repair. But leaving these considerations aside, the age of a building will not necessarily reduce the rental value if it is otherwise performing its function satisfactorily. What is much more likely to reduce the value of a factory is antiquated layout and restricted access to the property and to individual buildings, causing manufacturing and transport difficulties.

State of repair

Industrial properties are assessed direct to rateable value and in these **9–06** circumstances the tenant or ratepayer is deemed to be responsible for repairs to the property. As a result the fact that a property is in general disrepair is not, in itself, sufficient to reduce the rateable value, but there comes a point at which the cost of undertaking the repairs needs to be considered in conjunction with the rental value of the building in good repair. If these repairs are not able to be carried out at reasonable cost there will be a case for arguing a permanent diminution in the rental value of a building. The same argument may well apply when structural defects are discovered which restrict the use of a building. In these cases the "hypothetical landlord" is deemed to provide the buildings and would in consequence be obliged to accept a reduced rent.

Size

9–07 The size of the property will not itself be proof of diminishing levels of value. The proof, if this is so, will come from the evidence of the market. But as most larger factories are not rented there has been a tendency for larger factories to be valued at a lower rate overall than smaller units. Such allowances are more apparent in large general purpose factories than specialised properties, such as vehicle manufacturing plants and chemical works which are generally large enterprises, in order to benefit from the economies of scale in the production process. Certainly there is a tendency for larger factories to be demolished and redeveloped or split into smaller units when they are vacated, which tends to show that the value of the site or buildings is maximised when dealt with in these ways.

The comparative or rental basis

9–08 The basis of assessment in factories valued on this basis—the vast majority of industrial properties—will ultimately depend on the rental evidence available in the locality. For the 1995 revaluation the "tone" of values will be derived from rental levels at April 1, 1993 (the antecedent date) and this "tone" will be applied to the physical facts at April 1, 1995.

The "tone" of values results from a consideration by the Valuation Officer of the rental evidence obtained by the issue of forms of return which ratepayers are obliged to complete under penalty and which provide details of the lease or leases under which rented properties are held. In the majority of cases, the start of a lease or the date of a rent review will not coincide with the antecedent date and the rent will need to be adjusted to reflect this.

In the case of rented properties, the rent actually paid is clearly the best indication of the likely rateable value, if it has been agreed on an "arms length" basis, but a number of adjustments still have to be made.

First, the terms of the lease need to be considered carefully. The majority of leases exclude tenants improvements. Factory units, particularly those constructed on a speculative basis, are frequently

124

let in a shell condition with only basic services supplied to the property, leaving the tenant to fit out the premises to his own requirements. As a result, electrical services, sprinklers, air conditioning, partitioning, mezzanine floors, and office and storage enclosures, car parks and hardstandings, are frequently provided by the tenant and the rent value of these items, where they result in additional value, must be added to the basic rental value of the property to arrive at the appropriate rateable value. It is particularly important to consider any rateable plant and machinery which may be found at the property.[1]

The lease terms may or may not disclose whether any "concessions" were granted by the landlord to the tenant on taking the lease in the form of rent-free periods, fitting-out periods or the payment by the landlord for fitting-out work. It is expected that the effect of these concessions will have considerable relevance in negotiations on the 1995 revaluation assessments.

In cases where an industrial property is not rented, it is necessary under the comparative method to "fit" the property into the established "tone" of values which may not be apparent until some time after the revaluation date. This is a subjective exercise, particularly in the case of larger or unusual properties. Factual information at the revaluation date needs to be established, and any subsequent additions and demolitions need to be separately noted. In these circumstances the actual date of any appeal may be relevant. Rateable plant will need to be considered in the light of the 1994 Plant and Machinery Regulations.

The contractor's basis of valuation

In the case of specialised properties which are seldom if ever let, and **9–09** no rental evidence is available, the contractor's basis of valuation is used.

It is generally recognised that there are five stages in the process which are:

(1) To estimate the cost of replacing the subject property, comprising the buildings, structures, rateable plant and machinery, site works and site services at prices ruling at the antecedent valuation date and on the facts at the date that the revaluation comes into effect.

(2) To make allowances for obsolescence and other factors, to produce an adjusted replacement cost.

---

[1] See section 9–15 below.

(3) To add the market value of the land for its current use to arrive at an effective capital value.

(4) To apply the prescribed decapitalisation rate to convert the adjusted capital value into an annual value.

(5) To consider the resultant valuation and to make any further adjustments necessary.

Whether the property is valued on a rental or comparative basis or a contractor's basis, the purpose is the same, to arrive at the rateable value of the property.

This method of valuation has been called "a method of last resort", but it has been, perhaps over-criticised. In *Eton College (Provost & Fellows) v. Lane V.O. and Eton U.D.C.*[2] the Lands Tribunal decision contained the following passage:

> "Provided a valuer using this approach is sufficiently experienced, and is aware of what he is doing, and knows just how he is using his particular variant of the method, and provided he constantly keeps in mind what he is comparing with what, we are satisfied that the contractor's basis provides a valuation instrument at least as precise as any other approach."

Certainly this form of valuation is not for the squeamish or inexperienced valuer, but the existence of stages 2 and 5 above make it a much more flexible method than is sometimes suggested.

The allowances in stage 2 can include, redundancy, unremunerative expenditure, age, changes in technology and methods of operation and the "final look" in stage 5 can take into account location, layout and site disadvantages. It is an opportunity to compare with what might be appropriate in the property had been assessed on a comparative basis. The prescribed decapitalisation rate for the 1995 revaluation is 5.5 per cent.

End allowances

9–10 The question of whether an end allowance is appropriate for disabilities is a vexed one, but if the valuer considers that there are disabilities which have not already been reflected in the preceding valuation and which should be taken into account in the overall valuation there are a number of decided cases which give authority to this view:

---

[2] *Eton College v. Lane and Eton UDC* [1971] J.P.L. 577.

(1) Sloping Floors, redundant plant and buildings (*Royal Bathrooms v. Maudling (V.O.) 1984*).

(2) Sloping site, piecemeal development, vehicle circulation (*Alvis (V.O.) v. Paver (V.O.) 1970*).

(3) Obsolescent buildings and divided site (*Linoleum Manufacturing Co. Ltd v. Gilbard (V.O.) 1968*).

(4) Congested access (Re the appeals of *Hooper (V.O.) 1985*).

(5) Divided Site (*Bowater PKL (U.K.) Ltd v. Worssam (V.O.) 1985* and *Austin Motor Co. v. Woodward (V.O.) 1968*).

(6) Restricted access, isolated position (*Hunt Kennard & Co. Ltd v. Sital (V.O.) 1982*).

(7) No Electricity Supply (*Williams v. Dickinson (V.O.) 1979*).

(8) Isolated Position (*Chilton v. Price (V.O.) 1991*).

(9) Nuisance from adjacent use (*Roleguide Ltd (T/A Container Services v. Dawson (V.O.) 1991*).

In most cases, however, end allowances are agreed between the parties by negotiation. An appearance before the Lands Tribunal can be an expensive way of resolving such an issue.

RATING OF PLANT AND MACHINERY

The law prior to 1925

In order to understand fully the position as regards the rating of plant **9–11** and machinery it is necessary to appreciate the situation prior to the Valuation and Rating Act 1925 which was entirely founded on case law. In many areas the presence of machinery and plant was ignored, or only taken into account when it was permanently affixed to the freehold, whilst in other areas regard was had to the whole of the equipment necessary to carry on the trade.

Two of the most important cases relating to plant and machinery were:

(1) *Kirby v. Hunslet Union A.C.*[3]

(2) *Smith (S.) & Sons (Motor Accessories) v. Willesden Union A.C.*[4]

and these will be considered briefly.

---

[3] *Kirby v. Hunslet Union AC* [1906] A.C. 43; 75 L.J.K.B. 129; 94 L.T. 36; 70 J.P. 50; 22 T.L.R. 167; [1904–1907] All E.R. Rep. 710; 1 Konstam 225; L.G.R. 144 H.L.

[4] *Smith (S) & Sons (Motor Accessories) v. Willesden A.C.* (1919) 83 J.P. 233; 89 L.J.K.B. 137; 121 L.T. 244; 17 L.G.R. 492.

The case of *Kirby v. Hunslet* concerned premises where the business carried on was that of a jobbing engineer and the machinery comprised a steam engine with shafting and pulleys, drilling and milling machines, lathes, etc., none of which was permanently fixed to the freehold. The case went to the House of Lords, and in each court the recorder was upheld in his contention that the question to be answered was: "What was the rent which a hypothetical tenant would give for the engineering works as a combination of land, buildings and scheduled machines?"

The case of *S. Smith & Sons v. Willesden* was heard some years after *Kirby v. Hunslet*, and possibly the result played some part in the decision to amend the law with regard to the rating of plant and machinery. The decision of the King's Bench division was that the net annual value was to be ascertained by estimating the rent that a tenant would pay for the property equipped with machinery on the assumption that the landlord would provide both the buildings and machinery, and the tenant's bid would have regard to both factors. The problem, therefore, briefly resolved itself into the question of what rent would the tenant give for the combination of buildings and machinery, and this is still the question to be answered today, except that the machinery and plant to be taken into account is limited by legislation.

The law subsequent to 1925

9-12 The unsatisfactory position following the decision in *S. Smith & Sons v. Willesden* was substantially amended by section 24 of the Valuation and Rating Act 1925, which for the first time, listed those items of plant and machinery which are assumed to be part of the hereditament. This Act applied only to England and Wales; in other parts of the United Kingdom separate rules were applied.

In Scotland, the principal Act governing the rating of plant and machinery was the Lands Valuation (Scotland) Act 1854, as amended by The Lands Valuation (Scotland) Amendment Act 1902. There were various subsequent amendments to the legislation, culminating in the Valuation (Plant and Machinery) (Scotland) Order 1983 which will remain effective in determining the rateable value of any hereditament before April 1, 1995. The 1983 Order only applies to trade, business or manufacturing premises. In other types of premises all items of plant and machinery "affixed or attached to the lands or heritage" are rateable.

In Northern Ireland, the principal Act governing the rating of plant and machinery was the Annual Revision of Rateable Property (Ireland) Act 1860, which was applied in conjunction with the provisions of the Landlord and Tenant (Ireland) Act 1860 (s. 17). For many years only motive power plant was valued, but various changes were made culminating in the Rates (N.I.) Order 1977, which effectively changed the law to that which subsisted in England and Wales.

9-13

The list of plant and machinery which originally appeared in the Schedule 3 to the Rating and Valuation Act 1925 was amended in Plant and Machinery Orders of 1927, 1960 and 1964. Further amendments were made under the provisions of section 5 of the Rating and Valuation Act 1961 and the Pipelines Act 1962.

This preceding legislation, incorporating the additions and amendments made over the years was re-enacted under the new non-domestic rating system in the form of the Valuation for Rating (Plant and Machinery) Regulations 1989, and was made under powers in Schedule 6 to the Local Government Finance Act 1988.

In 1991 the Wood Committee was appointed with the following terms of reference:

> "To consider the present law and practice in regard to the rating of plant and machinery in the United Kingdom, to make recommendations as to the principles that should be prescribed to comprise the extent of rateable property, with a view to removing inconsistencies and harmonising the law and practice in all parts of the United Kingdom; and to make proposals for giving effect to the recommendations."

So for the first time the same rules and regulations would apply to the whole of the United Kingdom.

The Committee's report was published in March 1993 as Command Paper 2170. After consultation with interested parties, the Government accepted the vast majority of the recommendations. In March 1994, the draft Valuation for Rating (Plant and Machinery) Regulations 1994 was published as a consultation document, prior to being laid before Parliament, now enacted as the Valuation for Rating (Plant and Machinery) Regulations 1994.[5]

These Regulations apply to England and Wales, but a similar set of Regulations apply to Scotland in accordance with (legislation not yet in place).

In Northern Ireland, there has been no general rating revaluation since 1976, and industrial properties currently enjoy 100 per cent rate relief, so any new Regulations will have very limited effect until the next revaluation takes place in 1997.

---

[5] S.I. 1994 No. 3199.

THE VALUATION FOR RATING PLANT AND MACHINERY REGULATIONS 1994[6]

9-14 These Regulations, together with the parallel Regulations for Scotland, and when appropriate for Northern Ireland will, be used "for the purpose of determining the rateable value of a hereditament for any day on after April 1, 1995, in applying the provisions of subparagraphs (1) to (7) of paragraph 2 of Schedule 6 to the Local Government Finance Act 1988.

The text of these regulations is reproduced in full[7] because its length and complexity make it difficult to memorise, nor can it be abridged. In practice, when making a survey or valuation of any hereditament likely to include plant or machinery it is necessary to have available a copy of the current Regulations.

The wording of subparagraphs 2 (a) and (b) in the introduction to the 1994 Regulations is similar to that of the 1989 Regulations. The overriding principle to be applied is:

(a) If the item is mentioned in the Regulations it is *rateable*.
(b) If the item is not mentioned, it is *not rateable*.

The assessment of any property made up to March 31, 1995, will be governed by the 1989 Regulations in England and Wales and the 1983 Order in Scotland.

One further change has been introduced, the 1989 Regulations did not apply to the assessments of properties valued on a profits basis. The Government has decided to apply the rules on the rating of plant and machinery to all valuation methods with effect from April 1, 1995.

THE PLANT AND MACHINERY REGULATIONS CONSIDERED

9-15 The 1994 Regulations divide rateable plant and machinery into four classes. It is necessary to consider each class separately and discuss the salient points which arise from an examination of the regulations, particularly when these differ from the previous 1989 Regulations.

---

[6] S.I. 1994 No. 2680.
[7] P & M Regulations Appendix, pp. 224 *et seq.*

Class 1 plant

Class 1 describes and Table 1 lists items of plant and machinery used **9–16** or intended to be used mainly or exclusively with the generation, storage, primary transformation or main transmission of power in or on the hereditament. Table 1 should be read in conjunction with the list of accessories printed after Class 2. The items "transformer" "primary transmission of power" and "main transmission of power" are defined in a rating context; comments on each form of power are set out below.

Electrical power

The 1994 Regulations make an important change in the rateability of electrical plant. The limit of rateability is now "the first distribution board". Straightforward examples of the limitations of rateability are set out in the diagrams below, but the general rules are that the line of main transmission within a hereditament starts at the following points:

(a) If power is generated within the hereditament—at the point of generation.

(b) If power is supplied from an external source—at the point or points at which the power passes from the supplier to the customer.

(c) If power is generated on the property and also supplied externally—at both points.

In summary, where power is generated on site or there is more than one grid intake point, there will be more than one "first distribution board".

It has been thought helpful in the following diagrams to indicate the difference in rateability between the 1989 Regulations and the 1994 Regulations.

Fig. 9.1. Simple factory installation.

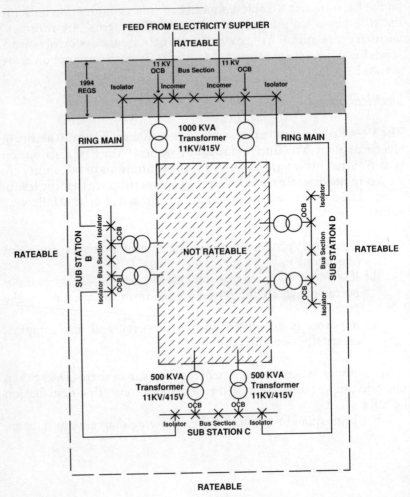

9-17 The limitation of rateability as a result of the changes introduced in the 1994 Regulations is most important and in the case of electrical power can be discerned from an examination of a schematic diagram of the electrical circuits. Primary transformation of power also includes "conversion" and "rectification" as well as "transformation" but, to be rateable, the plant must be within the line of main

132

Erratum

Sweet & Maxwell would like to apologise for an error which has occurred within Chapter 9. The three diagrams on pages 132 to 134 have been incorrectly titled and should read as follows:

9.1. Factory with main ring
9.2. Factory with power generating plant (simplified diagram)
9.3. Simple factory installation

Fig. 9.2. Factory with ring main.

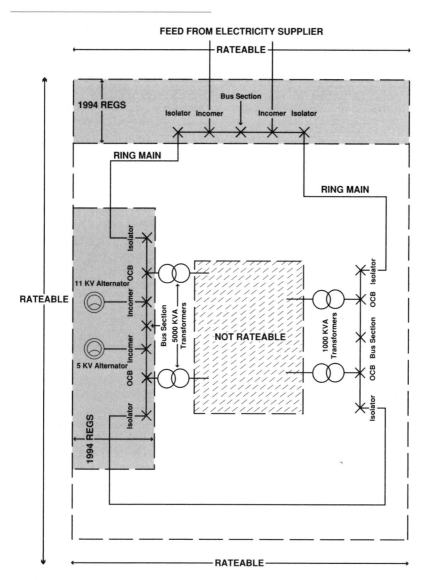

transmission of power (in practice this is frequently not so) *and* be a named item in Table 1.

In the case of transformers, there is an added limitation that any transformer which forms an integral part of an item of plant and machinery for manufacturing operations or trade processes is

133

Fig. 9.3. Factory with power generating plant (simplified diagram).

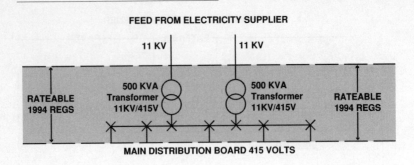

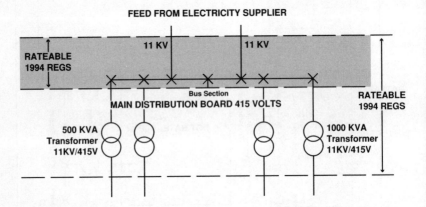

excluded. An example would be a transformer forming part of the equipment for an electric arc furnace (in practice it is highly unlikely that such a transformer would be situated *before* the first distribution board).

Transmission by shafting or wheels

Examples of power transmission by these means are now relatively rare but occasionally (as in flour mills) power transmission by way of lineshaft and or belting is to be found driven by a water wheel or turbine. If the shafting is driven by an electric motor this motor is *not* a prime mover, which is an engine or other device by which a natural source of energy is converted into mechanical power.

Hydraulic or pneumatic power

The Wood Committee recommended that air compressors and **9–18** hydraulic pumps should be excluded from rateability on the grounds that the power produced was a resuscitation of electrical power (after the first distribution board) rather than the creation of new power. The Government resisted this change.

As a result the opportunity to rectify the unsatisfactory position in the 1989 Regulations was foregone. The electric motors which drive air compressors and hydraulic pumps tend to be included (although they are not prime movers) because they are an integral part of the item under consideration. There is no provision (as in the case of electrical power) for air compressors and hydraulic pumps which form an integral part of plant for manufacturing operations or trade processes to be excluded.

Air compressors which are used for a genuinely "process purpose" however, are not rateable (*Ind Coope Ltd v. Burton-on-Trent Borough Council and Thomas (V.O.)*.[8] "Process" air compressors frequently (but not invariably) compress air to less than 7 bar (100 lbs/square inch), such as those which provide air for fermenting. In this case the air is an ingredient in the finished product.

Class 1 plant

Steam boilers are mentioned in Table 1. In the majority of cases it will **9–19** be obvious whether a boiler is mainly used for "power purposes" (for example to drive a steam turbine, or to provide steam for hammers in a forge) or for process and/or heating purposes where other circumstances may apply (rateability under Class 4) but there may well be cases where there is genuine doubt about the predominant use of the plant in question.

In the absence of case law on the subject, the way to proceed may well be on a "heat value" basis. The valuer will need specialist advice to arrive at a satisfactory answer in these cases.

To reflect changes in technology, the 1994 Regulations include, for the first time, aero generators, wind turbines, solar cells and solar panels in Table 1 to Class 1.

---

[8] *Ind Coope Ltd v. Burton Upon Trent BC and Thomas (V.O.)* [1961] J.P.L. 192; 8 R.R.C. 173; 177 E.G. 287 L.T.

Class 2 plant

9–20 Class 2 describes and Table 2 lists, items of plant and machinery which is used or intended to be used mainly or exclusively in connection with the heating, cooling, ventilating, lighting, draining, supply of water and the protection from hazards to the land or buildings of which the hereditament consists.

The 1994 Regulations significantly expand the number of items included in the listing under "Protection from Hazards" compared with those listed under Protection from Fire in the 1989 Regulations.

A number of these items were already rateable, either under Class 4 in the 1989 Regulations or as site improvements, but the inclusion of security equipment in general and the word "computers" in the list of accessories means that considerable attention will need to be given to these changes by rating valuers.

The list of accessories is in two parts. The items listed in paragraph 1 relate to plant which is rateable under Class 1 and those in paragraph 2 relate to plant which is rateable under Class 1 and Class 2. It will be noted that there are numerous items in the table of accessories which are included as a result of their function and which would not otherwise be rateable. Particular note should be taken of the limitation on rateability under which items which are used for manufacturing operations or trade purposes, which would otherwise be included under this class, are thereby excluded. This limitation has given rise to most of the case law on this subject.

In *Union Cold Storage Ltd v. Southwark Assessment Committee*,[9] refrigeration plant in a cold store was excluded from rateability on these grounds, although the insulation in the cold rooms was found to be part of the building. In *Burton-on-Trent Borough Council v. Bass Ratcliffe and Gretton and Thomas (V.O.)*[10] it was held that three Lancashire Boilers were not rateable under Class 1a (now 1) or 1b (now 2) on the grounds that the heat was used to regulate the conditioning process going on within the casks in the ale conditioning warehouse.

Valuation considerations on Class 2 plant

9–21 Many of the items listed in Table 2 and the list of accessories form part of the normal building services. In the case of a hereditament

---

[9] *Union Cold Storage Co. Ltd v. Southwark Assessment Committee* (1932) 16 R. & I.T. 160. 3. D.R.A. 55. 66.
[10] *Burton on Trent Borough Council v. Bass Ratcliffe & Gretton Ltd and Thomas* [1961] R.V.R. 310; 8 R.R.C. 149; 177 E.G. 435; [1961] J.P.L. 190 L.T.

valued on a rental basis they would generally be deemed to be included in the rental value adopted for the building of which they form part. On the other hand, it may be appropriate to consider whether the level of building services found in a building justified an increase or a reduction in the basic rental value of a serviced building. The practice of adding a bland fixed percentage of a fixed amount for heating, sprinkler installations or for air conditioning plant is to be deprecated. Those systems can vary widely in nature and complexity, and need thorough understanding before "short cuts" are attempted. The valuation of Class 2 plant demands the highest degree of expertise from rating valuers; it is also the class which receives the least amount of attention in rating valuations.

Sprinkler installations

It has become common practice to value sprinkler installations separately from the buildings or plant structures which they serve. Sprinkler installations are tailor-made to serve the requirements of the individual occupier and vary considerably in nature and complexity. In the case of chemical works and other high hazard installations, consideration should be given to the extent to which the installation has been installed to protect the "land or buildings of which the hereditament consists" or to protect machinery and plant which is used "mainly or exclusively as part of manufacturing operations or trade purposes".

Plant and machinery installed to overcome a disadvantage

Certain service plant may be installed to overcome a disadvantage; **9–22** for example, sewage treatment plant and machinery may have to be installed because mains drainage is not available. Adjustments to the overall value of the hereditament may need to be made to take these factors into account.

Technological change, manufacturing requirements, health and safety regulations

These factors have in many cases resulted in the need to replace building services well within the economic life of the buildings which they serve. There is an increasing need to take into account obsolescence as well as any enhancement in value as a result of these changes.

Dual purpose plant

An overriding consideration is that a plant which fulfils a land or building service function, but which is predominantly used for manufacturing operations or trade purposes should be excluded from rateability.

Security equipment

The inclusion of security equipment under the heading "Protection from Hazards" will need careful consideration. The words "cameras, display screens and controls, sensors and relays" were omitted from the Regulations laid before Parliament.

Class 3 plant

9-23   Class 3 of the 1994 Regulations brings together those items which are to be found in Classes 2, 3 and 5 of the 1989 Regulations with some fairly significant amendments which will be noted below.

This class covers plant and machinery which is installed for the conveyance of goods and passengers and the transmission of power and communications signals.

Paragraph (a) railway and tramway lines and tracks

The working of Class 3 of the 1989 Regulations has been extended by the addition of "associated fixed accessories and equipment". This will include, for example, signalling equipment.

This type of plant is relatively easy to identify but care should be taken that the lengths of track to be valued are capable of beneficial use.

In the case of narrow gauge tramway track, which is commonly found in mineral producing hereditaments; only the permanent lengths should be valued, as temporary lengths near working faces are frequently moved.

Paragraph (b) lifts, elevators, hoists, escalators and travelators

9-24   The wording of Class 2 of the 1989 Regulations has been altered and amended by the addition of the words "hoists, escalators, and travelators" and the exclusion of the words "mainly or usually used for passengers". As a result goods lifts are now rateable.

In valuing this type of plant, all builders work, such as the lift shaft and any penthouse will normally be treated as part of the building.

In the case of hereditaments valued direct to rental value, enhancement of the value of the upper floors to reflect the presence of a lift will normally avoid the need to value lifts as a separate item.

Paragraph (c) and (d) power and communications equipment

The privatisation of the electricity and communications industries has brought forward the rateability of "cables, wire and conductors" together with attendant "posts, towers, masts, mast radiators, dishes, antennae, ducts, conduits, valves, pumps, meters and switchgear" together with their foundations and supports, which are used or intended to be used in connection with the transmission, distribution or supply of electricity or communications signals. There is an exclusion of this plant and equipment within "premises", but this is defined as any hereditament "*other* than one used or intended to be used mainly or exclusively for the transmission, distribution or supply of electricity and communication signals".

Paragraph (e) pipelines

Certain pipelines were rateable under Class 5 of the 1989 Regula- **9–25** tions. The 1994 Order makes certain important changes. In particular, the rateability of pipelines has been extended to include lengths *within* premises up to and including the first control valve or to the last control valve from the premises as the case may be together with "associated fixed accessories and equipment".

In the case of an extensive cross-country pipeline the additional lengths to be valued may not be significant, but pressure reducing equipment situated immediately before the first control valve *into* a property, which will now be rateable for the first time, could have a more substantial impact on an assessment.

Pipelines between immediately adjacent properties, which have also escaped rateability hitherto, will also need careful consideration.

In the 1994 Regulations, the definition of a "mineral field" has been extended to include natural and landfill gas extraction and the definition of "premises" now includes a natural gas storage or processing facility or gas holder site.

Case law

The original decision to rate pipelines was made following the decision in *Lever Brothers, Port Sunlight v. Bright (V.O.)*[11] when the

---

[11] *Lever Bros., Port Sunlight Ltd v. Bright and Bebington Corporations* [1961] R.V.R. 70; 112 L.J. 44; 108 E.G. 798; [1962] J.P.L. 189; 9 R.R.C. 164 L.T.

Lands Tribunal held that certain steam pipes were not rateable as they were neither conduits (pipes or channels for the conveyance of liquids) nor structural.

9-26 *English Clays Lovering Pochin & Co. Ltd v. Davies (V.O.)*[12] clarified what was included in the definition of "quarry" (in section 180(B)(b) of the Mines and Quarries Act 1954) as "surface" (including building structures and works thereon surrounding or *adjacent* to the quarry)" and occupied together with the quarry for the purpose of, or in conjunction with, the working of the quarry, the treatment, preparation for sale ...or removal from the quarry of the minerals or products thereof gotten from the quarry". The word "adjacent" in this context was not confined to places adjoining but included places "in close proximity", the degree of proximity depending on the circumstances. There were alternative findings in this case which should be noted, but they did not affect the decision that the pipes were not rateable.

In *Rugby Portland Cement Co. Ltd v. Hunt (V.O.)*[13] it was held that 70 miles of external pipeline was rateable because it and the slurrying plant were not part of the equipment of the quarry but was part of the company's manufacturing plants elsewhere.

Finally, in *Air Products Ltd v. Case (V.O.)*[14] where the appellants occupied a property immediately adjacent to a customer, it was held that none of the connecting pipelines were rateable as they came within exclusion (c) of Class 5(1) of the 1989 Regulations. This decision now needs to be re-examined in the light of the 1994 Regulations.

Class 4 plant

9-27 Class 4 encompasses what may conveniently be regarded as process plant which is in the nature of a building or structure. In the 1994 Regulations the list of items has been substantially reduced in length, but the effect is somewhat less marked because the list has been prepared on generic rather than specific lines. For example, chambers and vessels are listed without qualification by their mode or category of use.

The purpose of listing the items in 2 Tables (Tables 3 and 4) remains the same as in the 1989 Regulations. Table 3 lists plant and machinery in the nature of a building or structure without further

---

[12] *English Clays Lovering Pochin Ltd v. Davis (V.O.)* [1966] R.A. 475; R.V.R. 607; (1966) 12 R.R.C. 307.
[13] *Rugby Portland Cement Co. Ltd. v. Hunt (V.O.) (1969)* 16 R.R.C. 42.
[14] *Air Products Ltd v. Case (V.O.) (1970)* 16 R.R.C. 194.

qualification. Table 4 lists process plant which is in the form of a container.

The proviso at the head of Class 4 has been amended in two ways compared with that of the 1989 Regulations. First, there is no longer an exclusion of items which are moved or rotated by motive power as part of the process of manufacture. Secondly, the size-limit for inclusion in Table 4 has been increased from 200 to 400 cubic metres. This increase in size-limit will take out of rateability a significant number of items which were assessed up to March 31, 1995, particularly when coupled with the less stringent test for removal of the item. Provided that the item in question can be removed from one site to another the mode of its removal is not crucial, assuming the surrounding structure is not demolished, but an item in Table 4 which is less than 400 cubic metres in volume may still be rateable if the conditions of clause (d) of the proviso to Class 4 cannot be satisfied.

As before, any part of a rateable item which is not in the nature of a **9–28** building or structure will be excluded from rateability. Non-structural ancillary equipment and moving parts are not rateable, and structural items in Table 4 which move or rotate are likely to be exempt if the overall size excluding foundation settings and supports is below the 400 cubic metre size-limit.

The detailed amendments of Table 3 bring in "bunds", the addition of "flues" to chimneys, and "ducts" are added to the item "flumes and conduits". The entries in the 1989 Regulations for ship construction and repair are amended to "shiplifts and building berths" in accordance with current shipbuilding practice. The disappearance of the word "racks" will cause few tears to be shed. Racking systems will henceforth only be rateable if the system forms the external wall of the building which encloses it.

In addition, separate entries for aerial ropeway supports, elevators and hoists, fan drifts, telescopes (except radio telescopes), weighbridges and windmills are not found in the 1994 Regulations, although some of these items re-appear under different classes. As before, items which are not rateable under Classes 1, 2 and 3 may be rateable under Class 4 if they are a named item and are in the nature of a building or structure.

In Table 4 of the 1994 Regulations, no new items are added but one **9–29** or two specific items including "Bessemer" (but not other converters) forges and dry cleaners for coal are no longer listed. The remaining changes from the 1989 Regulations are rearrangements of the existing wording and the removal of specific applications of an item.

The 1994 Regulations are likely to have a tendency to reduce the scope for argument on Class 4 plant, but there are always going to be borderline cases, and with the increase in the size-limit, those items just over the limit will be substantial and expensive.

Items which may be in the nature of a structure which are not named and which cannot be identified adequately by one of the generic items in the Regulations are not rateable (for example, the heat exchangers in *B.P. Refinery (Kent) Ltd v. Walker (V.O.)*.[15]

It is therefore sometimes necessary to go back to first principles in deciding whether or not an item is rateable, and the following paragraphs should be studied in this context.

The identification of named items

9-30 Problems can arise in comparing "structural" items found on the hereditament with the list of items named in Class 4. These difficulties can generally be resolved by proceeding in the following way:

(a) Identify and put a name to the individual items of plant under consideration.
(b) Decide whether each item is a single item or a combination of similar or diverse items.
(c) Ascertain whether any single item can or cannot be identified with a "named" item in Class 4.
(d) Consider whether the exceptions from rateability at the head of Class 4 are appropriate.

If the item is found to be rateable as a result of these tests, the next stage is to:

(e) Isolate any non-structural parts and exclude them.

Case law

Reference should be made to the Lands Tribunal decision in *B.P. Refinery Ltd v. Walker (V.O.)*, where it was argued by the Valuation Officer that the complex comprising a primary distillation unit was a "still" and should be rated as a single item. The Lands Tribunal found and the Court of Appeal affirmed that this was incorrect and that the constituent parts should be examined separately. In the same case condensers were mounted in banks with steel supports and formed a functional entity. The Lands Tribunal found, and the Court of Appeal

---

[15] *BP Refinery Ltd v. Walker (V.O.)* [1954] 2 Q.B. 305; [1957] 2 W.L.R. 907; 121 J.P. 231; 101 S.J. 391; [1957] 1 All E.R. 700; 50 R. & I.T. 182; 1 R.R.C. 300 C.A.; (1954) 47 R. & I.T. 771 C.T.

affirmed that although they were connected together they were neither collectively nor individually a structure. Finally, a heat exchanger (not named in Class 4) although similar in function to a condensor (which is), was held not be adequately described as a condenser and was, therefore, not within Class 4 and thereby not rateable.

What is a structure?

The two classic judicial interpretations of what is meant by a **9–31** "structure" were given by Lord Denning and Lord Jenkins in *Cardiff Rating Authority v. Guest Keen Baldwins Iron & Steel Co.*[16] The extracts given below should not be regarded as a substitute for reading these judgments in their entirety.

In Lord Denning's words:

> "A structure is a something of substantial size which is built up from component parts and is intended to remain permanently on a permanent foundation but it is still a structure even though some of its parts may be moveable ... A thing which is not permanently in one place is not a structure but it may be in the nature of a structure if it has a permanent site and all the qualities of a structure save that it is on occasion moved on or from its site."

Lord Jenkins said, *inter alia*:

> " ... the things in question must in relation to this hereditament answer the description of buildings or structures, or at all events be in the nature of buildings or structures. That suggests built or constructed things of substantial size; I think of such size that they either had been ... or would normally be, built or constructed on the hereditament as opposed to being brought onto the hereditament already made. It further suggests some degree of permanence in relation to the hereditament ... I do not, however, mean to suggest that a thing is necessarily a conclusive test in all cases or that a thing is necessarily removed from the category of buildings or structures ... because by some feat of engineering or navigation it is brought to the hereditament in one piece ... the question whether a thing is or is not physically attached to the hereditament is a relevant consideration but I cannot regard the fact that it is not so attached as being in any way conclusive against its being a building or structure ... nor can I regard the fact that a thing has a limited degree of motion when in use either in relation to the hereditament, or as between different parts of itself, necessarily prevents it from being a structure ... if it otherwise possesses the characteristics of such ...".

---

[16] *Cardiff RA v. Guest Keen Baldwin Iron & Steel Co. Ltd* [1949] 1 K.B. 385; [1949] L.J.R. 713; 65 T.L.R. 159; 113 J.P. 78; 93 S.J. 117; [1947] 1 All E.R. 27; 47 L.G.R. 159, 42 R. & I.T. 2 C.A.; affirming 64 T.L.R. 1 [1948] 1 All E.R. 830.

The tests for rateability as a "structure"

9–32 As a result of the guidance of these judicial interpretations and the subsequent interpretations of them by the Courts, the following tests can be made to establish whether an item of plant is in the nature of a building or structure:

- The method of construction
- The size and weight of the item
- The degree of attachment
- The degree of permanence

All these tests are subject to the item being identified as a "named" item in Class 4, and subject to the limitations of rateability set out in the proviso to Class 4.

Method of construction

(a) Items of plant which are built up on site from basic materials are almost invariably rateable, but may be excluded if they are too small to add significantly to the rental value of the hereditament.

(b) Items of plant which are built up on site from prefabricated parts may be rateable but are subject to tests of size and weight, the degree of attachment and the degree of permanence.

(c) Items of plant which are fabricated off site and brought to the site in one piece are subject to the same tests as in (b) above, but the limitations on rateability set out in Class 4 are particularly relevant in these cases. Items which are excluded by reason of their size may still be rateable because of the degree of attachment to the land or buildings or structures.

The size and weight of the item

9–33 (a) The size and weight of an item of plant will be a question of fact in each case, but note exclusion (d) in Class 4. Foundations, settings and supports (which may be rateable in their own right) and anything which is not an integral part of the item should be excluded from the calculation of the cubic capacity.

(b) The weight of an item does not affect the question of rateability as such, but if it involves a special feat of engineering or transportation to bring it to the site this is likely to lend "weight" to the view that it is rateable. The Motor Vehicles (Authorisation of

Special Types) General Order 1979 currently govern what would be classed as an "abnormal indivisible load".

Degree of attachment

(a) This was formerly thought to be of importance, and if an item of plant is readily removable by normal means of lifting and transportation it is submitted that this should remain a valid test, but in *Elliot's Bricks Ltd v. Hartley (V.O.)* [17] the Lands Tribunal member said:

> "I do not consider the degree of attachment to be a vital ingredient of rateability. In fact the tanks are substantially attached to the land by their own weight ... I do not consider the removability of the tanks to be a conclusive factor in deciding what is a structure ... in view of their size and weight this would involve a special feat of engineering or transportation even taking account of improved techniques at the date of the proposal."

(b) Items which in themselves are not rateable, become so if the degree of attachment makes them take on the nature of a structure: *Lever Brothers, Port Sunlight Ltd v. Bright (V.O.) and Bebington Corporation;*[18] *Shellmex and B.P. Ltd v. James (V.O.).*[19]

The degree of permanence

(a) Permanence can be of place or of time. With regard to place, the Lands Tribunal has held that a floating dock (a named item) which was regularly moved to different positions within a dock basin was not a structure as it had no permanent site and no degree of permanence in relation to the hereditament. *Vickers-Armstrong (Shipbuilders) Ltd v. Thornton (V.O.).*[20] On the other hand, it has been noted that a degree of movement on or from its site will not be an impediment to the treatment of an item as a structure, as in the *Guest Keen* case.

(b) With regard to time in the *Elliot's Bricks* case the Lands Tribunal member stated: "As to permanence ... I do not consider that an

---

[17] *Elliot's Bricks Ltd v. Hartley (V.O.)* [1990] R.A. 161.
[18] See n. 11 *supra*.
[19] *Shellmex and BP Ltd v. James (V.O.)* (1960) 8 R.R.C. 135, [1961] R.V.R. 106, 177 E.G. 62.
[20] *Vickers - Armstrong (Shipbuilders) Ltd v. Thornton (V.O.)* [1965] 11 R.R.C. 66.

intention to remove, or make way for alterations ... or in the advent of a change to another fuel is sufficient reason for considering that the tanks as at the date of the proposal were not a permanent feature of the hereditament."

MINERAL PRODUCING HEREDITAMENTS

9–34 Section 64(1) of the Local Government Finance Act 1988 defines a hereditament as a property which is liable to a rate or one which would fall to be shown as a separate item in the list. Included in those properties are:

(a) land,
(b) coal mines,
(c) mines of any other description.

It should be noted that under the 12 month Permanency Rule a moveable property, such as a contractor's hut, is not normally rateable. However, in mineral hereditaments such items as plant and machinery, contractor's huts and spoil heaps (see *Dick Hampton v. Lewis*[21] are considered to be permanently attached to the land and are therefore rateable.

Prior to the 1988 Act coal mines operated by British Coal were assessed on a formula basis but from April 1, 1990, all collieries have to be assessed according to the statutory basis for a rating valuation as set out in paragraphs 2(1) of Schedule 6 to the Act, *i.e.* the hypothetical tenancy.

However, due to the absence of evidence of royalties for coal since the Coal Act 1938, collieries are placed in one of five different categories; category one representing the more attractive collieries to the hypothetical tenant whilst category five represents the least attractive, royalties are then applied in descending order of value. Royalties are explained below.

Assessment

9–35 With most non-domestic properties it is safe to say that their assessment will be based on a comparison with similar hereditaments either directly or indirectly, but due to the lack of the

---

[21] *Hampton (Dick) (Earth Moving) Ltd v. Lewis* [1976] Q.B. 254, [1975] 3 All E.R. 946, [1975] 3 W.L.R. 357, 119 Sol Jo 658, 73 L.G.R. 503, [1975] R.A. 269 C.A.

availability of comparisons the best evidence for the assessment of mineral producing hereditaments will normally be the rents passing.

Under a mining lease several different kinds of rents may be payable, these being:

(1) Surface rents
(2) Royalties
(3) Minimum rent
(4) Way leaves.

Freeholders will look upon mineral workings on land as an added bonus to the existing income from that land, thus retaining the existing income known as surface rent until it is worked for minerals. At the same time a rent often above existing rental value, will be asked for the area of land where processing plant is sited.

To ensure that mining operations are carried out a minimum rent is set which must be paid annually (even if no mining takes place), this is set at between 25 per cent and 30 per cent of the total royalty income expected.

Royalties are paid for each cubic metre or tonne of mineral worked, the amount paid varies with the type of mineral and whether it is won by deep mining or surface extraction.

A general guide to royalty values would be 5 per cent to 20 per cent of the selling price per tonne. The total rent paid will be royalty per tonne multiplied by the annual tonnage.

Way leaves are payments made to a third party for the privilege of transporting minerals under land in their ownership from the place of working to the place where they are brought to the surface. This payment can be a fixed annual sum or can be based on the annual tonnage passing under the land.

Similar arrangements can be made for surface operations.

Owner-occupied operations

If a mine or quarry is owner occupied then the assessment will be **9–36** based on the rent which might reasonably be expected, that is compared to an existing rent for another hereditament.

In such cases care must be exercised as allowances to the royalty rate being compared must be made for any disabilities between the two hereditaments, such as inferior quality, dirt inclusions, faults, etc., also physical differences such as overburden, ease of working and proximity to markets.

As stated previously due to the lack of comparables, passing rents are usually the most suitable evidence to be used for assessment, but as with all other non-domestic hereditaments, tone of the list adjustments will need to be made in addition to the above allowances for disabilities.

Plant and machinery

9–37 Plant and machinery may be considered to be part of a mineral hereditament and must not be assessed separately, but as part of the whole hereditament. Not all plant and machinery at a mine or quarry is considered to be part of the hereditament, and it is necessary to establish if items of the plant and machinery are to be assessed by referring to the Plant and Machinery Regulations which set out a comprehensive list of items to be included under five classes. If an item of plant and machinery is not included in any of these classes it is not part of the hereditament and will not be part of the assessment. Those items which do form part of the hereditament are normally assessed by the contractor's method of valuation.

It is argued that the hypothetical tenant would not pay rent for plant and machinery exceeding operational requirements, and thus if these items are capable of handling, say, 100,000 units per annum but the actual output is, say, 75,000 units per annum, then the effective capital value of the plant would be 75 per cent of the full value even though this seems contrary to the *rebus sic stantibus* principle.

Specified land

9–38 Land which is specified for the purpose of winning, working, grading, washing, grinding and crushing of minerals is known as "specified land" and as such is important in the assessment of mineral hereditaments as the Non-Domestic Rating (Miscellaneous Provisions) Regulations 1989 provides for a 50 per cent reduction on specified land.

It should be noted that this reduction is applied to the land only and not to any structures or buildings thereon.

Landfill and waste disposal

9–39 On the cessation of mineral workings it is common practice for the resultant void to be filled with imported materials and a tipping charge made. This charge can be in the form of an annual rent or a royalty based on tonnage, cubic metres or lorry load. The annual rent and royalty charges will depend upon such matters as the lease restoration clause, planning consent conditions, type of infill material and market demand and supply. When such landfill takes place it will be liable to a rate charge, it is not considered to be specified land and will not attract the 50 per cent reduction.

Quinquennial reviews

Under the Rating Acts, rating lists are to be reviewed every five years, **9-40** however, as the output from mines and quarries will more than likely change from year to year, the Acts make provisions for an annual revision of the assessment of mineral hereditaments. The usual method of assessment is to use the previous calendar year tonnage, January 1, to December 31, as the basis for the rating year April 1, following, with adjustments being made at the end of the rating year if the actual output is different. When it is known that the hereditament will cease working during the rating year, that is, the projected tonnage will not be achieved, the above procedure is still followed to assess the rateable value of the hereditament, but the occupier will only be liable for the payment of rates up to the time of cessation of working (see *Amey Roadstone Corporation Ltd v. Gilbard*[22]).

Example

A royalty of 40 pence per tonne has recently been agreed by ABC Sand and Gravel Co. XYZ Sand and Gravel Co. operates a quarry in the same district but the sand and gravel is of slightly inferior quality, has poor access and is at a greater distance from market outlets.

The annual output is expected to be 200,000 tonnes but the plant is capable of processing 250,000 tonnes per annum.

Analysis of ABC Sand and Gravel

Royalty payable	40p
Adjust for increase in value since date of valuation list	−2p
	38p
Adjust for disabilities	−3p
Equivalent "tone of list"	35p

---

[22] *Gilbard v. Amey Roadstone Corporation Ltd* (1974) 73 L.G.R. 43; [1974] R.A. 498 C.A. reversing [1973] J.P.L. 491.

Assessment XYZ Sand and Gravel

		Unadjusted R.V. £	R.V. £
Mineral 200,000 tonnes @ 35p		70,000	35,000*
Buildings		1,500	1,500
Plant C.V.	300,000		
80% capacity	0.8		
E.C.V.	240,000		
@ 5.5%	0.55	13,200	13,200
Land occupied for specified operations		1,200	600*
		85,900	50,300

*Value reduced by 50 per cent in accordance with Non-Domestic Rating (Miscellaneous Provisions) Regulations 1989.

10

Assessment of Licensed Premises

LICENSED PREMISES GENERALLY

It states the obvious to say, in a chapter devoted to licensed premises, **10–01** that the distinguishing factor about this class of property is the fact that it is licensed. But in this case the obvious is, at present, technically not true.

The fact is that property as such is not licensed. It is the occupier who is licensed. A licence to sell intoxicating liquor is granted to a particular person to trade in particular premises. This qualification does, effectively, make the premises licensed because it is fairly safe to assume that a property considered suitable for one licensee will also be considered suitable for another person adjudged fit to carry on the licensed trade. There are indications, however, that the Government are currently looking into the concept of a two part licence whereby both the property and the occupier would be licensed. This change is not likely to make any significant difference to the consideration of rating valuation.

The licensing justices for a licensing area enjoy the statutory power to grant licenses within their area. Generally speaking, new licences are not easy to obtain and in most areas the assumption is that the status quo will continue. To an extent, therefore, licensees are each enjoying what amounts to a share in a statutory local monopoly.

"Licensed property" covers a wide field. Public houses form the biggest category and this chapter is primarily directed towards this class. Licensed clubs, licensed restaurants, licensed hotels and off-licences are considered separately at the end of the chapter.

The question of clubs can be resolved quickly. For clarity it should be noted that the above comments concerning licences do not apply to club premises. These are registered to permit the sale of liquor to members. In *Aberaman Ex-Servicemen's Social Club*[1] the High Court held that bar takings were personal to a club and should be disregarded in making an assessment. Clubs are valued for rating on a comparative basis per square metre and they do not therefore come within the remit of this chapter.

In simple, classical valuation terms therefore, there is a limited supply of licensed premises and there is every likelihood that the supply will not increase. This will have an effect on value. Whilst the licensee may change, it is a normal assumption in the market that the licence will continue and can therefore be a factor in the assessment of the value of the property.

EVOLUTION OF VALUATION METHODS

Effect of licence

10-02 Accepting the fact that a licence does affect value, it is then necessary to consider whether such an increment of value should be taken into account in rating. The doctrine of *rebus sic stantibus* applies and the hereditament must be valued as it stands and as it is used—licence and all. In the case of *Dodds v. South Shields Assessment Committee*[2] judicial approval was given for taking the existence of the licence into account.

The issue is then a case of determining how the licence should be taken into account. The valuer is seeking to establish a rental value (payable from year to year) at the specified valuation date. Public houses are a class of property which is readily found in the market but unfortunately the actual rental market for public houses is very complex.

The major matter to be accommodated is the presence in the market of the brewers themselves. Brewery companies started out as manufacturers of brewed liquors. They soon discovered, however, that securing the retail outlets for their products gave them a significant power in the market for liquor and the ability to profit from the monopolistic characteristics of the licensing system. This resulted in brewery companies generally buying all licensed premises with any significant potential trade. The industry developed the concept of the "tied tenancy" whereby a public house would be let by the brewery to a tenant (who was the licensee) at a rent (so that the

---

[1] *Aberaman Ex-Servicemen's Club and Institute Ltd v. Aberdare U.D.C.* (1947) 40 R. & I.T. 576.
[2] [1895] 2 Q.B. 133.

tenant/licensee was self-employed in his or her "own" pub) but with a condition in the tenancy agreement requiring all liquor to be bought from the landlord.

A captive market such as a string of public houses all required to buy their stock from a particular brewer, not only guaranteed volume for the brewer, but also enabled a price for liquor to be fixed which did not have to take account of competition from other brewers seeking to put their products into the houses.

This state of affairs has, of course, changed in recent years, but it was developing as the normal method of trade as modern rating and valuation precedents were being created. It is therefore useful to follow the historical development to better understand today's situation.

Hypothetical bidders in the market

In the case *Bradford-on-Avon Assessment Committee v. White*[3] it **10–03** was held that the house to be valued had to be considered independently of, and without reference to, any agreement which tied the publican to a brewer. The public house was to be considered as free. The brewers were not to be ignored but were to be treated like any other tenant, from year to year and with no personal contracts limiting the ability to trade at the house.

The *"Bradford"* ruling was generally applied by valuers in estimating the rating assessment by basing it upon the rent which a free tenant would give and taking no account of a brewer's interest as a manufacturer. The brewer's bid was therefore ignored until the matter was challenged and reversed in *Robinson Brothers (Brewers) Ltd v. Houghton and Chester-le-Street Assessment Committee.*[4] This case set the precedent that competition amongst brewers should be taken into account. In the House of Lords, Lord Macmillan said in his judgment:

> " ... the brewer who leases the premises because he thinks he can make money by sub-letting them to a tied tenant is influenced by perfectly legitimate business considerations, he offers the rent which he thinks it worth his while to pay to obtain the tenancy. Why should the rent which he is prepared to pay be excluded from consideration in fixing the market value of the tenancy? ..."

Having now an established approach which permitted the intro- **10–04** duction of the evidence of brewer's bids the method of doing so must

---

[3] [1898] 2 Q.B. 630.
[4] (1937) 26 R. & I.T. 228.

be considered. The case of *Dodds v. South Shields A.C.* already referred to, set the precedent that the fact of the licence must be reflected in the valuation. The case also, however, rejected the use of the accounts of the business being carried on as evidence. It was held that looking at the actual profits was a "dangerous novelty" and there was ample evidence as to the value of a more direct kind-comparison with other similar rented licensed premises.

Five years after the *Dodds* case the doctrine was liberalised to some extent. In *Cartwright v. Sculcoates Union*[5] the House of Lords held that evidence of the profits which the premises could command could be considered because these profits would be taken into account by the hypothetical tenant in formulating a rental bid.

In his judgment Lord Davey set out a commonsense approach:

> " . . . you have in each case to find out in the best way you can what is the rent which a tenant may reasonably be expected to give, and if the best way under the particular circumstances is to ascertain the use which a tenant might expect to be able to make of the premises, the facility afforded by the premises for the carrying on of a trade appears to me to be a primary and elementary consideration in the case. If you are to take into account the fact that the premises command a trade, you must surely ask what trade? Is it a large trade or is it a small trade? And I do not know myself any better test of what trade they may be expected to command than the trade which they actually do command. It is not that you rate the profits, it is not that you rate the man's skill and judgement or discretion in the mode of carrying on the business, but you have to ascertain what sort of a trade the hypothetical tenant, as he is called, may reasonably expect to be able to carry on on these premises as an element in determining the rent he would be willing to offer."

This sets out the case that there is no "better test" for ascertaining the trade which the hypothetical tenant "may reasonably expect to be able to carry on" than the trade which the premises "actually do command".

Use of actual trade

10–05 Even though case law was turning towards the admissibility of trading results as evidence for valuation this was still considered as inferior and the rule was that it should not be used if comparative evidence was available.

It must be recognised, however, that the availability of this preferred comparative evidence was diminishing. Brewery companies were acquiring public houses and were gathering together

---

[5] [1900] A.C. 150.

154

estates of, generally, freehold properties which they let on tied tenancies. The evidence which these lettings represented, being within the "tied" system, was far removed from the rental definition required for a rating assessment. Thus, whilst evidence of "real" rents is obviously better than a rent deduced from the profits, or even simply the takings of the business, these latter considerations became more and more usual because the trade was the only viable evidence.

The courts, which had originally rejected trading evidence, finally admitted that it could not be ignored. It was held in *Parr v. Leigh Union*[6] that if evidence of receipts and expenses is given it must be accepted by the court.

In the gathering acceptance of the doctrine that actual trade in a **10–06** public house is proper evidence of value, one important distinction must be drawn. The actual trade is nothing more than evidence and is simply a part of the process of estimating value. The evidence only points to the level of trade which might reasonably be expected to be achieved through the occupation of the premises. Collins L.J. in his judgment in the *Robinson Brothers* case added a cautionary word on this point:

> " . . . in fixing the rent of chambers in one of the Inns of Court, the facility for carrying on the legal profession in them is an element, and an important one, but the actual income of the tenant is not. The chambers command no more rent when let to the Attorney-General than they would do if let to a young barrister just called who does not as yet pay his expenses."

Whilst it would appear that the effective way of making valuations of public houses is by reference to actual trade achieved as evidence of value the alternatives need to be considered.

If actual trade is to be ignored or in some way regarded as improper or unreliable then the problem becomes more difficult because there is no reliable method of determining the potential trade of a public house by measuring any physical factor. A direct comparative approach of rent per square metre is impracticable. Inspection of the pub trade reveals large buildings with a few customers and some tiny premises full of customers. Any area based comparison must fail in the absence of a means of fixing differential prices for popular and profitable premises compared to the unpopular—a trade based comparison is the only reliable method.

Another alternative which has been attempted in the past has been an approach to rental value based on either capital cost or capital

---

[6] (1905) 1 Konstam 211.

value. These approaches have been steadfastly rejected by the courts as such figures have been shown not to have a consistent relationship with rental values.

Valuation Officer's right to trade information

10–07 Paragraph 5 of Schedule 9 to the 1988 Act states that:

> " . . . a Valuation Officer may serve a notice on a person who is an owner or occupier of a hereditament requiring him to supply to the Officer such information as is required by him for the purpose of carrying out functions conferred or imposed on him by or under this (Act) . . ."

The right of powers of the Valuation Officer were less well defined under earlier legislation.

In *Watney Mann Ltd v. Langley (V.O.)*[7] a friendly test case to obtain a judicial ruling on the valuation officer's powers under the then section 58 of the 1948 Act, which was largely a re-enactment of section 40 of the 1925 Act, it was held that the power for notices to be served on occupiers requesting "such particulars as may reasonably be required" did entitle the valuation officer to request trading information.

Earlier ambiguities have been swept away by paragraph 5 and the valuation officer is now entitled to "such information as is required".

VALUATION METHODS

Bradford method

10–08 Referring back to the case law dealing with the appropriateness of evidence, the ruling in the *Bradford-on-Avon A.C. v. White* case gave rise to the *"Bradford"* method of valuation. This judgment held that personal contracts between brewers and tenants had to be ignored (but brewers as competitors for the tenancy were not to be excluded). This rather convoluted logic was generally interpreted by valuers, estimating the rating assessment, as the rent which a free tenant would give.

The approach of valuers had to change 40 years later when the judgment in *Robinson Brothers (Brewers) v. Houghton & Chester-le-Street Assessment Committee* was delivered. The effect of the

---

[7] [1963] R.A. 431.

opportunity for brewers to let houses on tied tenancies now had to be included in the evidence.

The significance of the tied trade system on profitability is, at its simplest, the difference in the prices which the brewer, as the supplier of liquor, can charge the tied tenant as compared with the discounted prices which will be offered to a free trader who can go to whichever brewer from which he or she wishes to obtain supplies. This discount and captive market has two effects. The tied tenant obviously pays more for beer (thereby increasing the brewer's wholesale profit) but, of course, as a consequence, pays a lower rent as a reflection of the restriction contained in the tenancy agreement (and the lower retail profit which will be made when selling the beer). In making *"Bradford"* valuations an amount was added to the tied tenant's trading figures to represent the discount which a free tenant would enjoy. After *"Robinson"* the valuation method became *"Bradford plus"* and a further addition was made to give recognition to the "overbid" a brewer would make—to secure the opportunity to let the house to a tied tenant—in competition with other brewers.

This method was unsatisfactory if only because it relied on two notional additions which could only be justified, ultimately, on the basis of the experience of the valuer.

Direct method

The limitations of *"Bradford plus"* were eventually superseded by the acceptance in the courts of what became known as the "direct method". This approach to valuation effectively held sway from the mid-1940s until the end of the 1973 valuation list in 1990. **10–09**

The name "direct" simply describes the method's direct approach to the brewer's profits, and from them, the rent which would be offered. The method evolved considerably over the years it was in use. In its final form it has become, in academic terms, an extremely confused valuation, unashamedly mixing its methods and defying its own logic.

The concept involved determining the appropriate tied rent for the house being valued. This was calculated on a liquor sales volume basis. To this tied rent was added an element for the brewer's wholesale profit which, as discussed above, the tied tenancy guaranteed. This profit too was calculated from the liquor trade in volume terms. The two figures added together totalled the return which the brewer would enjoy from the house.

A percentage of this amount would then be taken (the "brewer's bid") to be the rent the brewer would offer. The choice of this bid was, of course, crucial and many valuation judgments were wrapped up in that decision. The typical range of bids during the life of the 1973 valuation lists was 30 per cent to 50 per cent.

10–10   When the "direct method" was first proposed the above would have described the concept quite reasonably. Changes in trading over the years, however, had to be incorporated. These changes were simply tacked on at the end. It was only custom and practice (and certainly not academic valuation erudition) which caused the direct method to survive.

Food became more and more important in public house trading over the 40 years from 1950—and indeed has continued to grow in significance throughout the 1990s. The rental element to account for the opportunity for catering, together with other "dry" elements (such as accommodation) was added to the assessment produced by the direct method simply as a percentage of the gross takings which the dry trading could achieve. This is, of course, an entirely different theoretical approach to that adopted for the "wet" trade in the direct method. The mix up was further compounded by the introduction of an addition for gaming machines. And this was just that, an addition. A flat rate figure for having a gaming machine—to all intents and purposes treating these machines as rateable plant! Fortunately the direct method did not survive the 1990 revaluation.

Overbid method

10–11   In preparing to make the valuations for the 1990 rating lists, the Valuation Office concluded that the direct method had outlived its usefulness. Ignoring the arguments, suffice it to say here that the "overbid" method was born. This has many similarities with the direct method—at first sight. It is, however, founded on an entirely different concept. Regretfully the "mix and match" illogicalities of the direct method survived the change.

The overbid approach simply stated that a house would command a certain tied rent (calculated from the volume of wet trade and turnover of the dry trade) which must be less than the open market free rent. The additional rent which the brewer would bid (in order to secure the property and therefore obtain the tied rent) must be a proportion of the wholesale profits which the brewer could anticipate from being able to tie the house. This proportion was the "overbid" and was added to the tied rent. To this figure was also added (as in the direct method) a further amount for any gaming machines.

In settling assessments in the 1990 rating lists the Valuation Office and the industry engaged in considerable argument to settle upon mutually agreed methods for determining the tied rents and overbids. In the finally applied valuations overbids ranging from nil to 27.5 per cent of the calculated profits were added to the tied rents.

The common thread through both the direct and the overbid **10–12** methods was the reliance, for the greater part of the valuation, on liquor volumes. In other words these were barrelage valuations and the experienced eye of a licensed property specialist would sum a house up with the number of barrels of beer it could be expected to sell. The suitability of this approach was, however, being eroded virtually simultaneously with the introduction of the 1990 revaluation.

In its wisdom, the Monopolies and Mergers Commission published its report *"The Supply of Beer"* in 1989. The Government reacted with the Beer Orders and the consequence was—as far as this rapid run through licensed property rating is concerned—that it was no longer possible for the Valuation Office to obtain reliable information concerning the level of trade in pubs simply by serving return forms on the brewers asking for the volumes supplied. A combination of the Beer Orders and European Community legislation now meant that a rigorous imposition of the tied system was no longer possible. So liquor could now legitimately find its way into pubs other than from the brewery which owned them.

As brewery companies could no longer provide reliable information on anything other than managed houses, and as non-brewing public house companies sprang up who bought their liquor where it best suited them, it became apparent to the Valuation Office (rightly or wrongly) that the only information which was going to be usable was the turnover (in money) at the pub. So it was to the publican that return forms for the 1995 revaluation were sent.

PUBLIC HOUSE VALUATIONS

Trade based valuations

The use of turnover is already established as a valuation approach. **10–13** Indeed it has found considerable favour in the past. Rentals were, and are, being contested as a percentage of gross turnover. Free houses had been valued for rating in both the 1973 and 1990 lists as a percentage of "gross takings from all sources" although this had not been challenged in the Lands Tribunal on either a qualitative or quantitative basis.

An objection to the use of turnover as a comparative basis is the

159

proportion of turnover taken up by excise duty. This can, of course, "move the goal posts" on the overnight say so of the Chancellor of the Exchequer. This problem is largely overcome by the fact that we are valuing in the frozen economic (and duty) circumstances of the antecedent valuation date. Whilst we must take into account physical changes after that date, the valuation must always be related economically back to the antecedent valuation date—including, if relevant, changes in excise duty.

A description of such valuations as a "method" in the sense of the concept of the direct "method" and the overbid "method" would be an attempt to invest simplicity with some complex mystique it does not deserve. But in simple terms in all the relevant circumstances, the rateable value will be a given percentage of the gross takings.

Before examining those relevant circumstances it must be stressed that, just because the starting point of the valuation is the monetary turnover at the house does not mean that it is a "profits" valuation.

Valuation to rateable value by reference to profits is a common method of assessment. It can be used to make a public house valuation. The valuations which will now be discussed are not profits valuations. They are comparative valuations in which the unit of comparison is the pound of turnover, as compared with the more usual unit of comparison, the square metre.

10-14 The comparative analysis relies on the very straightforward concept that all the evidence of public house rents fixed at the antecedent valuation date can be converted into a percentage of the turnover of the house at the same time. In a perfect world of a perfectly negotiated and perfectly informed market there would be, if not one single rate per cent, at least a rational pattern of rates that, perhaps, would provide evidence of a relationship with the quantum of turnover.

Perfection is seldom achieved—and certainly not in rental analysis. In considering any public house rent as evidence of a basis in terms of a percentage of gross takings it is suggested that the following points, at least, are relevant.

The rent must be converted so as to be in terms of rateable value. Thus, the domestic accommodation (if any) must be excluded.

- Any element of landlord's repairs must be excluded.
- The question of term and review period must be addressed in order to reflect properly the requirement for the rent to be (in rating terms) that which would be commanded "from year to year" on the assumption that it will continue.
- The rental must not be subject to any trading restrictions such

as a tie (in the old fashioned sense) or some more modern device now found in pub letting agreements.

Having "cleaned up" the rent in terms of rateable value the other part of the analysis must be similarly examined—that is the turnover. It is not sufficiently simple to look at the top line of the profit and loss account for the takings.

The use of actual trading information as evidence for public house **10–15** valuations has already been discussed above. In general terms it has been recognised that valuers should use their skill and experience to decide the level of trade a particular house should achieve—but in making this decision the actual trade is the best possible evidence.

Likewise in devaluation, assessing the turnover against which to analyse the rent to produce a rate per cent, it is necessary to start with the actual turnover and then examine it more deeply.

Looking at trade over a number of years gives better depth and can indicate circumstances which are out of the ordinary (thus, if one year is markedly out of line with the rest then examination of that year might throw up factors which should be taken into account). A very typical event which can have a marked effect on trade is the change of licensee. The traditional scenario is that of the older person coming up to retirement who is happy to let trade look after itself. The new broom who follows comes with an enthusiasm and motivation which transforms the takings.

Publicans are often blamed for poor trade. They are accused of running down towards retirement (as above); of being drunkards; of encouraging too much riff-raff (who discourage polite drinkers); or of keeping the riff-raff out (so only leaving polite drinkers, who don't drink very much); and so on.

It should be remembered that the converse can be true too. Some **10–16** publicans can succeed where others fail. Some publicans can achieve a level of trade which outstrips all expectations for the pub in question. Again obvious examples of this are the local hero (such as a footballer) who in retirement from the playing field takes a pub to which the loyal and curious flock. Another distortion in this direction can be the fame of the house rather than its landlord. A pub which appears regularly in a TV soap opera is an example of this. Twice weekly on the box can result in coach parties turning up just to have a pint. A useful reference in this regard, is the judgment of Lord Davey in the *Sculcoates Union* case.

For both devaluation and, ultimately, valuation, it is essential to determine the "fair maintainable trade" for each house. The term is well chosen: fair means impartially just; maintainable, to keep in a steady state. The fair maintainable trade can be considered to be the business which can reasonably be expected to be achieved by an experienced publican taking account of the trading practices and normal competition in the locality. As will be discussed below, the fair maintainable trade must also be split between the different types of trade carried on in most pubs today.

10–17 Having thus refined both the rent and the turnover, it is possible to determine just what percentage the rent is in terms of rateable value, compared with the fair maintainable trade. The results of the analysis, however, do not produce a pattern of nicely ordered percentages that can be employed to calculate rateable values. It is still necessary to take account of many individual points which apply to every pub in differing degrees. The following are examples of some of the factors which should be taken into account. They convey the process of thought that a valuer must follow through in considering each property.

Factors tending to increase profitability	*Factors tending to decrease profitability*
1. The building Modern construction Easy to run with few staff Opportunities for functions, etc. Provision of proper catering kitchen	**1. The building** Very large with redundant space Old and expensive to maintain Many rooms requiring big staff No suitable catering facilities
2. The location Prominent main road position Central to "pub minded" catchment area Supply of customers all day Good staff available locally	**2. The location** Out of the way—no passing trade Inappropriate character for neighbourhood Trade only available for part of the day Staff difficult to find and expensive
3. The trade Little local competition Ability to charge high prices No need for promotions Food can be sold profitably Entertainment charged for Car park encourages customers Emphasis on lager and "designer" beers	**3. The trade** Considerable competition Prices kept down by competition Requirement for promotions & marketing Food provided at or near cost Entertainments provided free Car park adds to maintenance bill Emphasis on bitters and milds

The above pointers convey the process of thought that a valuer must follow through in considering each property.

10–18 There is a mention of food in the above table. The sale of food in public houses is now a very important part of the trade. It is not too long ago that the pub which sold food was the exception. Pressures of competition, and the price of beer, have changed this. Licensees now realise that the profit on a sandwich or a cup of coffee can make non-liquor sales a very attractive alternative to pulling pints. Nothing in life is absolutely simple though. Running effectively neck and neck with the growth in dry trade has been the strengthening of environmental health legislation. A publican must now be both careful and responsible in the handling of food—and in the provision of a proper kitchen in which preparation takes place.

The turnover in a pub (and thus its profits) come from markedly different streams of income: primarily liquor and food. There may also be accommodation; almost certainly machines—gaming machines (AWP or "amusement with prizes", the traditional one armed bandit, now a flashing electronic double amputee), quiz and video machines (SWP or "skill with prizes"), juke boxes, pool tables, vending machines (with very lucrative lines being installed in the lavatories in some pubs), pin tables, etc; entertainment, either charged for by way of an entrance fee, or through increased prices on the night, or simply provided as a "service" in the hope that it will encourage better patronage and a consequential increase in sales; and anything else which an enterprising publican can think of to encourage the sale of drink.

The amount of rent which might be bid for the opportunity to **10-19** engage in any of the above types of trade will, of course, vary when considered as a percentage of the takings. Indeed, in the case of entertainments, for example, it is not untypical for a publican to pay considerable amounts for entertainers and to make no specific charges to recover this outlay. On top of the cost of the entertainment itself there may be other costs which inevitably arise—doormen for example. This is all done in the hope that sufficient extra liquor will be sold to make the expenditure worthwhile. These are circumstances where the valuer must consider adjusting the fair maintainable trade.

If part of the actual takings is only achieved by an above average expenditure (e.g. on entertainments) then it follows that the profit from this part of the takings will be less than "normal". If the house is then to be compared with one which trades entirely "normally" an appropriate deduction from the actual takings must be made to render them into terms of "fair maintainable trade".

It is impossible to provide any really meaningful examples of public house valuations. But if only to impart some degree of familiarity a valuation for the 1995 rating lists will look something like this.

Fair maintainable wet trade:

£100,000 @ 8.5%   8,500

Fair maintainable dry trade:

£50,000 @ 6.5%   3,250

Total rateable value: £11,750

ALTERNATIVE USE VALUATIONS

10–20 In the 1967 Act (section 20(2)) public houses were defined as:

" ... a hereditament which consists of or comprises premises licensed for the sale of intoxicating liquor for consumption on the premises where the sale of such liquor is, or is apart from any other trade or business ancillary or incidental to it, the only trade or business carried on at the hereditament."

This definition was necessary for the operation of section 20(2)(c) which provided for the volume of trade carried on in a public house (as defined) to be a "relevant factor" in determining the rateable value. This subsection gave authority to the practice of annual reviews of assessments for pubs. With the repeal of the 1967 Act, both the definition of a public house and this special treatment afforded to pubs (whereby the assessment could be changed in response to variations in trade) were lost. Changes in rateable value can now be sought only to reflect a material change in circumstances.

Whilst there have been well established valuation methods recognised and used by practitioners acting for both the ratepayers and Valuation Office (direct method for the 1973 lists and overbid method for the 1990 lists) it became clear that assessments so produced were, in some cases, seriously out of line with assessments derived from alternative valuation methods.

Typically public houses in shopping centres began to show assessments based on trade which were less than those based on shop values. This was in contrast to the situation during the life of the 1963 lists where public houses in shopping parades had rateable values in excess of the adjoining shops and arguments on behalf of ratepayers could be pursued profitably if it was possible to show that, in accordance with the definition of a public house, the hereditament was *not* a public house (but, say, a restaurant) and therefore fell to be valued on a comparative area basis. The relative values reversed for

164

the 1973 and 1990 lists and the argument became that of, for the ratepayer, showing that the public house should rather be valued on the trade basis than on a zoned shop basis.

The Valuation Office has profferred the argument that public **10–21** houses are no longer statutorily defined for rating purposes and, as compared with shop uses, a change to public house use falls within Class A3 of the Use Classes Order 1987, so putting public house, wine bar, restaurant, cafe or shop all into the same mode or category of occupation. Thus, the argument is that obviously the highest potential bid must dictate the value.

To counter this is the long standing principle of rating: you value what you see (*rebus sic stantibus*) and not the potential or development value. The current case law which deals with this argument all falls within the 1967 Act. These cases can provide useful pointers. The latest Lands Tribunal case, at the time of writing—*Jones (V.O.) v. Toby Restaurants (South) Ltd*[8]—concerned precisely this point and in his decision, the member (Mr C. R. Mallett) said:

" ... I find that the hereditament was used as a public house and could not be used for any other purpose without significant changes to its physical state."

However, two cases at Valuation Tribunal concerning post-1990 revaluation proposals have subsequently rejected the precedent of this case on the grounds that the Valuation Tribunal, " ... feel that we cannot consider any case law relating to public houses predating ...".[9]

As these decisions have both been appealed to the Lands Tribunal it remains to be seen how this argument will develop.

One speculation of interest is how this situation will evolve following the 1995 revaluation. If the basis adopted for 1995 turns out to better reflect the market as a whole it may be that there will be no significant difference between the two approaches—particularly when the general stagnation in shop rents in some places over the life of the 1990 lists is taken into account.

---

[8] [1992] R.A. 87.
[9] The Local Government Finance Act 1988.

LICENSED RESTAURANTS

10-22 The question of definition of a public house has been addressed above. This problem also arises in the case of a restaurant. What distinguishes a restaurant from a public house? Indeed, these days, one can sometimes ask what distinguishes a shop from a restaurant given the number of shops seeking to increase turnover by setting areas aside for the sale and consumption of coffee and snacks.

In simple terms one might reasonably argue that a restaurant is a place where food is sold for consumption on the premises. Such premises may also be licensed. The type of licence is important and providing the licence is not a "full on licence" then the property can be considered to be a restaurant and not a public house. Some premises do, however, enjoy full on licences but trade in a style which makes designation difficult.

Given that a particular hereditament is clearly a licensed restaurant then it is necessary to consider whether the existence of the licence has any effect on the value. In rating theory this can be rephrased as "would the hypothetical tenant bid any more for the benefit of the licence as compared with the unlicensed building?" The answer is beset with ifs and buts. The primary factor is the place of the property in the market as a whole and the pressure from competition in the locality (not just restaurant competition but also alternative uses within the concept of *rebus sic stantibus*).

10-23 At the top end of the scale, for a restaurant serving those who consider themselves gourmets, a licence is an absolute essential. Even so this does not invariably warrant an increase in value, for the hereditament may have alternative retail uses of equal or greater value, and might be unlettable as a restaurant were a licence not available. At the other end of the scale an establishment having, or intended for, a less select type of customer may gain nothing from a licence, this trade being satisfied by public houses.

A practical approach to valuation is therefore necessary. The careful consideration of all the circumstances, information and evidence available is essential. Thus, where there is ample rental evidence, that evidence must take precedence over anything less direct. One would expect such an approach, or the use of assessments settled on adjoining properties, to be best expressed in comparative terms by a price per square metre. A valuation based on such a method can then be reviewed (on the "stand back and look" common-sense check) with reference to the accounts (if available) and the style and character of the premises. The number of covers that can be accommodated such as to maintain the quality of the business being conducted and the physical arrangement of the kitchens (for example the traditional approach behind private swing doors or an open cooking space across a counter as adopted by "fast food" outlets) are factors which might be relevant in some circumstances—and should certainly be considered in comparing restaurant with restaurant.

Finally, one must consider the liquor trade. If this is a predominant part of the business there may be some justification for adding to the valuation but the question is how? If liquor trade is dominant, is it a public house? If "restaurant" or "retail" values outstrip public house values then the question of an addition for the licence is irrelevant.

HOTELS

The term "hotel" covers an enormous spectrum. Indeed, many public **10–24** houses sport the name hotel but are only regarded as such when some undefined line is crossed: demarcation relating to the number of bedrooms; the style of the restaurant, the predominance (or otherwise) of the bar and the overall style of the trade. Whilst it is difficult to define an exact set of criteria to distinguish pubs from hotels there is absolutely no doubt about a very large number of hereditaments. These in themselves vary widely in size, type, market and profitability.

In view of the individuality of hotels the classical approach is generally through the accounts by a formal profits valuation, particularly in the case of larger hotels. For smaller hotels it has become usual for comparative valuations to be used, based either on a percentage of gross takings or a room or bed space basis. In view of the fact that rents are so scarce for hotels, the comparison is generally being made with other hotels where assessments have been agreed. These assessments will most probably have been made using a profits approach. The comparison then becomes in effect a comparison of profitability. This factor must be kept in mind when different hotels are being considered against a basis which has become established. The application of a price per bedroom or bed space on a particular hotel can only be done safely if the source of the basis is properly compared with the subject. Hotels vary in virtually every possible respect over a very wide range.

Three particular trade characteristics must be judged.

- Accommodation
- Restaurant
- Bar

First, the accommodation business, this more than any other aspect, defines a hotel as such. How many rooms are there? What is the quality, what are the facilities? What type of guest is the hotel aiming to attract? Are there going to be seasonal problems?

10–25 Guests in bedrooms have to be supported with a restaurant. This is the second important characteristic and again, it is important to consider just how the restaurant facilities fit into the market as a whole. The range of quality of hotel restaurants is at least as wide as that for hotel bedrooms. A particular concern will be the degree to which the hotel is known for its catering to non-residents.

The third aspect of the trade which can be a useful comparative consideration is the bar. Does the hotel trade, in any sense, as a public house? Does it have an important bar trade providing a good draw for non-residents?

The highly competitive hotel market of recent years has caused many businesses to extend themselves into the "leisure and fitness" fields. Small swimming pools and miniature gymnasiums have been opened in many hotels. These fitness suites can do good business in their own right, usually attracting a locally based membership who pay a subscription to use the facilities (and perhaps to enjoy some spin-off from the social cachet which an exclusive club can offer). Such leisure facilities do also, of course, increase the attractiveness of the hotel in the highly competitive market of selling bedrooms.

In considering an hotel comparatively, the significance of all the ancillary elements must be weighed. Parking space, banqueting and function rooms, entertainment facilities, conference facilities, business support services, golf, private beach and many other ideas join the leisure and keep-fit suites, already discussed, in the quest for business.

Lastly, it is relevant to revert to the question of a licence. Whilst hotels have been considered here with public houses, a hotel does not, of course, have to be licensed to sell intoxicating liquor. If there is a licence its type will be relevant (residential licence, restaurant licence or full-on licence). The relevancy of the licence and its type is the influence it brings to bear on the assessment of the level of business which the property can achieve and how that will affect the valuation, no matter which approach to estimating rateable value is chosen.

OFF-LICENCES

Today an off-licence is almost invariably a shop. Very few public **10–26** houses now have an off-sales counter. The grant of off-licences has become very much more liberal than in the past. Supermarkets and department stores have entered the field.

In considering an off-licence shop for valuation the approach should be that for any other shop. The only factor which differs from the normal is the question: does the licence have any effect on the value?

In view of the availability of licences, and the considerable competition between such shops in the High Street, it is generally accepted that an addition to the unlicensed shop assessment to account for an off-licence is not warranted.

11

Garages and Service Stations

BACKGROUND

11-01 Historically, garages and petrol filling stations were often sited together and usually run as one business. Today, although both motor related, they are considered to be totally different businesses with little in common, and when sited together can be the cause of conflict with car sales impinging on forecourt movements and the forecourt detracting from the impact of the car showroom. Increasingly the two businesses are run by different operators. Most large motor groups have sold off their petrol filling stations or converted them into car sales areas. The motor dealers objective is focused on selling new and used cars where the purchaser is considering a major purchase, and then to providing service and parts aftercare. Petrol sales are a "distress" purchase whilst the shop will rely on impulse purchases.

PETROL FILLING STATIONS

11-02 Turning first to petrol filling stations, the oil companies have continued to increase their share of the retail petrol market, although some large independent operators, who have sufficient muscle, are carving themselves a niche. Perhaps the most important development in the retail petrol business is the growth of the superstore petrol filling station. Although there have been filling stations next to superstores for many years they were originally built when operators had surplus land after satisfying their requirements for the store and parking and very often they were run as loss leaders. Now the big four food retailers insist on a petrol filling station being incorporated in all their new developments and it is estimated they will soon capture 20 per cent of the retail petrol market. Even more ominously for the petrol retail industry is Tesco's decision to develop stand alone petrol filling stations with large convenience stores. Sainsbury's have now followed Tesco's lead in what they describe as a pilot study and you can be sure that other operators will follow. For some years the oil companies have been powerless to exert any influence on the market owing to the over supply of product which means the superstore operators, who are buying large quantities of product, can negotiate very low prices particularly when they use their own transport to pick up the product from the terminal. This allows them to undercut the market at the expense of the oil companies who not only have to compete on price in the wholesale market when supplying the superstores but also watch helplessly as their own retail sites suffer the effects of competition. The individual operators, who may be tied to an oil company on inflexible supply terms are being squeezed in the middle by both the oil companies who are not over anxious to reduce their profit margins even further by giving price support and the superstore operators, and other large chains who have the buying power to purchase product at the right price.

The number of sites has continued to fall; from 20,640 in 1986 to 18,000 in 1993 and although there was a spurt of interest in the late 1980s when petrol sales were rising and oil companies were anxious to maintain their market share, the pace of closures has increased with many oil companies now disposing of their lower volume sites. Sites which only a few years ago were considered to be reasonable volume sites, perhaps achieving 2,250,000 litres per annum, are no longer of interest to oil companies and are being disposed of. They are looking for sites capable of in excess of 4,500,000 litres where economies of scale can be achieved with large loads delivered and a good return on investment through high sales volume. Many oil companies are also becoming more regionalised preferring to concentrate on sites which are within a reasonable delivery distance of their terminals.

As mentioned, the cost of developing a petrol filling station is now very high and therefore few companies will consider developing a site unless it was likely to achieve in excess of 4,500,000 litres. Whilst it is still true that the best location for a filling station is the first site going out of town, on the left hand side of the road, it also has to be visible, have convenient access and be large enough to appear spacious. Purchasing petrol is a "distress" purchase and consequently filling stations have to make the task of purchasing petrol as easy as possible. Even if the site has the attributes mentioned above it

171

still may not be viable if the level of competition is too fierce, particularly if there is a nearby superstore with a petrol filling station.

In order to arrive at the value of a filling station one has to look at the various elements which are as follows:

- Petrol sales
- Shop sales
- Car wash/jet wash
- Any other activities such as outside car display, lubrication bays, etc.

Petrol sales

11–03 In practice for rating valuations, the rental value of petrol sales is determined by reference to a nationally applied scale relating rental value to throughput. For this purpose all grades of fuel are aggregated without adjustment for different types and grades of fuel.

The scale applied for the 1995 revaluation was agreed between the Valuation Office and the United Kingdom Petroleum Industry Association and this is applied to the "maintainable" volume of sales. "Maintainable" volume is derived from the actual throughput.

It is dangerous to rely too heavily on existing petrol throughput and where possible previous years throughput should be compared. Throughput for the last three years or even better five years should be sought. It is possible to manipulate the throughput of any particular site by the pricing at the pump. That is why one has to look at the underlying profitability which is not only governed by the volume of sales but also the retained profit margin. If trading accounts are available then this is a useful check. It is therefore necessary to adjust the actual volume of sales to arrive at a "maintainable" volume which is the volume that could be achieved if a sensible pricing policy were adopted and normal opening hours were kept and furthermore one has to assume a reasonable standard of management. What is defined as a sensible price is hard to define but it does presuppose that a reasonable profit margin is retained and would probably mean a price which is the average for the area. This may result in a "maintainable" volume which is higher or lower than the actual throughput achieved.

11–04 In arriving at the "maintainable" volume it may be necessary to adjust the actual volume to reflect the effect of superstores on the volume of sales and profitability. Where a site is forced to reduce its prices to compete, the adjustment applied to the actual volume could be as great as 40 per cent where there is a substantial difference between the normal unaffected price and the prices charged by the nearby superstore.

The reliability of the valuation depends on the assumptions made as to the "maintainable" volume achievable from the site and the possibilities of this being maintained in the future bearing in mind such outside influences as highway schemes and competition such as superstores. Unless the valuer is experienced in this field the risks can be great.

Adjustments may be required by way of an end allowance to take into account the following:

- 24 hour opening
- Credit card sales outside the "normal" band
- Agency sales in excess of 10 per cent
- Customer accounts

Opening hours between 7am to 11pm are considered normal and consequently 24 hours opening will increase running costs. Credit card sales, agency sales and customer accounts above an average level will warrant an end allowance in accordance with a pre-determined formula to reflect their impact on profitability.

Once the "maintainable" volume has been determined an appropriate value per gallon or litre is applied, which increases exponentially as the volume increases to reflect the fact that profitability increases at a faster rate than turnover owing to the fixed nature of the costs of running a petrol filling station.

Shop sales

It is normal to apply a rate per litre to reflect the fact that there is a **11–05** correlation between shop sales and petrol throughput with a maximum and minimum rate per square metre. This is usually expressed in pounds (sterling) per square metre for every 25,000 litres of maintainable throughput. Ancillary accommodation such as offices, stores and kitchen are taken at a lower percentage of the rate applicable to the shop. Obviously convenience stores and other shops which do not necessarily rely on the petrol buying motorist do not fall within this valuation approach. Such areas as toilets, meter cupboards and compressor rooms do not fall to be valued.

Car washes

11–06 Car washes are given a band of rateable values depending on facilities, location and competition. It is necessary to look at the potential of the site and the buildings clear of all non-rateable plant. The valuer has then to decide which class the car wash falls in, which will depend on its location, whether it is housed within a purpose built structure, whether it is well laid out and has good access and circulation, competition and the likely demand from the residential areas close by.

Other activities

11–07 Workshops are valued on the basis of a rent per square metre whilst car display spaces are valued on a rent per space basis.

Motor dealerships

11–08 The motor manufacturers and distributors still control, to a large extent, the method of car sales in the country. The franchised dealer who sells a car will very often retain a source of business from the purchaser by servicing the car and providing spare parts in successive years. Second-hand car sales are becoming increasingly important to the profitability of motor dealerships and very often more money is made from second-hand cars than from new car sales although the latter lends the business an air of respectability. Although there have been recent improvements in the motor retailing business, the over capacity in production of cars has meant intense competition which impacts on the profitability of manufacturers who in turn try and claw back some of the profit that the retailers are making by restricting margins, etc. Whereas cars once needed servicing every 500 miles, many cars now only need servicing every 10,000 to 12,000 miles and what is more, modern motor cars are much more reliable. Workshops have therefore become smaller, the drive for increased profitability has meant that parts departments have also become smaller, with many parts being sourced directly from the manufacturer or from larger distributors. Showrooms have also become smaller and seldom are used cars displayed inside a showroom. Apart from the reduction in the requirement for covered space, site areas for dealerships will become smaller owing to the fact that manufacturers are moving onto centralised stocking and are trying to build cars to order rather than stockpiling cars and awaiting demand. It is likely that the need for storage compounds is therefore going to recede.

174

Outside display areas have become more important and there is **11–09** now a trend to make them more attractive rather than just an area of tarmacadam. Modern dealerships have moved out to the edges of towns, often where the retail parks are located, where there is room to build purpose built facilities with a high standard of parking and circulation space. Outmoded garage premises with poor parking facilities will struggle to satisfy the requirements of the modern dealership.

The motor retailing industry is becoming increasingly concentrated in the hands of the plc groups who are looking for large turnover sites in the bigger towns and the smaller dealers, particularly those situated in small towns and villages, are being forced out by competition or are having their franchises terminated by the manufacturers/distributors. It now seems likely the European Commission will dismantle the franchise system, perhaps in some years time, which will allow free competition and multi-franchised sites. This can only mean an even bigger market share for the large retail groups.

GARAGES AND SERVICE STATIONS

When valuing motor dealerships the showroom space will command **11–10** the highest rental value and this is often related to non-food retail values. The workshops and parts areas will have a lower value but a significant value will be attributable to the used car display areas.

12

Valuation of Public Utility Undertakings

GENERAL PRINCIPLES

12–01 Public utility undertakings are those public or private concerns, whether operating for a profit or not, which supply services to the public. These services are normally in the field of public transport or public supply, as of gas, electricity, water, etc. Often the hereditaments which these undertakers occupy comprise or include a network of pipes or wires which extend into many rating areas.

Many of the principal utility undertakings have now ceased to be rateable in the normal way, although most of the industries concerned have continued to contribute to the national non-domestic rate on the basis of various complicated formulae.

Prior to 1990, these formulae specified how the rateable values for the undertakings were calculated and how this value was to be apportioned to the various rating districts.

In 1990, the national non-domestic rate in the pound (sterling) was introduced and the complex task of apportioning rateable values for these undertakings to the various charging authorities (now billing authorities) became unnecessary. Central rating lists for England and Wales were introduced so that one entry could be made for the whole statutory undertaking throughout the country. In addition, the central rating lists contain the rateable values of telecommunications hereditaments, Tyne and Wear Metro, Docklands Light Railway and certain long distance pipelines which are valued by conventional methods. The Central Valuation Officer who is the chief executive of the Valuation Office Agency is responsible for compiling and amending, as necessary, the central rating list.

What properties are deemed to be included in the formula assessment are specified and defined in the Central Rating Lists

Regulations 1994[1] and the Non-Domestic Rating (Railways, Tele-communications and Canals) Regulations 1994.[2] These generally specify the "relevant hereditaments" occupied by the named under-taking or utility which are included in the formula assessment and included in the central rating list, and that there are certain "excepted hereditaments" which are assessed in the normal manner and included in the local rating lists.

The following are the definition of "relevant hereditaments" and "excepted hereditaments" for each industry.

"RELEVANT" AND "EXCEPTED" HEREDITAMENTS

Electricity industry

Relevant hereditaments comprise: **12–02**

(i) In the case of National Power plc, Powergen plc and Nuclear Electric plc:

Hereditaments (other than excepted hereditaments) wholly or mainly used for the purposes of the generation of electrical power or for ancillary purposes.

(ii) In the case of National Grid Company plc:

Hereditaments (other than excepted hereditaments) wholly or mainly used for the purposes of the generation trans-formation and transmission of electrical power or for ancillary purposes.

(iii) In the case of:

Eastern Group plc
East Midlands Electricity plc
London Electricity plc
Northern Electric plc
NORWEB plc
MANWEB plc
Midlands Electricity plc

---

[1] S.I. 1994 No. 3121.
[2] S.I. 1994 No. 3123.

Scottish Power plc
Seeboard plc
Southern Electricity plc
South Wales Electricity plc
South Western Electric plc
Yorkshire Electricity Group plc
Hereditaments (other than excepted hereditaments) wholly or mainly used for the purposes of the functions of a public electricity supplier or for ancillary purposes.

12–03 Excepted hereditament means any hereditament consisting, or comprising of premises used wholly or mainly:

(a) as a shop or other place for the sale, display or demonstration of apparatus or accessories for use by consumers of electricity (any use for the receipt of payments for the use of electricity being disregarded);

(b) as office premises of a designated person, where those premises are not situated on operational land of that person; or

(c) for both of the foregoing purposes; or

(d) for the generation of electricity primarily by means of wind or tidal power.

The valuation formula for the central rating list is set out in The Electricity Supply Industry (Rateable Values) Order 1994.[3] This order also includes the valuation formula for certain small independent power generators which are not included in the central list.

Hereditaments occupied for the purposes of electricity generation by persons other than National Power plc, Powergen plc, or Nuclear Electric plc; and the generating plant uses wind, tidal or water power as its source of energy; or has a declared net capacity of 500 kilowatts or more, are valued by formula at £5,810 RV per MW of capacity for wind or water power generators or £11,620 RV per MW of capacity for fuel burning generators. The entries for these hereditaments are contained in the local rating lists not the central rating list.

---

[3] S.I. 1994 No. 3282.

Railways

Relevant hereditaments comprise:

12–04

(a) In the case of the British Railways Board, Rail Track plc, London Underground Limited and Docklands Light Railway Limited:

Hereditaments (other than excepted hereditaments) used wholly or mainly for the purposes of the parts of the designated person's undertakings which are concerned with carriage of goods or passengers by rail, providing railway services or heavy maintenance services or for purposes ancillary to those purposes (including the purpose of exhibiting advertisements).

(b) In the case of The Tyne and Wear Passenger Transport Executive, Greater Manchester Metro Ltd and South Yorkshire Supertram Ltd:

Hereditaments (other than excepted hereditaments) used wholly or mainly for the purposes of the appropriate undertaking, or for the purposes ancillary to those purposes (including the purpose of exhibiting advertisements).

Excepted hereditament means a hereditament consisting, or comprising of:

(a) premises used as a shop, hotel, museum, or place of public refreshment;
(b) premises used wholly or mainly as office premises occupied by a designated person which are not situated on operational land of that person;
(c) premises or rights so let out as to be capable of separate assessment;
(d) premises (other than premises used on connection with the collection and delivery of parcels, goods or merchandise conveyed or to be conveyed by rail) used wholly or in part for purposes concerned with the carriage of goods or passengers by road transport or sea transport or with harbours, or for purposes incidental to such purposes.

The valuation formula for the formula-assessed hereditaments is contained in the Railways (Rateable Values) Order 1994.[4] It should be noted that British Rail, Rail Track and London Underground are assessed by formula and included in the central rating list. Docklands Light Railway and Tyne and Wear Metro are valued by conventional methods and are included in the central rating list. Greater Manchester Metro and South Yorkshire Supertram are valued by conventional methods and are included in the local rating lists.

Water supply

12–05 The relevant hereditaments are hereditaments (other than excepted hereditaments) used wholly or mainly for the purposes of a water undertaker under Part III of the Water Industry Act 1991 or for ancillary purposes. The water undertakings which constitute designated persons are as follows:

Anglian Water Services Ltd
Bournemouth and West Hampshire Water plc
Bristol Water plc
Cambridge Water Company
Chester Waterworks Company
Cholderton & District Water Company Ltd
Colne Valley Water Company
Dwr Cymru Cyfyngedig
East Surrey Water plc
Eastbourne Water plc
Essex and Suffolk Water plc
Folkestone & Dover Water Services Ltd
Hartlepool Water Company
Mid Kent Water plc
Mid Southern Water plc
Mid Sussex Water plc
North East Water plc
North Surrey Water Ltd
North West Water Limited
Northumbrian Water Ltd
Portsmouth Water plc
Severn Trent Water Ltd
South Staffordshire Water plc
South West Water Services Ltd
Southern Water Services Ltd
Suffolk Water Company plc

---

[4] S.I. 1994 No. 3284.

Sutton District Water plc
Tendring Hundred Water Services Ltd
Thames Water Utilities Ltd
Three Valleys Water plc
Wessex Water Services Ltd
West Kent Water plc
Wrexham Water plc
The York Waterworks plc
Yorkshire Water Utilities Limited

Excepted hereditament means a hereditament consisting, or **12–06** comprising of premises used wholly or mainly:

(a) for the manufacture, storage, sale, display or demonstration of apparatus or accessories for use by consumers of water (any use for the receipt of payments for the use of water or sewerage services being disregarded); or

(b) as office premises of a designated person, where those premises are not situated on operational land of that person; or

(c) for both of the foregoing purposes.

The valuation formula for the central list entry is contained in The Water Undertakers (Rateable Values) Order 1994.[5]

Telecommunications

Relevant hereditaments comprise, for British Telecommunications **12–07** plc:

All hereditaments occupied by posts, wires, underground cables and ducts, telephone kiosks, switchgear and other equipment not within a building, or by easements or wayleaves, being property used for the purposes of telecommunications services;

and for Mercury Communications Limited:

All hereditaments occupied by posts, wires, underground cables and ducts, telephone kiosks, towers, masts, switchgear and other equipment or by easements or wayleaves, being property used for the purposes of telecommunications services.

The valuation formula for the central list entry is contained in the

---

[5] S.I. 1994 No. 3285.

Telecommunications Industry (Rateable Values) Order 1989.[6] The British Waterways Board and Telecommunications Industry (Rateable Values) Revocation Order 1994[7] provides that with effect from April 11, 1995 all properties occupied by British Telecommunications plc and Mercury plc will be assessed under the normal rules for rating.

However the "relevant hereditament's" occupied by the following telecommunications companies: British Telecommunications plc, Mercury Communications plc, BR Telecommunications Ltd, Energies Communications Ltd and AT & T (U.K.) Ltd will be included in the central rating list from April 1, 1995. The relevant hereditaments in these cases are occupations by posts, wires, underground cables and ducts, telephone kiosks, towers, masts, switching equipment, or other equipment or easements or wayleaves being property used for the monitoring, processing or transmission of communications signals for the provision of telecommunications services.

British Gas

12–08 Relevant hereditaments comprise hereditaments (other than excepted hereditaments) used wholly or mainly:

(a) for the purposes of British Gas plc acting as a public gas supplier; or

(b) for the purposes of the supply, installation or maintenance of gas appliances, or for ancillary purposes; or

(c) for more than one of the foregoing purposes.

Excepted hereditament means any hereditament consisting, or comprising of premises used wholly or mainly:

(a) for the manufacture of plant or gas fittings;

(b) as a shop or other place for the sale, display or demonstration of apparatus or accessories for use by consumers of gas (any use for the receipt of payments for the use of gas being disregarded);

(c) as office premises, where those premises are not situated on operational land of British Gas plc; or

(d) for more than one of the foregoing purposes.

---

[6] S.I. 1989 No. 2478.
[7] S.I. 1994 No. 3281

The valuation formula for the central list entry is contained in the British Gas plc (Rateable Values) Order 1994.[8]

British Waterways

Relevant hereditaments (other than excepted hereditaments) **12–09** comprise:

(a) Waterways (including cuts and culverts, locks, gates, sluices, pumps, feeder conduits and weirs);
(b) Aqueducts, basins, bridges, embankments, reservoirs and tunnels;
(c) Lighthouses, beacons, buoys, breakwaters, boatlifts and other structures designed to aid navigation;
(d) Docks, wharves, piers, jetties, pontoons, moorings, slipways and buildings used for the floating storage of craft; or for the provision, maintenance or servicing of inland waterways and plant and machinery in connection therewith;
(e) Clay pits, dredging and other waste disposal tips;
(f) Other land, buildings or parts of buildings and structures used for the provision or servicing of facilities for traffic by inland waterways or in harbours, or for ancillary purposes.

Excepted hereditament means any hereditament:

(a) consisting of, or including a dock or harbour undertaking carried on under authority conferred by or under any enactment;
(b) consisting of premises so let out as to be capable of separate assessment;
(c) consisting of premises used as a shop, museum, car park, warehouse, place of public refreshment or as a workshop or premises for maintenance or repair or for the hiring or storage of craft; or
(d) consisting of office premises.

The central list value formula is set out in the British Waterways Board (Rateable Values) Order 1989.[9]
The British Waterways Board and Telecommunications Industry (Rateable Value) Revocation Order 1994 provides that all properties

---

[8] S.I. 1994 No. 3283.
[9] S.I. 1989 No. 2472.

occupied by British Waterways will, with effect form April 1, 1995, be assessed under the normal rules of entry.

Statutory docks and harbours

12-10 Dock and harbour undertakings are not included in British Waterways Central List formula assessment but they are also valued by reference to the formula set out in the Docks and Harbours (Rateable Values) (Amendment Order 1994).[10] The rateable value of these undertakings is equivalent to 9 per cent of the relevant income of the undertaking adjusted to tone it back to the level of values in line with the Retail Price Index for September 1992. The relevant income is all income failing to be included in the profit and loss account of the undertaking except for income in respect of pilotage, income from investments or loans, rents for separately assessed hereditaments or sums received in respect of the disposal of land.

It should be noted that not all dock and harbour undertakings are included in the local rating list and if it is in more than one charging authority area, the value of the whole undertaking is inserted in the charging authority area which contains the larger or largest physical area of the undertaking.

It should be noted that not all dock and harbour undertakings are valued in accordance with the 1989 Order. Article 3 of the Order specifies those undertakings to which the value formula does not apply. These include non-statutory dock and harbour undertakings and undertakings where the relevant income was less than £1,000,000 in 1993 and single business undertakings occupied by persons who use the dock or harbour exclusively or mainly for bringing or receiving goods.

(a) manufactured or produced by them;
(b) to be used in the manufacture or production of their goods;
(c) to be sold by them.

No method of valuation for these undertakings has been laid down in the Order, but it will be noted that the old rule established in the *British Transport Commission v. Hingley (V.O.)*[11] case that the profits basis must apply as a matter of law was rescinded in regulation 3 of the Non-Domestic (Miscellaneous Provisions) (No. 2) Regulations 1989 and it now provides that any evidence relevant to estimating the rent of these undertakings is to be taken into account.

---

[10] S.I. 1994 No. 3280.
[11] [1961] 2 Q.B. 16; [1961] 2 W.L.R. 370.

Accordingly rental, profits or contractor's test valuation approaches can be used for these undertakings.

Long distance pipelines

Whilst these are not public utility undertakings they can be included **12-11** in the central rating list.

The relevant hereditaments are cross-country pipelines (within the meaning of the Pipelines Act 1962) situated within the area of more than one charging authority.

The designated persons whose relevant hereditaments appear in the central lists are as follows:

Barking Power Limited
The BOC Group plc
BP Chemical Limited
BP Oil U.K. Limited
BP Exploration Operating Company Limited
Conoco Limited
Conoco (U.K.) Limited
Esso Petroleum Company Limited
Esso U.K. plc
Fina plc
ICI Chemical and Polymers Ltd
Kelt U.K. Ltd
Kinetica Ltd
Manchester Jetline Ltd
The Rugby Group plc
Shell Chemicals U.K. Limited
Shell U.K. Limited
United Kingdom Oil Pipelines Limited
Walton-Gatwick Pipeline Company Limited

Whilst these pipelines are included in the central list there is no statutory formula laid down to determine the method of valuation. A conventional valuation approach, contractor's test basis will therefore be appropriate.

13

Community Properties

Educational Establishments

Schools in public occupation

13–01 Schools provided by local education authorities are very numerous and in an endeavour to avoid disputes between those authorities and the valuation officers, a working formula was prepared and informally agreed between the central and local government bodies concerned for the 1990 list.

Strictly, therefore, valuation of such schools ought to be made based on a contractor's test for each individual school. However, the agreed formula was based upon an examination of costs, as at 1988 for the 1990 list for building the various types of school, allowance being made in particular for age, obsolescence and excess capacity, and for the addition of sports halls, tennis courts, swimming pools and other accommodation which is not always found.

The formula is reconsidered at each revaluation and brought up to date in terms of building costs and current educational needs. The use of this non-statutory formula has been considered by the Lands Tribunal (*Dawkins (V.O.) v. Leamington Spa Corpn and Warwickshire County Council*)[1] and has been approved provided that it can be shown, as it was, that the result is correct in terms of a normal contractors test valuation.

The (1990) formula was based on the following guidelines:

Main school buildings	£570/m^2
Temporary classrooms	£240/m^2
Sports hall (standard)	£380/m^2

At the time of writing comparable figures for 1995 have yet to be agreed.

---

[1] [1961] R.V.R. 291; 32 D.R.A. 195.

The valuation follows the contractor's test approach with the buildings, sports facilities and land being valued in the normal way.

A suitable superfluity deduction is made where the actual number of pupils falls short of the standard number of scholar places, a figure determined by a consideration of classroom floor areas. Reductions are made overall for disabilities and age, these being set out in the agreed formula. The full formula is not reproduced as it runs to several pages and is of limited general interest. However, copies for those concerned can be obtained by application to the Valuation Office or Local Authority Valuers Association.

Schools not in public occupation

These vary from small nursery schools and kindergartens to large **13–02** prestigious public schools of national repute. No one system of valuation will be applicable. In the simplest cases the premises will probably have started life as a dwelling house, subsequently "converted" to school use by the addition of, for example, some more toilets. This type of school will probably be best valued by reference to the value of broadly similar houses, perhaps enhanced a little to reflect the benefit of planning consent for change of use and the adaptations. Alternatively, a modified contractor's test could be done basing effective capital value on sale prices for similar properties.

There may, rarely, be direct rental evidence available. Comparisons based upon the number of scholar places may be possible, but as the space and facilities available vary so much in practice such comparisons tend to be of limited use.

Preparatory schools tend to be a little larger, and often include boarding accommodation which is not assessed for non-domestic rates because it is regarded as domestic property and may be banded for Council Tax. For the larger establishments some form of contractor's test offers the most likely route to value.

The larger public schools and other private establishments of **13–03** considerable size will usually include one or more large houses often adapted for boarding pupils together with purpose built classrooms, gymnasium, playing fields, chapels, theatres, and practical education workshops and laboratories. There is no statutory provision for a formula approach, although the preparation of a full contractor's test valuation is a laborious exercise fraught with countless practical problems. There have been a number of appeals to the Lands Tribunal dealing with the assessment of public schools and reference can usefully be made to the cases of *Shrewsbury School v. Hudd (V.O.)*,[2]

---

[2] [1966] R.A. 439.

Shrewsbury School v. Shrewsbury Borough Council and Plumpton (V.O.),[3] and the rather later case of *Eton College v. Lane (V.O.) and Eton Urban District Council.*[4] The appropriate rate of interest was a major issue in *Westminster City Council v. The American School in London and Goodwin (V.O.)*[5] and in *Imperial College of Science & Technology v. Ebdon (V.O.) & Westminster City Council (Court of Appeal).*[6] For the 1995 list the rate of interest set at 3.67 per cent in the Non-Domestic Rating (Miscellaneous Provision) (No. 2) Regulations 1994.

The principal parties in the valuation disputes (the Valuation Office and the Independent Schools Joint Council) have informally agreed a simplified form of contractor's test to be applied to public schools and in the majority of cases the result of applying this basis has been that agreement is reached without either party having to undertake a full valuation on a strict contractor's test, and has therefore avoided the expense of appeals. Details of this unofficial formula can be obtained, at the time of writing, from the office of the Chief Executive Valuation Office Agency, and any surveyor who is called upon to advise a public school is advised to obtain a copy. The application is usually limited to schools which are members of the Council, but similar schools can be valued on the basis to maintain comparability. As with valuations of schools in public occupation, adjustments are required in the form of additions for specialist buildings and extras, and deductions for age and disability. It will be observed that fresh negotiations will be needed at future revaluations to update the guidelines, valuations in any event then being to net annual value.

Many of the schools referred to above are charities or not conducted for profit and relief may be possible.

Universities and colleges

13-04 As with the larger public schools these vary widely in age and accommodation. A similar approach involving the Valuation Office and representatives of the universities has resulted in a formalised contractors test approach to valuation using agreed levels of values and allowances, and the statutory decapitalisation rate of 3.67 per cent. Whilst this approach has limited disputes it has not entirely eliminated them. The nature of universities is such that the buildings

---

[3] (1960) 53 R. & I.T. 497.
[4] [1971] R.A. 186.
[5] [1980] R.A. 275.
[6] [1986] R.A. 233 (C.A.).

are often scattered about, leading to separate assessments for which, in many cases, a contractor's test is clearly not appropriate. Some of the older university buildings justify very generous allowances for age and disabilities (mainly provided for in the agreed approach), and there is a necessity to discount to some extent the over elaboration of old buildings erected in times long past when such ornamentation was deemed appropriate. On the other hand some modern buildings can be essentially basic in design, whilst others are within a prestigious setting where some elaboration is deemed proper. Some universities are not represented on the committee which conducted negotiations with the Valuation Office, and are therefore valued on a strict contractors test, but keeping an eye on other comparable establishments using a price per place comparison.

The former polytechnics which have become universities are also valued on a contractor's test basis similar to formula adopted for the older universities.

PUBLIC BUILDINGS, HOSPITALS AND INSTITUTIONS

Some public buildings, such as municipal offices, can be conve- **13–05** niently dealt with by comparison with other similar rented accommodation in the town, on a rental value per square metre basis, but this does not apply to many of the buildings of more individual character such as town halls, libraries, museums, clinics, etc. Such properties as these are seldom, if ever, rented and the only practicable approach is by way of the contractor's test. This of course involves first estimating the structural or effective capital value and then applying a percentage thereto. Many of the buildings which have to be dealt with are so old (sometimes of historic interest) that there is inevitably great difficulty in arriving at a fair and proper effective capital value. If the buildings concerned are priced out at appropriate rates per metre cube in accordance with their quality of construction, the resultant figure is often out of all proportion to their utility value. If, therefore, such a method is used it may be necessary to make generous allowances for age, obsolescence or unnecessary extravagance and further allowances may be justified for very high rooms conducive to heating problems, and for occupation disadvantages.

Some assistance in arriving at the effective capital value may come from considering a "substituted building" providing substantially the same useful accommodation but shorn of all necessary embellishment, over-high rooms, waste space and bad planning. It is, however, the actual building which has to be valued and the difficulty

189

of reconciling the actual with the substitute is such that the method is probably only useful as a check; not least amongst the problems presented is that of actually designing a substitute—a task for which most valuation surveyors are not qualified. The rate per cent to be finally applied has been set at 5.5 per cent if it is not an education or hospital property (The Non-Domestic Rating (Miscellaneous Provisions) (No. 2) Regulations 1994).

Many public buildings occupy prestigious sites in central commercial zones. The site value element in the effective capital value needs to reflect the value of the site for the purpose for which it is in fact used, not its value cleared and available for some alternative more valuable purpose. It is the actual building together with the site which has to be valued, and the one cannot be separated from the other in considering its worth.

Hospitals

13-06 From April 1, 1991, hospitals occupied by NHS Bodies and Trusts became liable for non-domestic rates and lost their Crown exemption. They are therefore valued in the normal way. Unless there is rental evidence the normal method of valuation will be the contractor's basis using the statutory decapitalisation rate of 3.67 per cent (The Non-Domestic Rating (Miscellaneous Provisions) (No. 2) Regulations 1994). Parts of the hospitals may be exempt if they are used for the disabled (Schedule 6 (16) to the Local Government Finance Act 1988). In addition parts of some hospitals may be domestic and banded for Council Tax purposes if it is used for long stay patients who have no other residence or for staff accommodation if it is used as permanent living accommodation by staff. "On call" staff accommodation or short stay wards would be non-domestic. Ancillary accommodation such as kitchens, canteens, dining rooms, laundries, etc. which wholly serve long stay patients or permanent staff will also be regarded as domestic accommodation.

In recent years there has been a growth in the provision of private hospital facilities and clinics. These will mostly be purpose built to modern standards and a valuation on the contractor's test should be possible, relating actual building and site costs to the valuation list date.

Institutions

Institutions vary in character and range from adapted houses to large purpose built, hospital like, institutions. Since April 1, 1993, most of these types of properties used as old people's homes, nursing homes, children's homes, hostels, hospices, monasteries and convents will be domestic properties and banded for Council Tax and no entry will be made on the non-domestic rating list.

Village halls and community centres

There is no reliable rental evidence, and the capital costs of providing **13–07** the premises often comes from generous donations and grants which do not continue once the building is erected. The means of the occupying trustees will largely determine the rent they could afford to pay, and there is no competitor in the market. It follows that the assessment is usually low, and there is no particular method of arriving at such a value because profits do not exist and a contractor's test approach is likely to produce too high a resultant value. In the case of publicly run centres, supported on the rates, the above special considerations clearly do not apply, and a valuation will be made as for other public buildings.

14

Valuation of Miscellaneous Properties

ADVERTISING STATIONS

14-01 Advertising stations have long been regarded as presenting special problems and although for many years their assessment was governed by the Advertising Stations (Rating) Act 1889, new and amending provisions were found necessary in both the 1948, 1961 and 1967 Acts. The law on the subject is now contained in section 64 of the Local Government Finance Act 1988 stipulating that:

> "a right is a hereditament if it is a right to use any land for the purpose of exhibiting advertisements and:
>
> (a) the right is let out or reserved to any person other than the occupier of the land, or
> (b) where the land is not occupied for any other purpose, the right is let out or reserved to any person other than the owner of the land."

Thus, where advertising rights are let out they are to be treated as separately rateable hereditaments, it being provided that the assessment of the "host" hereditament to which the right attaches shall not contain any element of increased value arising from the use of the land for exhibiting such advertisements.

However, an addition can be made, where appropriate, to the rental value of the "bare right" to advertise in respect of structures, including hoardings, frames, posts, walls, etc., or signs erected by the occupier, in order to arrive at the assessment of the hereditament. Until the structure or sign is completed or the advertisement is displayed, whichever happens first, the hereditament is not to be regarded as being in rateable occupation, and if the structure is subsequently dismantled or altered this event will be regarded as a material change in circumstances (The Non-Domestic Rating (Alteration of Lists and Appeals) Regulations 1990).

Where the land on which the exhibition of advertisements takes place is not otherwise utilised, the person permitting the land to be used for advertising, or, if he cannot be found, the owner of that land, to be deemed to be the beneficial occupier of the hereditament (section 65(8A) of the Local Government Finance Act 1988).

Advertisements exhibited on any land forming part of railway or **14–02** canal premises are included in the formula valuations of the statutory undertaking concerned.

Thus, apart from the above exception, advertising rights where severed from the occupation of the land will be separate rateable hereditaments. In other cases they will continue to be rated with the parent hereditament.

In the majority of cases it will be found that a rent is passing (which must of course be considered in the light of the "tone of list" provisions dealt with elsewhere in this book), and failing that, it is seldom difficult to estimate the rental value by comparison. All rents should be carefully scrutinised as poster companies are sometimes able to secure sites at less than their full value.

It may be noted that many commercial firms are concentrating on television advertising and this may well have its long-term effect upon bill-posting as an advertising medium. A cautious approach to rents entered into some years ago may be justified on this account. Where comparison is made, full regard must be made to the publicity value of each site. Such factors as the following will have to be considered:

(1) where the advertisement is to be viewed from a highway, the importance of the highway, volume and type of traffic, and whether the advertisement can be seen by both pedestrians and road traffic;

(2) whether it has a return frontage and can be seen in both directions;

(3) the prominence of the position (*e.g.* it is naturally of great importance that the advertisement faces oncoming traffic in a "one-way" street) and whether it is overshadowed;

(4) if not illuminated at night, whether it benefits from road lighting.

It is a good plan to grade sites into classes according to position. It is **14–03** then possible to compare the sites having regard to their capacity, which is usually expressed in the number and size of the posters being displayed. In view of the fact that the value of a site will depend entirely on its position and aspect it will be appreciated that there are very wide variations in rents paid. However, modern rents may vary for each 16 sheet or 48 sheet which the site is capable of displaying. The modern tendency in advertising is to develop a site so that a single advertisement (48 sheet) is displayed in a bold frame in such a manner that it positively stands out and commands attention. Rents will always provide the best evidence of value and to deal with sites which have been purchased by the advertising contractor comparison with other rented sites will be the best approach.

In addition to the normal 48 sheet and 96 sheet sites there are special sites for "twin" advertisements and other high profile town centre sites especially in parts of the West End of London where substantial rents are paid.

The following are the usual sizes for single stations:

16 sheet	10 ft. by 6 ft. 8 in.
48 sheet	10 ft. by 20 ft. 0 in.
96 sheet	10 ft. by 40 ft. 0 in.

As will have already been appreciated where the contractor has erected the hoarding it is usual to add a percentage on capital outlay to the rent passing for the site in order to arrive at the rateable value.

INCORPOREAL HEREDITAMENTS

14–04 Incorporeal hereditaments are rateable subjects only when specifically included in a statute—*e.g.* tithe rent charge (rateable under the Poor Relief Act 1601, but derated under the Tithe Act 1936), sporting rights (assessed under section 64(4)(d) of the Local Government Finance Act 1988) and advertising rights now assessed under section 64(2) of the Local Government Finance Act 1988. Harbour tolls, ferry tolls, market tolls, highway tolls, telegraph wires, and so forth, are only rateable when the character of such easement or incorporeal right requires the occupation of land for the exercise of the right.

The value of such land is, therefore, enhanced by the exercise of such rights. The mere possession of an easement or right-of-way is not rateable unless it carries with it an occupation of land. Thus, in *R. v. Trent and Mersey Navigation Co.*[1] it was held that the granting of a licence to dig for minerals, the owner reserving the right to grant to

---

[1] (1825) 3 L.J.K.B. 140.

other persons a similar licence over the same ground, was not enough to make the licensee a rateable occupier—the owner would be rateable (see, *e.g. Andrews v. Hereford Rural District Council*[2]).

Sporting Rights

The Rating Act 1874 created rateability of rights of fowling, shooting game and fishing where such rights are severed from the occupation of land.

In section 64(4)(d) of the Local Government Finance Act 1988 "right of sporting" is defined as:

> "any right of sporting (that is to say, any right of fowling, of shooting, of taking or killing game or rabbits, or of fishing) when severed from the occupation of the land on which the right is exercisable."

In the case of sporting rights exercised over agricultural land, regard **14–05** must be had to Schedule 5(1) & (2) to the Local Government Finance Act 1988, whereby agricultural land is exempt from rating. If sporting rights are exercised over agricultural land and are not severed from the occupation of that land, the total rating exemption of that land prevents the assessment of the sporting rights.

The important word in the Act is "severed". Early cases[3] decided that where land is to let to a tenant and the sporting right over the land is reserved to the owner there is severance and the owner may be rated.

If the rights to shoot over farm land are enjoyed by the occupier of the farm, nobody can be rated for them, since there is no severance.

(a) Shooting rights. The most frequent type of sporting right arises where the owner of lands reserves to himself the right of sporting over the land let, and a farm agreement usually contains a clause to this effect in these cases. It should be noted that although section 64(4)(d) of the Local Government Finance Act 1988 defines sporting rights as including the killing of rabbits, the Ground Game Act 1880 gives the tenant of the land such a right. In these cases where the owner desires to exercise this right exclusively, it is not infrequently found that the letting of the land in the first instance is by way of a 364 day licence only to graze, etc., with the result that there is no severance and no rateable hereditament of sporting is created.

---

[2] [1963] R.V.R. 168.
[3] *Rogers v. St German's Union* (1876) 35 L.T. (N.S.) 332; *Towler v. Thetford Rural District Council* (1929) 99 L.J.K.B. 258; *Cleobury Mortimer Rural District Council v. Childe* (1933) 18 R. & I.T. 225; *Lord Hastings v. R.O. for Walsingham* [1930] 2 K.B. 278.

In deciding the question of value, the point arises as to the boundary of the hereditament as a sporting right, for it is usual in the case of a large estate that not only are the farm lands let to various persons, but they are divided by areas of woodland in the occupation of the owner. Thus, as the sporting right over the woodland is not a rateable hereditament, unless it is let by deed under seal, the value of the shoot as a whole is practically useless unless it includes such woodland where the game takes cover, etc. This particular problem was considered in a case[4] concerning the assessment of sporting rights in the Isle of Wight where the Lands Tribunal found that they were obliged to exclude from the assessment certain woodlands comprising four coverts which were almost essential to the shoot. In doing so, however, they refused to regard these woodlands as being in "hostile" hands such that the remainder of the shooting was almost valueless, and merely apportioned the value of the shoot as a whole to exclude the non-rateable woodlands.

14–06 It is common for an owner to let his shoot on a seasonal basis, and the rent paid for the whole may include rates, keepers' cottages, repairs to and provision of breeding boxes, hire of dogs, beaters, breeding grounds, etc. As will be seen later when the sporting rights are let, the rent paid less the value of landlords' services and corporeal portions is prima facie evidence of the rental for arriving at rateable value. Although in practice such evidence is often applied to the ascertainment of the rateable value of reserved sporting rights, it is open to doubt as to whether it is correct.

There are occasional rents paid for separate parcels of land, such as where the owner of a shoot desires to make a convenient area and include lands not owned by him. The rents paid may be far higher than the real value owing to the sporting tenant being more or less compelled to pay what is demanded: the farmer knowing that the sporting tenant has no option of taking alternative shooting, and the sporting tenant knowing that unless he pays what is asked he risks the farmer being in a position to shoot game driven from the sporting tenant's adjoining land. Therefore, any rents paid in these circumstances must be carefully examined before acceptance as evidence.

14–07 The position of the shoot is also important. Reasonable accessibility from a travel point of view must be considered, for members of a shooting syndicate would probably pay a higher figure per gun if it is possible for them to be within easy reach of their residence or business.[5] Freedom from trespass and disturbance by the public is most important. Rental and rateable values vary so enormously

---

[4] *Carters Trustees v. Woodward* (1958) R. & I.T. 102.
[5] See, *e.g. Illingworth v. Claro Assessment Committee* (1928) 7 R. & I.T. 305.

according to the nature of the shoot that sample values are of no practical guidance.

Where the sporting rights are let either by the owner direct or by the tenant of the land, the rent paid after adjustment, if necessary, for the items mentioned above is prima facie evidence of the rent for purposes of rateable value. It is important to note that the cost of adequate keeping is regarded as the hypothetical tenants' responsibility so that if the shoot is run down due to lack of keepering this should not affect the rating assessment.[6]

It is difficult to drive large areas of woodland, and the birds tend to nest near the edges, and thus for good shooting the woodland should preferably be split into spinneys of 5–10 hectares. Again, it depends on the type of game preserved. Partridges and the like are open-country game, and pheasants are both. Pheasants also prefer oak and chestnut trees which provide food. In many cases, of course, pheasants are reared by keepers in special pheasantries. It is impossible to ascertain with any detail the value over any particular parcel of land, but generally speaking in decreasing order of value come, woodland, arable, pasture lands and moors. Regard should be had to the average bag of game over a period of years, for this can materially affect rental values—indeed valuations based on average bag are not unknown.[7] Moreover, it is worthwhile noting that, for reasons quite unknown, game will never be found in certain woodland: whether this is according to the type of trees or underwood is a mystery.

Difficulties sometimes arise over the rateable value when the **14–08** owner of reserved sporting rights does not exercise his rights, either because he objects to the principle of killing game or he cannot find a tenant. In all these instances no general rule can be laid down, but each case is dealt with on its merits. It is suggested that the assessment should remain if the rights are still reserved from the letting of the land. It may be a question of quantum of rateable value in that no tenant can be found at a rent equal to the rateable value, or that the non-letting of the rights may only be a temporary difficulty. In these cases it is submitted that a rateable value is properly assessed.

The Lands Tribunal in *Olding v. Denman*[8] considered the assessment of sporting rights and made allowances for the fact that a high rent had been agreed in ignorance of the fact that a subsequent assessment might be based thereon.

(b) Fishing rights. In most cases the above rules are also applic-

---

[6] *Myddleton and Myddleton v. Charles* (1957) 51 R. & I.T. 106.
[7] See, *e.g. Fenwick v. Weardale Rural District Council* (1956) 49 R. & I.T. 38.
[8] (1951) 44 R. & I.T. 550.

able to fishing rights, but certain interesting points arise where the distinction between the rights as an incorporeal hereditament and as a corporeal hereditament is a fine one. In many cases the fishing rights are simply occupation of "land covered by water", where the owner has the fee simple of the whole or even only one-half the bed of the river with the right to fish from the bank of an adjoining owner's land. The hereditament is therefore rateable as "land covered with water". If, however, the "rights only" are let by deed under seal, they then become "fishing rights".

In many cases the owner of adjoining land owns to the middle of the water concerned, and unless he severs them (as required for rights of shooting) the rights are not separately valued but the assessment of the adjoining land has to be enhanced by the value of the fishing rights. This rule means exemption in the case of agricultural land. Rents, and rateable values, vary so much according to the type of water that any attempt to quote guidelines would only be misleading.

The assessment of an oyster fishery was considered in *Colne Fishery Co. v. Essex C.V.C.*[9] and the Recorder held that the fact that the public have rights of navigation along a river does not prevent the occupation of the bed of the river as a fishery being an exclusive one, subject to those public rights, and under those circumstances an oyster fishery was properly rateable.

Common rights

14–09 Rights of common as such are, of course, not rateable. Over all such land that under the Inclosure Acts is declared as common land, or wastes of the manor, the public have right of air and exercise, but in many cases the owners of adjoining lands have ancient rights of pasturage, etc., whilst the lord of the manor has rights such as taking surface minerals. In some cases the commoners have also right of taking minerals, cutting peat, etc. Again, the highway authority under the Highways Act 1959 have the right to take minerals for the repair of roads in the locality. In all these cases there is extreme difficulty in finding a person who is in exclusive and beneficial occupation of the right, and in deciding whether rateable occupation arises. If the latter is a fact, then rateability can only arise on occupation of land and not as a rateable incorporeal hereditament.

If a right of common is attached to land, and a tenant of such land would be prepared to pay a higher rent on account of such right, then the rateable value can properly be based on such higher rent.

Not infrequently the case arises of golf courses on commons, such

---

[9] (1931) 15 R. & I.T. 148 at 281.

as where conservators of a common grant a licence to a club giving them the exclusive rights to lay out greens and fairways. Nevertheless, in two cases[10] where golf courses were established in the New Forest, the Court of Appeal held that as the clubs had not exclusive rights to the land they were not in beneficial occupation and could not be rateable in respect of their courses. It is notable, however, that in neither case was the course enclosed and that the general public were not excluded, indeed although the clubs endeavoured to charge green fees no action was taken when players refused payment.

Markets

With regard to markets, case law is somewhat confusing owing to the **14–10** apparently illogical distinction which has grown up as between on the one hand franchise tolls which are not rateable, and on the other hand stallage, *i.e.* a payment to erect a stall, and piccage, *i.e.* a payment to erect a booth or tent which are accountable for rating purposes. Historically the exclusion of the former class of tolls stems from the fact that a "common market toll" payable to the lord of the manor for witnessing a sale not dependent upon occupation of the land forming the market. This exclusion was later extended to all payments made in respect of mere entry on the reasoning that the public must be presumed to have a right of access to a public market, accordingly any tolls payable as a result of charter or ancient custom must be regarded as being of a similar nature to "common market tolls": see *R. v. Mosley,*[11] and *Yarmouth Corporation v. Groom.*[12]

This distinction has been reaffirmed in subsequent cases[13] but the limited nature of the exclusion should be appreciated, for in a case where a local authority set up a cattle market under general statutory powers tolls payable on animals admitted were held to be rateable.[14] Likewise where the legal origin of the tolls does not give grounds for a presumption of their incorporeal character they will be rateable.[15]

In the case of markets provided by local authorities the contractor's **14–11** test is sometimes used, but generally the receipts and expenditure basis is adopted. In the case of *Taunton Corporation v. Sture*[16] the issue as to whether the valuation should be by reference to the

---

[10] *Peak v. Burley Gold Club; Harding v. Bramshaw Golf Club Ltd* (1960) 53 R. & I.T. 277.
[11] (1823) 2 B. & C. 226.
[12] (1862) 32 L.J. Ex. 74.
[13] *Horner v. Stepney Assessment Committee* (1908) 98 L.T. 450, and *Oswestry Corporation v. Plumpton* [1962] R.V.R. 44.
[14] *London Corporation v. Greenwich Assessment Committee* (1883) 48 L.T. 43.
[15] *Percy v. Ashford Union* (1986) 34. L.T. 579.
[16] (1958) 51 R. & I.T. 749.

accounts or the contractor's test was brought before the Lands Tribunal. In the course of the hearing the following valuation (reproduced omitting some detail) was put in on behalf of the corporation:

Valuation of Taunton Market

	£	£	£
Gross revenue			
Tolls and weighing		2,800	
Auctioneers' Fees		3,887	
Special Sales		1,700	
Car park		250	
Corn stall rents		250	
Produce market lettings		525	
Sundry other receipts		260	
			9,672
Working expenses			
Supervision and management:			
Salaries	1,355		
National insurance	75		
Superannuation	210		
Central administration:			
Expenses—proportion	550		
Audit fee—proportion	7		
		2,197	
Car park—wages		280	
Traffic control—wages		110	
Fuel, lighting and cleaning		2,740	
Administrative expenses including printing, stationery, telephone, etc.		651	
			5,978
			3,694
Tenant's repairs and renewals			
Repairs—3 years' average		71	
Insurances		16	
Sinking Fund:			
Tractor, trailer and load £750 7 years at 2.5%		100	
3 weighing machines £2,000 12 years at 2.5%		150	
Sundries		50	
			387
			3,307

Landlord's repairs and renewals		
Repairs—3 years' average	597	
Insurances	11	
	608	3,307
Sinking fund buildings, pens, etc., as valued by Valuation Officer £5,585—average life 75 years at 2.5	277	
		885
		2,422
Tenant's share		
Capital—chattels £4,000 and cash £1,000		
£5,000 at 20% (=£1000)		
or 10% of gross receipts (=£967)	say	1,000
Net annual value plus rates		1,422
Rates at 20s. 6d in £		720
		£702

Say, £700 RV.

A contractor's test valuation was put in by the Valuation Officer **14–12** whereby an effective capital value of £65,630 was computed which at 3 per cent gave £1,969 RV.

The Lands Tribunal preferred an approach by reference to the accounts but criticised on the receipts side the item relating to auctioneer's fees which was thought to be less than might have been charged. On the working expenses side, the Tribunal thought the item relating to supervision and management to be excessive. After adjustment the Tribunal considered that the accounts produced an assessment of £850. The Tribunal determined an assessment of £1,272 (half as much again) on the assumption that the local authority would pay a substantially higher rent or "overbid" to secure the hidden benefits brought to ratepayers from maintaining the market.

In two later cases concerning local authority markets at Hereford[17]

---

[17] *Hereford Corporation v. Taylor* (1960) 53 R. & I.T. 771.

and Oswestry[18] the "overbid" principle has been followed, the increases being 35 per cent and 25 per cent respectively, although in the latter case there were special circumstances in that it was planned to erect a new market elsewhere.

Markets in small country towns are often let to a local firm of stock auctioneers, when the rent paid will be prima facie evidence of value. In any event there is no rule requiring use of the profits approach even in the case of a statutory market.[19]

Cases arise where stallholders in a market are in such beneficial occupation as to create separate assessments in respect of each occupation. Reference should be made to *Soper and Rolin v. Exeter City R.A. and A.C.*,[20] where stall holders formerly paying tolls but subsequently paying weekly rent for the same pitch were held to be in beneficial occupation in the same way as occupiers of bookstalls on railway stations.

Tolls

14-13 Tolls in gross being incorporeal property and not expressly rateable by statute are not *per se* rateable. Where tolls are received in connection with and arising out of the occupation of land, however, they may be taken into account as enhancing its value. Thus, where the owner of a lighthouse[21] receives tolls from passing ships the tolls are not rateable, but it may be that the facilities afforded by the lighthouse for the earning of tolls will increase the rental value of the lighthouse. Rateable tolls can also arise in connection with toll bridges and private toll roads. In such cases the tolls are definitely linked with the occupation of land and the value of the tollhouse or gatehouse will be enhanced by the facilities which it affords for the collection of tolls.

As in the case of a shop, it is not the profits that are rated, but the facilities afforded by the premises for carrying on a gainful trade that can be taken into account.

Bridge undertakings and private road tolls can only be satisfactorily valued on the profits basis. In the event of information being lacking through non-production of the accounts, the best approach is to estimate the gross receipts by observation of the volume of traffic and thence take a direct percentage as the landlord's share or rent.

---

[18] *Oswestry Corporation v. Plumpton* [1962] R.V.R. 44.
[19] *Thrapston Market Co. v. Newton* [1968] R.A. 415.
[20] (1948) 41 R. & I.T. 382, *Brook (V.O.) v. Greggs plc* (1991) L.T. R.A. 61.
[21] But see para. 37.

Foreshores

If the owner of a foreshore, whether it be a local authority or **14-14** otherwise, derives benefit from the grant of licences, etc., and receives the revenue therefrom, rateable occupation will arise. In such cases it will probably not be practicable to plead that the land is dedicated to the public. This was demonstrated in the *Redcar* case[22] where part of the actual foreshore was one of seven hereditaments to be brought into assessment. The following extracts from the judgments are pertinent.

In his judgment Viscount Caldecote C.J. said:

> "I make no point of the fact that there is nothing to show any irrevocable dedication of this land and works and buildings to the use of the public, but in truth and in fact these hereditaments, taken as a whole, are not used so as to allow the public the free and unrestricted use of them ... So far as the foreshore is concerned, the corporation use it for the purpose not merely of providing amenities for the public, but of making a revenue towards the expense which they have incurred. It is not disputed that it is necessary, in order that the corporation should be rateable, that their occupation should be a beneficial one. I take the test which Brett L.J. laid down in *Hare v. Overseers of Putney*.[23] This test was that there is no beneficial occupation if by law no benefit can possibly arise to the occupier. Applying that test, I think the corporation fails."

Cassels J. said:

> "There is not in any of these hereditaments any statutory dedication to the public. The highest that it can be put is that the Redcar Corporation is a local authority, and in the conveyance of some of these lands there is a covenant to use the land for the public benefit. That does not mean that the public are in occupation of these seven hereditaments in the way in which in the *Brockwell Park* case it was said that the public were in occupation of the park. The Redcar Corporation are using these lands for the public benefit in what they are doing, and it is not suggested that they are in breach of their restrictive covenant, but the occupation is of value to the corporation and incidentally to those who hire the concert hall and the sites on the foreshore and to those who rent the shops."

---

[22] *North Riding of Yorkshire C.V.C. v. Redcar Corporation* (1952) 35 R. & I.T. 356 at 366, 376.

[23] [1871] 7 Q.B. 233.

14–15   The part of the foreshore in question was used for the erection of stalls for the sale of sweets and ices and for the carrying on of certain amusements, and hence was a source of revenue. In this case there was an excess of income over expenditure.

In relation to foreshores, generally, various ways of deriving revenue may be exploited, *e.g.* the hiring out of deckchairs, bathing-huts and tents, grant of licences to hawk chocolates, ices, etc., the grant of photographic rights, licences to permit donkey rides. Punch and Judy shows, licences to permit boating trips, the collection of parking fees and licences to occupy kiosks for various purposes. It may be, however, in respect of kiosks that there is a sufficient element of exclusive occupation to warrant separate assessments.

The only satisfactory method of assessment is by reference to the accounts, and it may be the case that expenditure will approach, if not exceed, revenue. Care, too, should be exercised that the accounts for several years be examined as a particularly wet season and a particularly dry season will show a very wide variation on the revenue side, whereas expenditure may remain fairly constant. The vagaries of the weather should also be reflected in the tenant's share, which will need to be substantial in view of the risks incurred. The reader is recommended to peruse the appeal to the Lands Tribunal in *Morecambe and Heysham Borough Council v. Robinson*[24] in which informative valuations were submitted and interesting issues resolved.

Cemeteries

14–16 Churchyards and extensions of churchyards under the Church Building Acts are, by the decision of the House of Lords in *Winstanley v. North Manchester Overseers*,[25] held to be rateable and are not entitled to exemption under Schedule 5, to the Local Government Finance Act, 1988, paragraph 11.

In these cases the method of arriving at the annual value would be the same as that adopted where a cemetery company is in occupation, *i.e.*, on the profits basis.

The net annual value has to be ascertained by means of a profits basis[26] and in the calculation of gross receipts the sales in each year from the disposal of land to private persons for family vaults, etc., must be included for that year, and the extent of the company's

---

[24] (1959) 52 R. & I.T. 577.
[25] [1910] A.C. 7.
[26] *R. v. Abney Park Cemetery Co.* (1873) L.R. 8 Q.B. 515.

occupation includes such portions disposed of.[27] From the gross receipts of the year previous to the assessment there would be deducted the working expenses and the tenant's share, usually estimated at 10 per cent of the gross receipts, owing to the amount of tenant's capital being small, the balance left then representing net annual value plus rates from which net annual value would be arrived at in the normal way. Such a hereditament is a wasting one, and there would obviously be little deduction for sinking fund in respect of renewals, although the company must, of course, keep the grounds and graves, etc., in tidy repair and condition.

In practice many churchyards occupied with "exempt" churches have been treated as exempt and are not included on the rating lists.

Crematoria

Due to the operation of town planning control and other restrictions **14-17** under the Cremation Act 1902, there is necessarily some element of monopoly and on this account there would seem to be good grounds for using the receipts and expenditure basis of assessment. On the other hand, a crematorium might equally well be treated much as other public buildings and be assessed by reference to the contractor's test. No decisive ruling has yet been given by the courts in this matter but in the absence of accounts the contractor's test has been held to be applicable to a new local authority crematorium.[28]

Leisure properties

The growth of time and personal resources available for leisure **14-18** pursuits renders this class of properties of increasing importance. Unfortunately for the rating valuer the provision of leisure facilities has been dominated by the owner/occupier entrepreneur, often in the guise of large corporations with extensive interests in more than one field. There is almost no rental evidence available, and what there is often proves to be unreliable in terms of market forces. The method of valuation most often adopted is therefore, of necessity, either the contractor's test or a profits basis, or some adaptation of either.

Wherever free market letting transactions occur, the evidence of the rent or rents arising is to be preferred to any other basis of

---

[27] *R. v. St. Mary Abbott's, Kensington* (1840) 10 L.J.M.C. 25.
[28] *Melville and Rees v. Airedale and Wharfdale Joint Crematorium Committee* (1963) R.V.R. 201.

valuation. Suggested approaches where this is not the case are given in the paragraphs which follow.

Cinemas and theatres

14–19 The cinema industry, once represented in every town and large village, has now contracted to a fraction of its former importance. The most valuable cinemas are now thought to be the new six to twelve screen multiplex cinemas which have small auditoria restricted to 250 seats each. Next in importance are the first run cinemas which have often been converted into multi-screen studios each with a much reduced seating capacity but offering patrons a better choice of programmes. Only in central London, or in holiday centres, is it usual to find the large super-cinema of former days. The seating capacity, once a measure of value in itself, is now largely an accidental survival of former days and mere size has little to do with the profitability and hence the rental value. In present circumstances, clearly a consideration of profits is likely to provide the best guide to value. But unfortunately it is often virtually impossible to obtain detailed accounts for each cinema, unless the large Corporations who own them are prepared to provide a detailed breakdown of their trading figures. It is, however, usually possible to eventually obtain a note of the gross receipts broken down into sale of seats and sales of sweets, cigarettes, etc. Failing actual figures the best estimate possible must be made by the valuer.

A few rented cinemas are to be found scattered throughout the country and the most practical approach, if sufficient rents are locally available, is to use those rents as a basis, making comparisons, not by way of number of seats, but by expressing each rent as a percentage of the gross receipts of that cinema. Gross receipts need to be defined—the price of admission includes VAT and may from time to time, include other direct government levies, such as the film levy, which obviously do not benefit the occupier who merely acts as a collecting agent. It is proper, therefore, to deduct all such direct taxation principles. Receipts from sales of sundries such as sweets and tobacco are normally taken at sale price less wholesale cost.

14–20 After considering the rental evidence, classified for further refinement of comparison into first run, second run and so on, it becomes possible to find a pattern which rents represent as a percentage of receipts; the average of such percentages can then be applied to receipts of non-rented cinemas as a starting point for valuation subject to refinement for quality, position, etc., in the normal way. Such a valuation is not a profit basis, but an application of a rental basis. In any case its accuracy can be tested by a full profit basis calculation if accounts become available.

Theatres present a different problem. Some are rented and hence provide a reliable basis, but comparison is difficult because the same problems arise as with cinemas in relation to the size and location of the properties, local circumstances dominate the demand and hence the profitability upon which value depends. A profits basis is recommended as the best approach where profits are actually made, but in many cases the theatre only survives because of a subsidy from public funds; in such cases the accounts do not really provide a basis for valuation. A contractor's test approach usually results in far too high a valuation. The valuer is left with taking a low percentage on the receipts as his best guide to the rent the occupier might perhaps be prepared to offer bearing in mind that a continued subsidy is likely. Generally speaking, the more secure the finances of the hereditament, the higher the percentage of receipts can be ventured by the occupier by way of rent. Thus, a central London theatre with a good reputation and a tradition of public support can pay pro rata a higher percentage rent than a marginal repertory theatre in a small provincial centre.

Bingo halls

Many former cinemas were converted into bingo halls and there is **14–21** some evidence that some of these bingo halls are no longer profitable. However, the mainstream operators have in many cases improved the environment in which bingo is played to attract a wider patronage. Once again profits provide the best guide to value. Comparison between properties, when necessary, must be done on the basis of a percentage of receipts.

Bowling alleys

As with many other "new" sports these enjoyed an initial burst of **14–22** popularity in the 1960s. The game declined in popularity in the 1970s, though some recovery was shown in the late 1980s. It is appropriate to look at the profits as evidenced by trading over the last year or two. There is some rental evidence, and this can be analysed by reference to a percentage of receipts or the number of games played per line per day to arrive at value per line to be applied to properties which are not rented.

Sports grounds

14-23 These vary from a more or less flat field to establishments capable of staging international events. In the very simple cases a straight-forward rental basis, based upon local evidence, for the field with additions for clubhouse, toilets and car parks is appropriate. Where the field has been specially prepared—levelled, drained, sown to special grass—the cost of such works need to be taken into account as enhancing the land value. A contractor's test is probably the best approach in such cases, remembering that an end allowance may be appropriate having regard to the ability of the occupiers to pay. It is a feature of sporting establishments that much of the work is often done by voluntary labour, and this community support also extends to providing funds for pavilions and other amenities. The ability of the club to use its premises for social activities as well as the actual playing of games will not influence the level of rent they can afford. If the occupying club is not operated for profit then there will be the possibility of discretionary relief from rate payments under section 47 of the Local Government Finance Act 1988. If the land is used for agricultural purposes and only incidentally for sport then this may entail a total relief from assessment as agricultural land; this relief will not be available if the sports use is significant (Schedule 5(2) to Local Government Finance Act 1988).

In deciding the extent to which any area of land can actually be used for organised sport it is necessary to have regard to the size of the pitch or court which will be needed. Prestige establishments will need to meet national or international standards of size, safety and ancillary accommodation. The following table sets out the accepted sizes of pitches and courts:

(All dimensions given in metres, although some sports actually specify dimensions in imperial measures.)

Football	International	100–110	×	64–75
	F.A. U.K.	90–120	×	45–90
	"Normal"	96–100	×	60–64
Rugby League		134	×	80
		(including 6m margins)		
Rugby Union		156	×	81
		(including margins & touch down)		
Hockey		100.58	×	61.265
		(including end and side margins)		
Bowls	square	36.58 min		40.234 max
	1 rink	5.486 min		5.79 max

Crown Green				
Bowls	square	36.58		
Lawn Tennis	single			
	International	36.58	× 18.29	
	County &			
	Club	36.58	× 18.29	
	Recreational	34.25	× 17.07	
	extra courts	add 15.24		County & Club
		add 14.63		Recreational
Badminton		16.8	× 8.54	
		7 m min height		
Cricket		125	× 119	
		(including 46 m boundary)		

For further detail, and other sports, readers are advised to consult the "Handbook of Sports and Recreational Design" produced by the Sports Council (Publishers: Architectural Press Ltd), to whom we are indebted for the above extracts.

In all cases spectator space, and circulating space around the actual **14–24** playing area will be required. In considering value such factors as all-weather surfaces, drainage of playing areas, level area for play, and good access must be considered. Adequate car parking is required either on the ground or very close by.

Once a body of information on current costs has been established it becomes possible to convert those costs into annual value (rent) per pitch by a process of averaging and taking a percentage thereon. Valuations can then be built up directly in terms of annual value per pitch plus appropriate additions for pavilions, stands, changing rooms, toilets, car parks, etc., based also upon costs.

Spectator sports

Horse racecourses

The horse racing industry is well organised and closely controlled in **14–25** all aspects by the Jockey Club, with statutory regulation under the Betting, Gaming and Lotteries Acts. It is established that the proper approach is by a profits basis but in practical terms this presents difficulties, arising in the main from the methods by which the sport is financed. There are very few courses which are rented from, *e.g.* the local authority, but the level of rent paid and the background negotiations make even this slender evidence not particularly reliable. Apart from the admission charges the income of a racecourse comes from grants made by the controlling bodies, the Betting Levy Board, and sponsors which together pay for many of the buildings (stands, jockeys accommodation, etc.), the race control equipment, veterinary attention, and the prize money. It follows that the normal accounts will not show anything like the true financial state unless these various grants can be fully reflected, and since much of the money provided goes to provide/maintain what is in rating terms the landlord's hereditament it is even more obscure. If a contractor's test is considered, these same grants make a cost approach to what has actually provided a theoretical exercise of little value. Many of the courses are not seemingly operated with profit as the primary motive, and this factor renders a strict profits approach unreliable. The valuer, therefore, has to use rents where these are available, profits basis where relevant, and for the rest a comparative basis resting upon a percentage of gross receipts. In extremis, a modified contractor's test might be utilised.

Totalisators on horse racecourses

14-26 Whilst not strictly appropriate to this section of the book it is convenient to include them here, close to the racecourses on which they operate. Totalisators are operated under statutory control by the Horserace Totalisator Board and pay for their accommodation on the course by way of a site rent and daily payments for various facilities provided. The valuation is therefore based upon such payments, plus an appropriate amount representing the rental value of any buildings placed upon the site by the occupiers.

Greyhound racecourses

These require a licence from the local authority, and whilst the major tracks conform to rules and regulations laid down by the controlling body for the sport there are a number of smaller tracks which are operated outside that control. Where there is a totalisator on the course it will be operated by the owner of the tract. The normal method of assessment is on the full profits basis, including tote receipts and expenses, but if full accounts are not available an approach using a percentage of gross receipts can be adopted.

League football grounds

The finances of many clubs are precarious but few go under. An assessment based strictly upon accounts can be helpful if regard is had to the cost of the premises and the estimated ability to survive due to likely public support. The immediate financial results will stem from the success of the team, which league it is in, and depends to a lesser extent to the actual ground, its situation in a supportive locality.

It has been accepted that a profits basis is appropriate, as would be a contractors test, but in each case the results need to be adjusted to reflect any excess capacity of the ground, the ability to pay, and the likely chance for additional revenue from television, advertising and sponsorship.

In many cases the actual occupier is the only hypothetical occupier, who needs to take the subject premises to continue in existence and the bargaining strength of each party to the rental negotiations should be taken into account.[29]

Some comparison between clubs may be possible on the basis of attendance figures within a league. In practical terms however there is no sure way to arrive at any assessment of a football league club's ground, professional judgment is needed on both sides to reach agreement on the rent a particular ground can stand irrespective of the transient success or failure of the club side.

Cricket grounds

Broadly the same considerations apply as for league football grounds **14–27** and it follows that a look at the accounts with a view to a profits basis valuation, combined with a look at a contractor's test, may well point to an acceptable assessment. In all cases it is necessary to have some regard to the ability of the occupier to pay a rent equal to the annual value.

Foreshores, funfairs and amusement parks

The first consideration, when this type of hereditament is situated **14–28** within a public park or open to public access, is whether there is in fact a rateable occupation, or whether the entire property will be exempt as a park, recreation ground, pleasure ground, public wall or open space covered by Schedule 5 (15), to the Local Government Finance Act 1988 being provided by, or under the management of, a relevant authority. This is largely a matter of act—if the amenity in question is ancillary to the public enjoyment of the principle hereditament then it will be part of it, and exemption follows. A

---

[29] *Tomlinson V.O. v. Plymouth Argyle Football Club Co. Ltd,* (1960) 53 R. & I.T. 297, C.A.

charge for admission is not in itself a disqualification, if it is clear that the public resort is first to the main hereditament and that use of the particular facility is incidental thereto. In broad terms, such specific properties as swimming pools and bowling greens within the boundaries of parks are likely to be exempt, but the same facilities alongside a public walk or foreshore are more likely to be rateable in their own right as separate hereditaments.

The ability to pay a rent depends first upon the financial results as shown in the accounts, and secondly upon the financial results to subsidise the facility. Where there is a regular subsidy it will be more useful to make a contractor's test valuation. If the occupier is a company or individual operating with a profit motive then a profits basis valuation is best, always providing of course that there is no rental evidence available—it is quite often found that the owner of the freehold is a local authority and the amenity is put up for tender annually.

Travelling fairs

These are unlikely to attract an assessment since their stay in one spot is almost always of a transient nature and does not involve rateable occupation of the site. However, it is possible that a site preserved mainly for this purpose may be rateable, the owner being the rateable occupier, there then being no exemption as "agricultural" land. The measure of value will be the rent or licence fee charged, which will be deemed inclusive of rates.

Holiday accommodation

14–29 The following sections deal with the less permanent forms of accommodation ranging from holiday villages to open camp-sites.

Holiday camps

In the main there are no difficulties in establishing rateable occupation, but valuation can be difficult. In the absence of rental evidence there is a choice between a profits basis and a contractor's test; the latter is preferred but a look at the accounts is helpful because upkeep is expensive and profitability is in decline. These factors will assist in deciding what obsolescence or end allowances may be appropriate in a contractor's test valuation. Since it is the common practice to let the chalets by the week there is no question of making separate assessments thereon, the operator will be rateable for the whole enterprise.

Holiday chalets, huts, cabins, etc.

Sometimes these are owner occupied, some are let off by the week or season, and some are grouped together and operated much in the same way as a holiday camp. The first question is therefore "what is the rateable hereditament?" Single owner occupier holiday properties are treated as dwellings and are banded for Council Tax. Where the owner retains control and lets it by the week as holiday self-catering accommodation, the property is treated as domestic providing the time of letting for short periods totals less than 140 days per annum. If, however, the period of letting exceeds 140 days per annum it is treated as a non-domestic property and valued on a profits basis.

In other cases where the paramount occupier of the group of units is the person who runs the self-catering holiday business, one assessment on the whole complex is appropriate and a simple profits basis valuation is likely to provide an adequate basis of assessment.

Holiday caravans and caravan sites

Holiday caravans, as distinct from touring vans, usually remain on **14-30** the same pitch throughout the season and usually remain there from one year to another. Any caravan which remains on the same pitch throughout the season will become a rateable chattel with the pitch on which it stands, and this rule applies even if the van in question was designed for and is capable of being used for touring. The law regarding the rating of chattels which are allowed to remain on land and are so used as to become occupied together with that land as a rateable hereditament has developed considerably in recent years. Reference should be made to *Field Place Caravan Park Ltd v. Harding (V.O.)*[30] in the Court of Appeal in 1966 which dealt with the rateability of caravans which remain on a pitch for some time, and to *Thomas (V.O.) v. Witney Aquatic Co. Ltd*,[31] in the Lands Tribunal 1972 where a floating clubhouse which moved about within the hereditament was held to be rateable. The Non-Domestic Rating (Caravan Sites) Regulations 1990[32] provides that where a holiday site exceeds 400 square yards, the Valuation Officer shall treat the entire site and rateable caravans thereon as a single hereditament in the rateable occupation of the site operator who thereupon becomes liable to pay the rates on both site and rateable caravans, recovering a due proportion from the various caravan owners by apportionment—

---

[30] [1965] R.A. 521; [1966] R.A. 393.
[31] [1972] R.A. 493.
[32] S.I. 1990 No. 673.

pitch rents being charged on an inclusive basis. The Valuation Officer is required to inform the site operator about the number of caravans included in the assessment, and the values thereof. Any person occupying a pitch on the site has a right to inspect the Valuation Officer's statement to the site operator.

The valuation of these composite hereditaments is best approached as being the sum of the pitch rents plus an amount being the assumed rental value of each caravan which can be derived from its capital value at a percentage, with specific additions for communal facilities such as shops, social rooms, etc; it is usual to regard the value of toilet blocks as being reflected in the pitch rents not therefore requiring further addition.

None of the foregoing applies to the valuation of residential caravans and their sites, which are treated as domestic properties under section 66(3), of the Local Government Finance Act 1988 if it is the sole or main residence of the occupier and is therefore banded for Council Tax purposes.

Camping sites

There are some sites which provide only the most basic accommodation for tents or touring caravans to make short stays. Only the site and any service buildings such as toilets thereon will be rateable, valuation being direct to rateable value, and based upon the rents received less expenses and tenants share.

Concessions

14-31 In any of the foregoing hereditaments the operators occasionally permit other traders to come in for the purpose of selling goods or providing services. For these licences it is usual to charge a fee. Such concessions do not themselves create rateable hereditaments, the fee received being an item included in the gross receipts and thereby reflected in a profits basis valuation. However, occasionally it may be found that the concessionaire requires to leave on the premises equipment (such as deckchairs, kiosks) which then involves the separate occupation of an area of the site and in these circumstances a separate rateable hereditament can be created which will be assessed using the concessionary fee as a guide to value.

15

Council Tax

INTRODUCTION

Since the introduction of the Uniform Business Rate in 1990, **15–01** residential property is no longer subject to a rate. The issue of domestic rating has been a highly charged political battleground for the last three decades and the debate surrounding the way in which domestic occupiers would contribute to the financing of local government has emerged through a series of White Papers and Green Papers as well as the Layfield Report of 1976.

For various reasons the Conservative Government, elected in 1979, committed itself to the abolition of domestic rates which resulted firstly in the ill-fated Poll Tax and ultimately the current Council Tax.

The Council Tax is something of a hybrid being neither a rate nor a poll tax but retains elements of both. It is now the only form of domestic property tax which elicits a contribution from residential owners and occupiers and no consideration of rating would be complete without covering this important area. This chapter will provide a brief historical outline of domestic property taxation and the current valuation rules concerning the Council Tax.

HISTORICAL BACKGROUND

Until 1990, occupiers of domestic property were subject to the rate, **15–02** being valued and treated in much the same way as non-domestic property but, in more recent years a number of factors did give rise to particular problems. As with most other types of property, the basis for the assessment of domestic rate liability was rental value and domestic property was valued in accordance with the definition of gross value as set out in the 1967 Act and its predecessors.

However the presence, particularly in the post-war era, of statutory controls as to rents payable by tenants of small and medium-sized residential properties made the rental valuation of domestic properties especially difficult. As these provisions have the effect of restricting such rents to levels substantially below full economic value (and of protecting tenants against eviction) the evidence which they provide is of little or no value in preparing valuations for rating. In particular in *Poplar v. Roberts*, the House of Lords established that a rent restricted under the Rent Acts was not the rent "reasonably expected" as defined for the determination of gross value.[1]

Thus, the Rent Acts have historically had two effects on valuation for rating of residential property. First, the proportion of owner-occupied residential property has steadily increased, and the privately owned unfurnished residence to let has almost disappeared (excepting those in the exceptional high value range). Secondly, the few rents which do occur are tainted for they cannot by definition represent the true market worth of the property concerned.

These problems have over the past half century increasingly manifested themselves to the extent that by the 1970s most informed professional opinion began to regard valuations on a rental value basis as being artificial and a switch to capital values as the best measure of assessment was felt to be long overdue.

For political reasons there has always been a tendency to shield occupiers of residential properties from the full impact of the rate burden. This end has been achieved in various ways, for example, by the under-assessment of residential properties in some areas in the pre-war revaluations, and more recently by differential rate poundages favouring private residential property, and by rate rebates.

In tracing the problem through the post-war era it is notable that under the 1948 Act a new method of assessment of residential properties was decreed, was found unworkable, and was eventually abandoned. Parliament then passed the 1953 Act, as a "stop-gap" measure, and under its provisions private residential properties were assessed at the 1956 revaluation on the basis of 1939 rental values.

At the 1963 revaluation the first post-war attempt was made to assess residential properties at their full current rental values on the same definition of "gross value" as for other classes of property, namely, the definition contained in section 19 of the 1967 Act. Lest this revaluation produced unacceptable harshness, reserve provi-

---

[1] [1922] 2 A.C. 93.

sions were enacted (not invoked but since repealed) enabling the Minister to introduce temporary derating on a county basis.

The 1973 revaluation attempted to update the figures in the 1963 **15–03** lists on the basis of full market rental values. In this process section 1(1) of the General Rate Act 1970, (to be read as section 19(2A) of the 1967 Act) was passed to enable evidence of actual rents to be translated to other classes of residence and to other areas. Notwithstanding this attempt to mitigate the problems caused by the absence of adequate open market rental evidence, the 1973 list figures hung together by a process of mutual leaning rather than truly representing 1973 rental values. This unsatisfactory situation was perpetuated by a combination of successive postponements of the revaluation originally due in 1978, and the use of the tone of list provisions enacted in section 20 of General Rate Act 1967.

The attention of readers is also drawn to the provisions of section 21 of the Local Government Act 1974 which prevented assessments of residential properties being increased to reflect the value of small improvements made after April 1, 1974, until their cumulative value exceeded 10 per cent of the existing gross value or £30, whichever was the lesser.

Moreover, the installation of central heating after April 1, 1974 was also ignored irrespective of its effect upon annual value under section 21(1)(a).

This section created all sorts of additional complexities particularly in circumstances where a proposal was served seeking a decrease in assessment due to new disabilities. In such cases the value of previously disregarded improvements had to be taken into account in determining the revised values.

For these and a whole host of other reasons, towards the latter period of the 1973 valuation list, domestic rating had fallen largely into disrepute and the search for an alternative became ever more pressing.

The eventual abolition of domestic rating can be traced back to the **15–04** 1970s, a period of high inflation and rapidly increasing local government spending with the consequence that rates paid by domestic occupiers became a very significant charge indeed.

As long ago as 1974 the Conservative Party, concerned with the increasing cost of local government finance and the perceived unpopularity of domestic rates, promised, in its election manifesto, to replace the rates with a more broadly based tax better related to ability to pay.

The commitment to the abolition of rates was followed by an examination of alternative methods of financing the cost of local authority services which resulted in the Layfield Committee Report of 1976. For a time nothing of much practical effect occurred other than the outpourings of various committees, and the production of Green and White Papers and consultation documents and the numerous deferrals of the general revaluation.

When eventually things did change, they changed at an alarming pace. In 1988, the General Rate Act of 1967 was repealed and replaced by the Uniform Business Rate, for non-domestic property, and the introduction of the Community Charge, which was essentially a personal charge rather than a charge on property, to be applied to individuals. Comparisons with the peasants revolt under Wat Tyler in 1381 might have seemed an exaggeration at the time but the Poll Tax, as it became known, did in fact result in widespread civil disobedience and disorder. At one point something in excess of £1 billion remained uncollected. To this day local authorities are still spending large sums of money chasing unpaid tax as well as high interest charges on the shortfall in income not forgetting the general impost of an extra 2.5 per cent on VAT which was necessary following the subsidy to reduce Poll Tax bills the year before abolition. Riots resulted in hundreds of arrests and injuries. Although, as far as we are aware, no one has been hacked to death as a result of the Poll Tax it did undoubtedly contribute to the downfall of Margaret Thatcher. Immediately her successor showed himself to be as keen to be rid of the Poll Tax as she was to be rid of domestic rates. The result was the abandonment of the Poll Tax and a firm commitment to introduce its replacement, the Council Tax, as soon as possible.

THE LOCAL GOVERNMENT FINANCE AND VALUATION ACT 1991

15–05 The Local Government Finance and Valuation Act of 1991 provided the necessary powers for the Council Tax valuations to be undertaken and, perhaps more significantly, abolished the existing capping restrictions giving the Secretary of State much wider powers and discretion to cap local authorities where he considers their expenditure to be excessive.

Capping powers are thought necessary to prevent the surge in local government spending that occurred with the introduction of the Poll Tax, with a rise of 25 per cent in the two years to April 1991.

Even though individual valuations were not contemplated, the banding of 21 million dwellings was a task of monstrous proportion and the Department of the Environment made it clear that the

Valuation Office would be assisted in this task by private practice valuers.

Areas of the country were divided up into parcels of 10,000–20,000 properties. Private firms were invited in September 1991 to register their interest in assisting with the banding of dwellings within these areas. In fact the private sector was offered the opportunity to tender for two-thirds of the work. Firms registering their interest were then required to go through a pre-qualification procedure to ensure that those who finally submitted tenders were professionally competent and had the capacity and financial viability to undertake the task. Once pre-qualified, firms then tendered for as many or as few blocks as they wished. The project began in December 1991 and was completed by May 31, 1992.

The Valuation Office was responsible for undertaking quality control on these outside valuations and the contracts contained stringent provisions to ensure accuracy. According to reports the amounts of the tenders varied from 20p to £10 per property, clearly dependant upon factors such as the density of dwellings and the degree of homogeneity within an area. There must have been many lower value regions in the country where Victorian terraced and inter-war semi-detached houses predominated where it could be determined without great difficulty that street after street fell into band A.

THE LOCAL GOVERNMENT FINANCE ACT 1992

In essence, the Council Tax retains the basic principle of the Poll Tax: **15–06** that the number of people contributing towards local government finance should be much broader whilst removing some of its less popular elements, including the 20 per cent minimum charge levied on full-time students and the Poll Tax register, for example. It is interesting to note that through the many years of debate on local government finance, the constant desire to maintain local accountability has effectively been overlooked as some six-sevenths of local government income is now centrally determined.

In some respects the Council Tax combines the concepts of both property tax and poll tax. Cynics might even suggest that it combines the disadvantages of both. Properties are banded in eight broad value bands in accordance with their open market value and a standard charge for each band is levied on the notional household of two adults, provided they are not otherwise exempt. The detailed provisions for the abolition of the Community Charge and the introduction of the Council Tax are contained in the Local Government Finance Act 1992.

The Act provided that from 1993 each billing authority should levy and collect the tax in respect of dwellings. Billing authorities are principally the district authorities who collected the Community Charge and the old domestic rates. "Dwelling" for Council Tax purposes remains as defined in section 115(1) of the General Rate Act 1967, but subject to certain exemptions contained in the Local Government Finance Act 1988, Part III.

> " 'dwelling-house' means a hereditament which, in accordance with Schedule 13 to this Act, is used wholly for the purpose of a private dwelling or private dwellings"

Section 66 of the Local Government Finance Act 1988 expands upon this definition and the Council Tax Exempt Dwellings Order[2] sets out a series of classes of property which are exempt for Council Tax purposes. These include unoccupied dwellings, halls of residence and dwellings owned by the Secretary of State for Defence for the purposes of armed forces occupation.

Composite hereditaments, caravans and moorings are also to be defined as dwellings.

Each household receives a single Council Tax bill with household occupiers being jointly and severally liable. Although information will be required about the occupants of a dwelling, no register of taxpayers is required.

BANDING

15–07 It is wrong to suggest that all dwellings were "valued" and it was not the intention of the 1991 Act that this should happen. It was surely the case that the majority of properties were banded at the desk by reference to key property types which are more or less representative of the main property types within a locality. These properties were subject to a detailed valuation and became key evidence in the case of appeals.

The definition of market value, to be used in the banding exercise was set out in regulation 2 of the Domestic Property (Valuation) Regulations 1991[3] and required the valuation to be made on the

---

[2] S.I. 1992 No. 613.
[3] S.I. 1991 No. 1934.

assumption of a sale in the open market, by a willing seller, with vacant possession given on completion. It was assumed that the interest was an unencumbered freehold, or 99 year leasehold at a nominal rent in the case of flats. A state of reasonable repair was assumed. The market value reflects current use value and did not include alternative or hope value, except for minor development permitted under the General Development Order. Size and layout, and presumably other physical features, were to be taken as existing at the time of valuation but the valuation is to reflect the level of values subsisting at April 1, 1991. Reasonable repair was taken to mean that which might reasonably be expected by a prospective purchaser having regard to the age and character of the property and its locality.

A Listing Officer for each billing authority was employed by the Inland Revenue and issued a valuation list based on capital values at April 1, 1991. This lists each dwelling and the value band applicable.

Standard bands are applied nationally in England, Wales and Scotland.

For England the bands are as follows:

Band		£		£
A less than		40,000		
B more than		40,000	and less than	52,000
C	//	52,000	//	68,000
D	//	68,000	//	88,000
E	//	88,000	//	120,000
F	//	120,000	//	160,000
G	//	160,000	//	320,000
H			more than	320,000

In Wales band A is up to £30,000 and band H is £240,000 and above. Scotland's top band starts at £212,000 with the lowest band up to £27,000 and the middle bands covering the range £45,000–£80,000.

Tax is payable in the proportions: 6:7:8:9:11:13:15:18 on the eight **15–08** bands, A to H. This means that the charge for the highest band is three times the size of the charge in the lowest band notwithstanding that the bottom value of band H is eight times the value at the top of band A.

Liability applies to anyone who is resident and has a freehold interest, is resident and has a leasehold interest, is a statutory tenant, or a licensee, in other words, the great majority of occupiers who are over 18 and not otherwise exempt. A 25 per cent discount is available for single residents and a double discount, 50 per cent for unoccupied dwellings and second homes.

People exempt from the Council Tax include students, student nurses, apprentices, youth trainees, those on income support, prisoners, elderly dependent relatives and the severely mentally handicapped. Exempt people are to be ignored for the purpose of determining the single person household discount.

Appeals from aggrieved persons are heard by the Valuation Tribunals, the same body responsible for the determination of appeals relating to the Uniform Business Rate.

Recovery powers are similar to those under the Community Charge, including distress and attachment of earnings orders. There were some initial transitional provisions protecting payers from large increases in liability.

There is provision within the Act for carrying out revaluations and altering the bands but there does not appear to be any intention to introduce any definite process of revaluation. Individual properties are revalued where there is a "material increase" or decrease in the value as a result of alterations, but this will only take effect when the property changes hands.

SETTING THE CHARGE

15-09 Billing authorities set the amount of the tax having regard to estimates of the total revenue expenditure for the coming year, reflecting contingency allowances, financial reserve provision and transfers from general fund to collection fund. From this aggregate total is deducted the aggregate of all payments into the general fund, including redistributed non-domestic rates, revenue support and additional grants from central government. This calculation will give the net budget requirement for the year.

The net budget requirement is then divided by the tax base to provide the basic amount of tax which would apply to a property in band D.

Much concern has been expressed about the disparities between values in different regions, so that poorer authorities which have a low tax base will tend, by definition, to be those same authorities with high spending requirements. In such cases the average charge equation would result in a high Council Tax charge. In theory the equation should be balanced by the grant support from central government which will help to reduce the net budget requirement. In practice, not everyone seems convinced that this happens.

This grant aid is determined for each authority in relation to its standard spending assessment, a detailed and complex formulation which makes adjustment for a whole range of more than a hundred different factors including the length of roads in the area, climate, altitude, demography, number of school children and so on, all of which are thought to have a bearing on the cost of provision of local authority services.

The 1992 Act further extended the Secretary of State's capping powers, no longer restricting them to local authorities spending more than £15 million, thus bringing an estimated further 80 or more authorities into the capping net. The general capping power is available where spending is deemed to be "excessive" and it is left seemingly to the Secretary of State to determine what is excessive.

CONCLUSIONS

Despite reports of widespread inaccuracies in original valuations and **15-10** large numbers of appeals, it would seem that the Council Tax has avoided the widespread unpopularity which greeted the introduction of the Community Charge. This may have more to do with the now extensive central government control of local government spending and the extent to which domestic taxation is effectively now subsidised rather than the inherent qualities of the tax itself. However, it does seem that the problem of domestic rating has now been resolved following three decades of debate and uncertainty.

After the massive initial valuation exercise, it is unlikely that the Council Tax will provide an area of significant work for valuation practitioners. The absence of regular revaluations means that once initial appeals have been resolved, valuations, other than for new properties, are likely to occur only upon change of ownership which is the only occasion upon which the valuation of individual listed properties is likely to take place, even here, valuation will only be significant in the case of a property which is placed close to the margin of one or other of the bands.

Appendix

Valuation For Rating (Plant and Machinery) Regulations 1994 (S.I. 1994 No. 2680)

Dated, October 16, 1994 and made by the Secretary of State for the Environment, as respects England, and the Secretary of State for Wales, as respects Wales, in exercise of the powers conferred on them by sections 143(2) of, and paragraph 2(8) of Schedule 6 to the Local Government Finance Act 1988, and of all other powers enabling them in that behalf, hereby make the following Regulations:

(1) These Regulations may be cited as the Valuation for Rating (Plant and Machinery) Regulations 1994 and shall come into force on April 1, 1995.

(2) For the purpose of determining the rateable value of a hereditament for any day on or after April 1, 1995, in applying the provisions of subparagraphs (1) to (7) of paragraph 2 of Schedule 6 to the Local Government Finance Act 1988:

(a) in relation to a hereditament in or on which there is plant or machinery which belong to any of the classes set out in the Schedule to these Regulations, the prescribed assumptions are that:

(i) any such plant or machinery is part of the hereditament; and

(ii) the value of any other plant and machinery has no effect on the rent to be estimated as required by paragraph 2(1); and

(b) in relation to any other hereditament, the prescribed assumption is that the value of any plant or machinery has no effect on the rent to be so estimated.

(3) The valuation officer shall, on being so required in writing by the occupier of any hereditament, supply to him particulars in writing showing what plant and machinery, or whether any

particular plant or machinery, has been assumed in pursuance of regulation 2(a) to form part of the hereditament.

(4)   (1) Subject to paragraph (2), the Valuation for Rating (Plant and Machinery) Regulations 1989(b) are hereby revoked.
      (2) The Valuation for Rating (Plant and Machinery) Regulations 1989 shall continue to have effect for the purposes of determining the rateable value of a hereditament for any day before April 1, 1995.

Schedule

Classes of Plant and Machinery to be Assumed to be Part of the Hereditament

Class 1

Plant and machinery specified in Table 1 below (together with any of the appliances and structures accessory to such plant or machinery and specified in the List of Accessories set out below) which is used or intended to be used mainly or exclusively in connection with the generation, storage, primary transformation or main transmission of power in or on the hereditament.
In this Class:

(a)   "transformer" means any plant which changes the pressure or frequency or form of current of electrical power to another pressure or frequency or form of current, except any such plant which forms an integral part of an item of plant or machinery in or on the hereditament for manufacturing operations or trade processes;
(b)   "primary transformation of power" means any transformation of electrical power by means of a transformer at any point in the main transmission of power; and
(c)   "main transmission of power" means all transmission of

225

power from the generating plant or point of supply in or on the hereditament up to and including:

(i)   in the case of electrical power, the first distribution board;

(ii)   in the case of transmission by shafting or wheels, any shaft or wheel driven directly from the prime mover;

(iii)   in the case of hydraulic or pneumatic power, the point where the main supply ceases, excluding any branch service piping connected with such main supply;

(iv)   in a case where, without otherwise passing beyond the limits of the main transmission of power, power is transmitted to another hereditament, the point at which the power passes from the hereditament.

TABLE 1

(a)   Steam boilers (including their settings) and chimneys, flues and dust or grit catchers used in connection with such boilers; furnaces; mechanical stokers; injectors, jets, burners and nozzles; superheaters; feed water pumps and heaters; economisers; accumulators; deaerators; blow-off tanks; gas retorts and charging apparatus, producers and generators.

(b)   Steam engines; steam turbines; gas turbines; internal combustion engines; hot-air engines; barring engines.

(c)   Continuous and alternating current dynamos; couplings to engines and turbines; field exciter gear; three-wire or phase balancers.

(d)   Storage batteries, with stands and insulators, regulating switches, boosters and connections forming part thereof.

(e)   Static transformers; auto transformers; motor generators; motor converters; rotary converters; transverters; rectifiers; phase converters; frequency changers.

(f)   Cables and conductors; switchboards, distribution boards, control panels and all switchgear and other apparatus thereon.

(g)   Water wheels; water turbines; rams; governor engines; penstocks; spillways; surge tanks; conduits; flumes; sluice gates.

(h)   Pumping engines for hydraulic power; hydraulic engines; hydraulic intensifiers; hydraulic accumulators.

(i) Air compressors; compressed air engines.
(j) Windmills.
(k) Shafting, couplings, clutches, worm-gear, pulleys and wheels.
(l) Steam or other motors which are used or intended to be used mainly or exclusively for driving any of the plant and machinery falling within this Class.
(m) Aero-generators; wind turbines.
(n) Solar cells; solar panels.

Class 2

Plant and machinery specified in Table 2 below (together with the appliances and structures accessory to such plant or machinery and specified in paragraph 2 of the List of Accessories set out below) which is used or intended to be used mainly or exclusively in connection with services to the land or buildings of which the hereditament consists, other than any such plant or machinery which is in or on the hereditament and is used or intended to be used in connection with services mainly or exclusively as part of manufacturing operations or trade processes.

In this class, "services" means heating, cooling, ventilating, lighting, draining or supplying of water and protection from trespass, criminal damage, theft, fire or other hazard.

TABLE 2

(a) *General*

Any of the plant and machinery specified in Table 1 and any motors which are used or intended to be used mainly or exclusively for driving any of the plant and machinery falling within paragraphs (b) to (f) of this Table.

(b) *Heating, Cooling and Ventilating*

(i) Water heaters.
(ii) Headers and manifolds; steam pressure reducing valves; calor-

ifiers; radiators; heating panels; hot-air furnaces with distributing ducts and gratings.

(iii) Gas pressure regulators; gas burners; gas heaters and radiators and the flues and chimneys used in connection therewith.

(iv) Plug-sockets and other outlets; electric heaters.

(v) Refrigerating machines.

(vi) Water screens; water jets.

(vii) Fans and blowers.

(viii) Air intakes, channels, ducts, gratings, louvres and outlets.

(ix) Plant for filtering, washing, drying, warming, cooling, humidifying, deodorising and perfuming, and for the chemical and bacteriological treatment of air.

(x) Pipes and coils when used for causing or assisting air movement.

(c) *Lighting*

(i) Gas pressure regulators; gas burners.

(ii) Plug-sockets and other outlets; electric lamps.

(d) *Draining*

Pumps and other lifting apparatus; tanks; screens; sewage treatment plant and machinery.

(e) *Supplying Water*

Pumps and other water-lifting apparatus; sluice-gates; tanks, filters and other plant and machinery for the storage and treatment of water.

(f) *Protection from Hazards*

Tanks; lagoons; reservoirs; pumps, hydrants and monitors; fire alarm systems; fire and explosion protection and suppression systems; bunds; blast protection walls; berms; lightning conductors; security and alarm systems; ditches; moats; mounds; barriers; doors; gates; turnstiles; shutters; grilles; fences.

List of Accessories

(1) Any of the following plant and machinery which is used or intended to be used mainly or exclusively in connection with the

handling, preparing or storing of fuel required for the generation or storage of power in or on the hereditament:

Cranes with their grabs or buckets; truck or wagon tipplers; elevating and conveying systems, including power winches, drags, elevators, hoists, conveyors, transporters, travellers, cranes, buckets forming a connected part of any such system, and any weighing machines used in connection therewith; magnetic separators; driers; breakers; pulverisers; bunkers; gas-holders; tanks.

(2) Any of the following plant and machinery which is used or intended to be used mainly or exclusively as part of or in connection with or as an accessory to any of the plant and machinery falling within Class 1 or Class 2:

(i)   foundations, settings, gantries, supports, platforms and stagings for plant and machinery;
(ii)   steam-condensing plant, compressors, exhausters, storage cylinders and vessels, fans, pumps and ejectors; ash-handling apparatus;
(iii)   travellers and cranes;
(iv)   oiling systems; earthing systems; cooling systems;
(v)   pipes, ducts, valves, traps, separators, filters, coolers, screens, purifying and other treatment apparatus, evaporators, tanks, exhaust boxes and silencers, washers, scrubbers, condensers, air heaters and air saturators;
(vi)   shafting supports, belts, ropes and chains;
(vii)   cables, conductors, wires, pipes, tubes, conduits, casings, poles, supports, insulators, joint boxes and end boxes;
(viii) instruments and apparatus attached to the plant and machinery, including computers, meters, gauges, measuring and recording instruments, automatic or programmed controls, temperature indicators, alarms and relays.

Class 3

The following items:

(a)   railway and tramway lines and tracks and associated fixed accessories and equipment;
(b)   lifts, elevators, hoists, escalators and travelators;

(c)   cables, wires and conductors, or any system of such items, used or intended to be used in connection with the transmission, distribution or supply of electricity other than such items, or parts of such items, which are comprised in the equipment of and are situated within premises.

In this paragraph, "premises" means any hereditament other than one used or intended to be used mainly or exclusively for the transmission, distribution or supply of electricity.

(d)   poles, posts, pylons, towers, pipes, ducts, conduits, meters, switchgear and transformers, and any associated supports and foundations, used or intended to be used in connection with any of the items included in (c) above;

(e)   cables, fibres, wires and conductors, or any system of such items, or any part of such items or such system, used or intended to be used in connection with the transmission of communications signals, and which are comprised in the equipment of and are situated within premises.

In this paragraph,

(i)   "premises" means any hereditament which is used, or intended to be used, mainly or exclusively for the processing or the transmission of communications signals excluding any part of such a hereditament within which there is equipment used mainly for the processing of communications signals;

(ii)   "processing of communications signals" means the conversion of one form of communications signal to another form or the routing of communications signals by switching; and

(iii)   "equipment used mainly for the processing of communications signals" includes;
—that part of any associated cable, fibre, wire or conductor which extends from the point of conversion or switching to the first distribution or termination frame or junction; and
—that part of any associated cable, fibre, wire or conductor which extends from the last distribution or termination frame or junction to the point of conversion or switching.

(f)   poles, posts, towers, masts, mast radiators, pipes, ducts and conduits, and any associated supports and foundations, used or intended to be used in connection with any of the items included within (e) above;

(g) a pipeline, that is to say, a pipe or system of pipes and associated fixed accessories and equipment for the conveyance of any thing, not being:

(i) a drain or sewer; or
(ii) a pipeline which forms part of the equipment of, and is wholly situated within, relevant premises;

and where a pipeline forms part of the equipment of, and is situated partly within and partly outside, relevant premises, excluding:

(i) in the case of a pipeline for the conveyance of any thing to the premises, so much of the pipeline as extends from the first control valve on the premises; and
(ii) in the case of a pipeline for the conveyance of any thing away from the premises, so much of the pipeline as extends up to the last control valve on the premises;

but not excluding so much of the pipeline as comprises the first or, as the case may be, last, control valve.

In this paragraph, "relevant premises" means a factory or petroleum storage depot, a mine, quarry or mineral field or a natural gas storage or processing facility or gas holder site. For this purpose:

(a) "factory" has the same meaning as in the Factories Act 1961;
(b) "mine" and "quarry" have the same meanings as in the Mines and Quarries Act 1954;
(c) "mineral field" means an area comprising an excavation being a well or bore-hole or a well and bore-hole combined, or a system of such excavations, used for the purpose of pumping or raising brine or oil or extracting natural or landfill gas, and so much of the surface (including buildings, structures and works thereon) surrounding or adjacent to the excavation or system as is occupied, together with the excavation or system, for the purposes of the working of the excavation or system;
(d) "petroleum storage depot" means premises used primarily for the storage of petroleum or petroleum products (including chemicals derived from petroleum) or of materials used

in the manufacture of petroleum products (including chemicals derived from petroleum).

Class 4

The items specified in Tables 3 and 4 below, except:

(a) any such item which is not, and is not in the nature of, a building or structure;

(b) any part of any such item which does not form an integral part of such item as a building or structure or as being in the nature of a building or structure.

(c) so much of any refractory or other lining forming part of any plant or machinery as is customarily renewed by reason of normal use at intervals of less than 50 weeks;

(d) any item in Table 4 the total cubic capacity of which (measured externally and excluding foundations, settings, supports and anything which is not an integral part of the item) does not exceed four hundred cubic metres and which is readily capable of being moved from one site and re-erected in its original state on another without the substantial demolition of any surrounding structure.

TABLE 3

Blast Furnaces.
Bridges.
Bunds.
Chimneys and flues.
Coking Ovens.
Cooling Ponds.
Floating pontoons, with any bridges or gangways not of a temporary nature used in connection therewith.
Flumes, conduits and ducts.
Foundations, settings, fixed gantries, supports, walkways, stairways, handrails, catwalks, stages, staithes and platforms.
Headgear for:
    mines, quarries and pits;
    wells.

Masts (including guy ropes) and towers for radar or communications signals.
Pits, beds and bays.
Radio telescopes.
Shiplifts and building berths.
Tipplers.
Transversers and turntables.
Well casings and liners.

TABLE 4

Accelerators.
Acid concentrators.
Bins and hoppers.
Boilers.
Bunkers.
Burners, converters, furnaces, kilns, stoves and ovens.
Chambers and vessels.
Condensers and scrubbers.
Coolers, chillers and quenchers.
Cupolas.
Cyclones.
Economisers, heat exchangers, recuperators, regenerators and superheaters.
Evaporators.
Filters and separators.
Gas producers, generators, purifiers, cleansers and holders.
Hydraulic accumulators.
Precipitators.
Reactors.
Refuse destructors and incinerators.
Retorts.
Silos.
Stills.
Tanks.
Towers and columns.
Vats.
Washeries for coal.
Wind tunnels.

INDEX